10.00

THE DREAM OF POLIPHILO

The Jungian Classics Series serves to make available again works of long-standing value in the tradition of C. G. Jung's psychology:

1
Aniela Jaffé: *APPARITIONS*
An Archetypal Approach to Death Dreams and Ghosts *(O.P.)*

2
James Hillman: *INSEARCH*
Psychology and Religion

3
Marie-Louise von Franz: *THE PASSION OF PERPETUA (O.P.)*

4
Victor White: *GOD AND THE UNCONSCIOUS*

5
Edgar Herzog: *PSYCHE AND DEATH*
Death-Demons in Folklore, Myths and Modern Dreams

6
Aniela Jaffé: *JUNG'S LAST YEARS AND OTHER ESSAYS (O.P.)*

7
Robert Stein: *INCEST AND HUMAN LOVE*
The Betrayal of the Soul in Psychotherapy

8
Linda Fierz-David: *THE DREAM OF POLIPHILO*

9
Cornelia Brunner: *ANIMA AS FATE*

10
John Weir Perry: *THE SELF IN PSYCHOTIC PROCESS*
Its Symbolization in Schizophrenia

THE DREAM
of
POLIPHILO
The Soul in Love

Related and Interpreted by
LINDA FIERZ-DAVID
Translated by
MARY HOTTINGER

SPRING PUBLICATIONS, INC.
DALLAS, TEXAS

Published 1987 by Spring Publications, Inc.;
P.O. Box 222069; Dallas, Texas 75222,
by arrangement with Princeton University Press.
Copyright 1950 by Bollingen Foundation, Inc.,
New York, N.Y. All rights reserved.
Printed in the United States of America

Cover designed by Mary Vernon with the design and production
assistance of Patricia Mora and Maribeth Lipscomb

International distributors:
Spring; Postfach; 8800 Thalwil; Switzerland
Japan Spring Sha, Inc.; 1-2-4, Nishisakaidani-Cho;
Ohharano, Nishikyo-Ku; Kyoto, 610-11, Japan
Element Books Ltd; Longmead Shaftesbury;
Dorset SP7 8PL; England

Library of Congress Cataloging-in-Publication Data
Fierz-David, Linda.
The dream of Poliphilo.

(The Jungian classics series ; 8)
Translation of: Der Liebestraum des Poliphilo.
Psychological interpretation of F. Colonna's
Hypnerotomachia Poliphili.
Reprint. Originally published: New York : Pantheon,
1950.
Bibliography: p.
1. Colonna, Francesco, d. 1527. Hypnerotomachia
Poliphili. I. Colonna, Francesco, d. 1527. Hypnero-
tomachia Poliphili. II. Title. III. Series.
PQ4619.C9Z72   1987   833'.4   87-18037
ISBN 0-88214-507-X

Contents

List of Illustrations   XI

Foreword by C. G. Jung   XIII

Title Page of the First Edition of the *Hypnerotomachia Poliphili*   XVII

INTRODUCTION   1

PART I

SECTION I: THE RUINED CITY   33

> His thoughts full of the divine Polia, Poliphilo falls asleep and dreams that he is lost in a wild, dark forest. By prayer, he finds his way out. He is startled by a wolf in a palm-grove. He comes to a ruined city of the ancient world. Poliphilo enters a porch and finds himself in darkness. His way back is cut off by a triple-tongued dragon. He roams about in gloomy vaults. Under a lamp he sees three golden statues. He finds the opening which leads out of the gloomy vaults.

COMMENTARY TO SECTION I   42

SECTION II: THE REALM OF QUEEN ELEUTERILIDA   66

> Poliphilo finds himself in a fertile plain. He meets five lovely maidens. They take him to the bath-house to bathe. Then to the court of Queen Eleuterilida. Banquet with the Queen and her ladies. The Queen appoints two of her attendants to be Poliphilo's guides and directs him to his next goal. The Queen's gardens and maze. The last garden and the golden obelisk. Poliphilo arrives at the three portals of Queen Telosia. He has to choose between them and chooses the portal of Mater Amoris. His companions leave him. He is fooled by Dame Love-Potion.

COMMENTARY TO SECTION II   77

SECTION III: THE TRIUMPHAL CHARIOTS   98

    Poliphilo is alone. Through an arcade of verdure he sees a group of youths and maidens. A nymph bearing a torch comes to be his guide. Poliphilo is enamoured of the nymph. She leads him to four triumphal chariots on which the place of the hero is taken by Europa, Leda, Danae, and a vase containing a vine. At the fountain of Narcissus. Can the nymph be Polia? She leads Poliphilo to the fifth chariot, that of Vertumnus and Pomona, and to the altar of Priapus. Then past Pan and Silvanus to the seashore. The temple of Venus Physizoa and its construction.

COMMENTARY TO SECTION III   109

SECTION IV: IN THE TEMPLE OF VENUS PHYSIZOA   131

    Poliphilo and the nymph are welcomed by the high priestess of the temple and her vestals. The nymph's torch is extinguished in the cistern. "I am Polia." Sacrificial rite and magic apparitions in the chapel. The heavenly feeding. The high priestess blesses Polia and Poliphilo. The nymph sends Poliphilo to visit the Polyandrion, which is dedicated to the triple-bodied Pluto. Cupid approaches. The lovers sail across the sea in Cupid's bark.

COMMENTARY TO SECTION IV   142

SECTION V: THE ISLAND OF CYTHERA   160

    Psyche, attended by nymphs and matrons, comes to welcome Cupid's bark to the island of Cythera. Polia and Poliphilo are led in Cupid's triumphal progress to the amphitheatre in the middle of the island. The image of Seraphis. The fountain of Venus is unveiled in the amphitheatre. The goddess speaks. Cupid transfixes Polia and Poliphilo with his arrow. Mars enters with the wolf. Nymphs lead the lovers to the fountain of Adonis. The grave of Adonis in the rose-bower.

COMMENTARY TO SECTION V   171

VIII

PART II

SECTION I: Polia's Story	**189**
Commentary to Section I	**194**
SECTION II: The Assumption of Polia	**210**
Commentary to Section II	**210**
EPILOGUE	**237**
PUBLISHER'S NOTE	245

List of Illustrations

1.	Poliphilo in the Forest	34
2.	Poliphilo and the Wolf	36
3.	The Ruined City	37
4.	Relief on the Plinth of the Winged Horse	38
5.	The Black Elephant	40
6.	Poliphilo Flees from the Triple-Tongued Dragon	42
7.	The Nymph Fountain	67
8.	The Five Sense Maidens	68
9.	At the Court of Queen Eleuterilida	71
10.	The Golden Obelisk on the Cube, Cylinder, and Triangular Prism	74
11.	The Three Portals of Queen Telosia	76
12.	Dame Love-Potion and Her Train	78
13.	Cosmic Emblem of the Alchemical *Opus* (from *Musaeum Hermeticum Reformatum*, Francofurti MDCXXVIII)	88
14.	Poliphilo Led by the Nymph	100
15/16.	The Fourth Triumphal Chariot	102-103
17.	The Altar of Priapus	105
18.	The Temple of Venus Physizoa	107
19.	The Central Lamp in the Temple of Venus	108
20.	The Torch Is Extinguished	132
21.	The Sacrifice of Roses and Sea-Shells	135
22.	The Heavenly Feeding	136
23.	The Polyandrion	137
24.	The Little Temple in the Polyandrion	139
25.	Plan of the Island of Cythera	161
26.	Cytheran Fashion-Plate	162
27.	Serapis in the Serpent Circle	163
28.	Plan of the Fountain of Venus	166
29.	Statue of Venus as the Mother of Cupid	169
30.	The Fountain of Adonis	170
31.	Polia Dragging Poliphilo into a Corner	190
32.	Poliphilo in Polia's Lap	191
33.	The Lovers with the Priestess of Venus	192
34.	In the Heaven of Venus	193

Foreword

It must be twenty-five years since the *Hypnerotomachia Poliphili* first came my way in the French translation published by Béroalde de Verville in 1600. Later, in the Morgan Library, New York, I saw and admired the first Italian edition with its superb woodcuts. I set about reading the book, but came to grief in the mazes of its architectural fantasies, which no human being can enjoy today. Probably the same thing has happened to many a reader, and we cannot but have a fellow-feeling with Jakob Burckhardt, who dismissed it with a brief mention, troubling himself little about its contents. I then turned to the *Recueil Stéganographique,* Béroalde's introduction to his translation. Through its obscure and noisy verbiage, I managed to catch a glimpse which aroused my curiosity and encouraged me to continue my labours, for labours they are in a case like this. Crawling on, chapter by chapter, I sensed, rather than saw, a growing number of details that I was to encounter later in my work on alchemy. Indeed, I cannot even say how far it was this book which put me on the track of alchemy. In any case, not many years later I began to collect the old Latin treatises of the alchemists. In the course of a close study of them lasting many years, I actually discovered that line of thought that we might call subterranean, and from which there sprang, not only the alchemists' images, but also Poliphilo's dream. What first found expression in the poetry of courtly love and the early Christian religious lyrics can be heard in it as a faint echo, along with a premonition of the future. Like every real dream, the *Hypnerotomachia* is Janus-headed; it is a picture of the Middle Ages just beginning to turn into modern times by way of the Renaissance—a transition between two eras, and therefore deeply interesting to the world of today, which is still more transitional in character.

Thus it was with no small interest that I read the manuscript sent to me by Frau Linda Fierz-David, for it is the first serious attempt to pluck the heart out of Poliphilo's mystery, and to unravel his crabbed symbolism with the methods of modern psychology. In my opinion, the writer's enterprise has been entirely successful. She has been able to show that the problem remains constant throughout the course taken by the action, and to demonstrate its personal and suprapersonal character while bringing to light its bearing on the world of that time. Many of her interpretations are not only definitive, they are illuminating, and bring an apparently outlandish and baroque romance, which was so eagerly read in the sixteenth and seventeenth centuries, once more within the immediate range of modern understanding. With an intelligence only equalled by her intuition, she has drawn a picture of that peculiar Renaissance psychology whose literary monument is the *Hypnerotomachia,* while giving that picture a timeless background in virtue of which it not only presents itself to the man of today in the freshness of its original colouring, but appeals to him directly by its imperishable and priceless psychological truth. This book owes not a little of its fortunate journey through seas as yet uncharted to the sensitiveness of the feminine mind, which, with tactful indiscretion, can take a peep behind the scenes of Francesco Colonna's ornate and impressive baroque façade. It was in virtue of this feminine gift that St. Catherine was consulted by the heavenly assembly "as was usually done in difficult cases," according to Anatole France's delicious account in the *Île des pingouins.* "On earth, St. Catherine had confounded seventy very learned doctors. She was versed in the philosophy of Plato as well as the Scriptures, and possessed rhetoric." Small wonder, then, that the writer of the present volume has succeeded in some dazzling interpretations which throw considerable light on the obscurities of Poliphilo's symbolism. It is precisely those labyrinthine ways in which the masculine mind sets traps for itself with its own vanities that have here been illuminated, and hence given a meaning for our own time.

The comments in the book, moreover, take us into the depths of the psychic problems which remain unfathomable to the modern mind, and therefore present it with a task. The book is not easy reading—indeed it requires some effort. But it is substantial and stimulating, and will reward the attention that comes halfway to meet it. In any case, I am grateful to the writer for the enrichment of knowledge and insight that her work has brought me.

C. G. JUNG

POLIPHILI HYPNEROTOMACHIA, VBI
HVMANA OMNIA NON NISI SO-
MNIVM ESSE OSTENDIT, AT
QVE OBITER PLVRIMA
SCITV SANEQVAM
DIGNA COM-
MEMO-
RAT.
✲✲✲
✲

Introduction

Poliphilo's Love Dream is a work of the early Italian Renaissance ascribed to a Venetian monk, Francesco Colonna. It would not have been very considerate to the reader to plunge him unprepared into the full title of the book, for it begins with an artificial and singular word invented by the author, which presides like some mysterious hieroglyph over the opening of his story. This artificial word, which is actually the main title of the book, is:

HYPNEROTOMACHIA

and is composed of the Greek words for dream, love, and strife. Thus what the present commentary deals with is "The Strife of Love in a Dream." That sounds mysterious enough, and if the author presents his dream to us under a title which is a Greek word coined expressly for the purpose, we can but infer that he does so in order to make us realize that it is concerned with supreme cultural values, Greek being, at that time, the language in which the most recent and distinguished culture was expressed. And in actual fact the *Hypnerotomachia* is a work of profound culture, rich in artistic feeling and vastly erudite. The highly imaginative nature of its contents, its manifold meanings, and the vivid sensuousness of its style have attracted cultivated readers at all times, and have had their influence on various domains of life and learning. Historians of art have turned to it again and again, for it abounds in architectural ideas and contains the first sketches of those idealized ruins which became so popular in later Renaissance art. Further, the elegant and profusely illustrated folio volume is a gem of earliest Italian book-making. In the course of the centuries, scholars and artists have striven to find the clue to its meaning, and the *Hypnerotomachia* was belauded or belittled by them according to the meaning, or lack of meaning, they found in it. It is true that the book, which claims, on the surface, to be a work of pure literature, is characterized by a peculiar kind of obscurity.

What the *Hypnerotomachia* relates is a mystery, i.e. it is the story of a mysterious action which has a secret purpose and in which the miraculous is the natural. To understand such a work on its face value is impossible. Like every mystery, it requires interpretation. In attempting to provide that interpretation, we must begin with a brief sketch of the time at which the *Hypnerotomachia* was written. It is of the greatest importance to know and understand the foreground behind which the mysterious action takes place.

The author's life belongs entirely to the Quattrocento, a century marked by a youthful, fierce, and splendid worldliness. The Sforza, the Medici, the Este, and the Montefeltre were in power, Boiardo and Macchiavelli were alive, and Aretino was young. There is, however, little need to recount names in order to conjure up a time on which European art and literature drew for so long. Though ridden by factions, Italy was at that time exceedingly prosperous. It was the age in which so many Italian cities took on that elegant gaiety which so much endears them to us today.

Venice, our author's native city, with a population of nearly 200,000 souls, was then at the summit of her power. In 1422 she possessed a fleet of 3345 vessels, forty-five of which were state galleys with crews totalling 36,000 men. The turnover of her trade amounted to some ten million ducats a year. As a city in which commercial interests reigned supreme, she was to a great extent free of internal factions. With her beautiful buildings, her stable and prudent government, her steady care for the public welfare, she was regarded as the supreme ornament of the age. The Venetian clergy was entirely in the hands of the state, to which the figure of the doge lent a spiritual element. Venice enjoyed general confidence by reason of her easy and clement government, for life there was more pleasant and secure than in any other Italian city.[1]

The Dominican order, to which Francesco Colonna belonged, had not yet passed through the thorough-going reformation it was to undergo at the end of the century under the influence of Savonarola. Since the order had, in 1425, obtained the right to receive gifts, it had acquired enormous wealth, and the slippered scholarship of the monks provoked the growing envy and even ridicule of their contemporaries.

The prevailing intellectual force in our author's lifetime was humanism.[2] The fire of the humanistic movement in Italy was short-lived—by the end of the fifteenth century it was practically spent. More than any other movement, humanism was remarkable for the contradictions inherent within it. It was noble-minded yet petty, aflame with sacred zeal yet shallow and artificial. It was *the* expression of the *Italianità* of the age, yet the language it spoke was Latin. It was Christian and pagan, medieval and modern at one and the same time. The conflicts inherent in humanism were manifested not only in the humanists' insatiable thirst for knowledge—the *cupiditas rerum novarum*—but also, and equally, in their ardent endeavour to blend new knowledge with established belief and in the creative idealism which inspired their conception of the redeeming function of classical culture.

[1] Cf. Jakob Burckhardt, *The Civilization of the Italian Renaissance.*
[2] Cf. V. Klemperer, "Italien," in *Die romanischen Literaturen von der Renaissance bis zur französischen Revolution* (*Handbuch der Literatur-Wissenschaft,* edited by O. Walzel, Athenaion Verlag, Berlin, 1924).

The Middle Ages had, of course, not been ignorant of the culture of the ancients. On the contrary, medieval scholars had eagerly studied it at all times. But in a case like this, what matters is not the knowledge of facts and the relative amount of that knowledge. Nor does it matter that there was a rich accretion of the purely fantastic in the medieval knowledge of the classics. It may well be that the fantastic element in medieval culture actually did less harm than the comparative lack of imagination which characterizes knowledge in our day. The point at issue here is the totally different attitude to the knowledge of antiquity taken up on the one hand by the Middle Ages, on the other by humanism. In the Middle Ages, that attitude was determined by religion; like all secular knowledge, the knowledge of the classics was subject to dogmatic valuation based on the reference to a Christian hereafter. But in proportion as the church was secularized, particularly in Italy, in the course of the Middle Ages, it forfeited its universal validity. When the certainty of salvation was undermined, absolutism in secular values began to totter. The loosening of that firm bond between all earthly life and the hereafter was equivalent to a dangerous liberation of feeling. Harassed and shaken by the collapse of the medieval world, the Italian humanists turned, in despair and longing, to their own past. They still felt the absolutely medieval need of a uniform standard of values, and since they could no longer find it in heaven, they dug it up out of the earth. Classical culture became for them the symbol uniting all their opposites.

How much the humanists really knew about antiquity, and how much they sensed beyond their knowledge, is difficult to determine. When they made a fresh start in the systematic exploration of the classical world, with the open mind forced upon them by necessity, they actually found themselves in a world where the medieval conceptions of good and evil were no longer valid. At that time, the Italian soil was rich in classical remains. Little had been touched or arranged in museums. The man who held a sculptured stone, a figure, a text in his hand felt the breath of virgin life fanning his face, and was moved by it to a degree we can hardly even imagine today. What was born of that emotion was a sense of life so free and natural that heights and depths were still—or once more—absolutely one.

The humanists' overwhelming emotion over their finds can only be explained by that fascination. Yet their writings give no adequate expression to it, partly because they still conform to the methods of medieval scholarship and partly because they are disfigured by personal passions, prejudices, and vanities. Hence the real significance of that fascination may perhaps be illustrated best by an actual incident, of no great moment in itself, recounted by Jakob Burckhardt.[3] In April, 1485, a rumour arose that the body of a young Roman girl, in a state of perfect preservation, had been discovered in a tomb on the Via Appia. Still blooming with the natural colours of life, the body was said to be like that of a girl of fifteen just dead—the eyes half open, the lips parted, the hair golden or gilt. The rumour caused a veritable pilgrimage to the tomb, for all believed that the miracle of beauty itself

---

[3] Cf. Jakob Burckhardt, op. cit. Cf. also Evelyn's *Diary* for January 25, 1645:
"In one of these monuments Pancirollus tells us that, in the time of Paul III, there was found the body of a young lady, swimming in a bath of precious oil, or liquor, fresh and entire as if she had been living, neither her face discoloured nor her hair disordered; at her feet burned a lamp, which suddenly expired at the opening of the vault; having flamed, as was computed, now 1500 years, by the conjecture that she was Tulliola, the daughter of Cicero, whose body was thus found, and as the inscription testified."
Cf. also Donne, "Epithalamion" (1613):
> Now, as in Tullia's tomb, one lamp burnt clear,
> Unchang'd for fifteen hundred year,
> May these love-lamps we here enshrine,
> In warmth, light, lasting, equal the divine.

would be revealed in this young Roman maiden's body. There were even a large number of artists who set out to paint the corpse. The crowds grew to such proportions that the authorities were compelled to intervene and have the body, which had in fact been discovered, secretly removed and reburied.

We can hardly believe that the goal of such a pilgrimage was the actual sight of the young body. Its true cause must rather have lain in the sense of another, larger life which, for the humanist, emanated from the very flesh and blood of antique humanity and which, seen from that standpoint, was so youthful and so near to wakening that even the man in the street could respond to it.

Hence if humanism has exercised so profound an influence outside of the Italian frontiers and down to our own day, the underlying reason would seem to reside not in a mere increase of knowledge, but simply and solely in the fact that, as a result of its attitude to classical civilization, it had, with all its wealth of learning, caught a breath of the very humanity of the ancients.

The author of the *Hypnerotomachia* felt the fascination of antiquity to such a point that he unswervingly followed the call of the past to its inmost heart. According to his own statement, it was a great love for a woman that showed him the way. Hence those critics who regard the book as a fragment of an autobiography are probably not far wrong. But it is an autobiography of the soul. Whether or how far it was connected with actual events, no one can tell.

Nothing certain is known about the author of the *Hypnerotomachia*. The tradition that he was the Dominican monk Francesco Colonna is, however, as old as the book and has only recently been questioned. In point of fact, the actual authorship of the book is a matter of complete indifference because its general human import far outweighs what is personal in it. The only thing that can be inferred with certainty from the contents of the dream is that the author was a monk. We may therefore briefly summarize here what is known of Francesco Colonna.

He was born at Venice in 1433, the son of a branch of the famous Roman family of Colonna, and there is evidence that he took his master's degree at Padua. He was only twenty-two when he entered the order. It is known that he spent the last fifty-six years of his life in the monastery of SS. John and Paul at Venice, where he died, highly honoured, at the great age of ninety-four. He was buried in the cloisters of the monastery.

The only evidence that he wrote the *Hypnerotomachia* and that the book is based on an actual experience of love is to be found in a contemporary note in a copy of the book discovered in an Italian monastery. Translated from Latin, this note runs:

"The writer's real name is Francesco Colonna. He is a Venetian who belongs to the Dominican order. Having lingered at Treviso by reason of his great love for a certain Hippolita, he gave her a new name, Polia, and, as can be seen, dedicated his book to her. This is confirmed by the initials of the chapters of his book for, placed side by side, they read:

POLIAM
FRATER FRANCISCUS COLUMNA PERAMAVIT

He is still alive in the monastery of SS. John and Paul at Venice."

In later times, many scholars investigated the existence of this Hippolita. And they actually succeeded in discovering the family and pedigree of a young lady of Treviso which seemed to correspond to what is told us in the *Hypnerotomachia*. The most recent French translator of the book, Claudius Popelin, who carefully examined all the earlier evidence, found none of it really convincing. The only fact that can be established is that a plague, mentioned in the *Hypnerotomachia,* was actually raging at Treviso at that time.[4]

The *Hypnerotomachia,* the first edition of which comprises four hundred and fifty folio pages of letterpress and illustrations, is subscribed as having been written "at Treviso, when Poliphilo languished in the sweet love-fetters of Polia, in the year 1467, on the first day of May." It was first published anonymously at Venice by Manutius, the most famous of Italian Renaissance publishers. Between 1499 and 1833 it was reprinted in all ten times. It obviously never lacked readers and was never forgotten; all kinds of interpretations were given to it and all kinds of ideas were taken from it.[5] It has given rise, in the course of time, to the most conflicting opinions—admiring, fervid, and blankly hostile—which merely go to prove how great are the difficulties it presents to the understanding.

It was on the whole the French alchemists of the sixteenth and seventeenth centuries who seem to have understood it best. This is evident from the fine French edition of 1600, made by Béroalde de Verville, who gave it another title: *Le Tableau des Riches Inventions Couvertes du Voile des Feintes Amoureuses, qui sont représentées dans le Songe de Poliphile, Desvoilées des Ombres du Songe et subtilement exposées par Béroalde (à Paris chez Matthieu Guillemot).* Béroalde's "subtle exposition" consists of a *recueil stéganographique,* i.e. an essay in cipher which forms the introduc-

---

[4] All these data, and the notes on the various editions which follow, are taken from Claudius Popelin's beautiful and scholarly introduction to his translation. This was published under the title *Le Songe de Poliphile ou Hypnérotomachie de frère Francesco Colonna* by I. Lisieux, Paris, in 1883. Popelin's introduction comprises two hundred pages and is particularly interesting for the humanistic aspect of the book.

[5] For instance, a special study of the influence of the *Hypnerotomachia* on French art and literature, which is mainly to be seen in matters of detail, may be found in the *Journal of the Warburg Institute,* Vol. I, No. 2, 1937: Anthony Blunt, "The *Hypnerotomachia Polifili* in 17th Century France."

tion to his translation. This *recueil* is a symbolic treatise on alchemy with a very beautiful frontispiece.[6] The work gains very much both from the treatise and the frontispiece, since they offer a very illuminating parallel in alchemy.

We might note as a curiosity that there is in English an incomplete translation of the *Hypnerotomachia*[7] dedicated to Essex, the favourite of Queen Elizabeth.

It is the architects and gardeners who have always shown the liveliest appreciation of the author of the *Hypnerotomachia*. Though he apparently never built anything, he is held in high honour among them and has sometimes been compared to the best Renaissance masters. And indeed, at the first glance, it is the architectural part of the book which is most striking. It is full of the most detailed descriptions of splendid buildings and gardens in the classical style. The large number of ground-plans, all with exact measurements, show it to be the work of an architect who knew his Vitruvius well. In this sense the author was a thorough humanist. Both in the text and the illustrations he envisaged a style in architecture which should familiarize his contemporaries with the ideal forms of antiquity, forms that were only partly created as he had conceived them by the mid-Renaissance. Claudius Popelin is of the opinion that Francesco Colonna must have known Leon Battista Alberti's work on architecture, although in his day it was not yet printed. One thing is certain, that the architectural fantasies of our author, even though some of them are gigantic in their proportions, may be compared with buildings created under Alberti's influence. Anyone familiar with Pienza or the church of San Francesco at Rimini, for instance, will be able to imagine what the Venetian monk had in mind when he wrote his book. His architectural digressions are extremely tedious, yet

[6] Reproduced in C. G. Jung, *Psychology and Alchemy*.
[7] A facsimile of the original was published by Methuen in 1904.

the ardour with which he raises noble piles, lays out gardens, and invents artistic fountains and dainty objects for use or show is touching and impressive, even to the layman. Here the humanist's heart is beating high for the coming rebirth of classical antiquity.

Béroalde de Verville, the alchemist translator of the *Hypnerotomachia,* dismissed these ideals as negligible. The thing that seems most important to many who know the book well was for him mere trifling. He regards all this architecture merely as a prudent cloak for the book's invisible yet visible meaning. For him, Francesco Colonna is a philosopher who is leading by the nose those readers who imagine that they can grasp the essence of the book by its externals. "The author is an alchemist," says Béroalde, "but in so secret a fashion that he almost uses the secret to conceal the secret." Here Béroalde is not far wrong, for the *Hypnerotomachia* is actually full of the obscure interplay of alchemical symbolism. It was architecture above all which gave alchemy its favourite symbols for the Hermetic vessel, which it is so difficult to construct and which contains the secret of the transmutation of matter. The alchemical aspect of the *Hypnerotomachia* will, however, be the subject of a brief discussion later.

For the writer of the book is no more an alchemist pure and simple than he is an architect pure and simple. His work is first and foremost a romance, and a romance of a perfectly definite type. In his introduction, Popelin spends a number of pages on a careful proof that the *Hypnerotomachia* is a slavish imitation of Boccaccio's romances. And he is perfectly right. But in this connection we must not think of the *Decamerone,* for in the early Renaissance it was far less famous than Boccaccio's love-stories; these derive in part from the medieval fabliaux, though they move in a totally different sphere, which the author of the *Hypnero-*

tomachia has also borrowed from them. Their scene is set in a heroic landscape among nymphs and youths of legendary, semi-divine descent.[8] Boccaccio was one of the founders of the rich classical mythology of the Renaissance. Not only the sense of dream, the motives, the cardinal position of Venus as the protectress of love, but even whole passages of the *Hypnerotomachia* are based on these romances of Boccaccio. And our writer has taken from Boccaccio the sensuous realism of his style, his joy in verdant nature, his delight in wealth and splendour and in the curled beauty of women.

With that, however, we have not yet traced the whole pedigree of the book. If Boccaccio's romance was, so to speak, its genial mother, the *Divina Commedia* was its austere father. To the *Divina Commedia* the *Hypnerotomachia* owes its basic structure, the conception of a journey through many regions under the leadership of a guide. True, quite apart from the vast difference in creative power, the differences between the incidents in the *Divina Commedia* and the *Hypnerotomachia* are so great that it would perhaps only be necessary to pursue the comparison in order to show how far apart were the ages in which the two works were written. In Dante's vision, the world is graded in heights and depths according to a precise and purely medieval hierarchy; for Colonna, the man of the Renaissance, the heights have already fallen in and the depths have risen up. Thus his path seems at first to lead straight ahead, since he no longer knows what are heights and what depths.

We need hardly ask how it was possible for the writer of the *Hypnerotomachia* to base his work so directly on others written a century before his time. Most of his contemporaries based their works in quite a similar way on the "three

---

[8] Boccaccio's three most important romances are *Ameto, Fiametta,* and *Il Corbacchio*. The *Hypnerotomachia* has borrowed most freely from *Ameto*. In subject, it also recalls Boccaccio's verse romances, and the name of the hero of the dream, Poliphilo, contains an echo of the names of two heroes of Boccaccio's early works, Filocolo and Filostrato.

crowns of Florence," Dante, Petrarch, and Boccaccio. Even the great humanist pope, Pius II, wrote a novel, *Euryalus et Lucrezia,* in the style of Boccaccio. But his imitation, like that of so many others, amounts to no more than a manner of writing current at a particular time. With Francesco Colonna (to simplify matters we shall continue to call our writer by this name) it is not a question of imitation in this sense of the word, for there is a similarity in the very point of departure which links him inwardly to his predecessors. For as in Dante, Petrarch, and Boccaccio, a profound experience of love stands at the beginning of all things. His work is also governed by the dominating, transcendent figure of a woman.

Thereby the *Hypnerotomachia* takes in, beside the humanistic and alchemical traditions, a third, namely the tradition of courtly love in the form in which it had been taken over from France and revived on Italian soil by the great Florentines.

Hence three conceptions are blended in one in the *Hypnerotomachia:* the humanistic conception of the revival of classical culture; the courtly conception of the love of women as a task; the alchemical conception of the transmutation of matter.

These three ideas, which are simply three facets of the one religious principle of transformation or rebirth, appear in the book as three superimposed strata, the humanistic being the upper or outermost, the courtly the middle, and the alchemical the lower. This order, however, must not be taken too literally, for the various strata or spheres interpenetrate. This figure of a stratification gives no more than a general impression.

The humanistic idea and its expression in Colonna in the guise of architectural theory have already been discussed. Our next step is to consider the idea of courtly love, which will prove to be of importance for the understanding of the book in its literary aspect. In speaking of "literature" in this context, we must not understand it in the modern sense, as purely conscious and aesthetic, but in the sense that literature had for the early Renaissance, as a valid expression of life really lived. Boccaccio, for instance, in spite of the apparent gaiety of his literary work, took it so seriously that in his old age it gravely troubled his conscience. To him, his romances were not merely writings; they were a fragment of life lived in pagan fashion, which, as a Christian, he was to repent in shame and despair when he came to die. In the same way, the literary form of the *Hypnerotomachia* is filled to the brim with life itself. Like a living body, it unites the inward and outward aspects of the ideas and views it unfolds, and is the expression of an experience in which the outer and the inner life interact.

The idea of courtly love as it appears in the *Hypnerotomachia* is a creation of French feudalism. The twelfth and thirteenth centuries in France saw the simultaneous development of the cult of the Virgin, the poetry of courtly love, and the predominance of noble women in political, social, and intellectual life. This emergence of the feminine principle in the church, in art, and in the forms of social life must be taken as merely simultaneous and no more. The poetry of courtly love and the predominance of women did not result from the cult of the Virgin, nor it from them. It was the spirit of the age which set its impress on every sphere of life and enabled the feminine principle to rise to peculiar power in all directions.

We are only concerned with the secular domain, and with that only in so far as it seems relevant to the understanding of the *Hypnerotomachia*. In the secular world, courtly love was at one and the same time a poetic idea, a science, and an ideal of courtly intercourse and the courtly life incumbent on both men and women. The ideal of capitalistic man in the nineteenth century, with its moral law of service to the community, was no less profound in its effect than the ideal of chivalry and the moral requirements of courtly love. For courtly love was first and foremost a moral commandment, and as such, it had the profoundest influence on the conduct of generations of human beings.

The doctrine of courtly love was established by the courts of love, which on occasion passed ingenious, realistic, and sensible verdicts on the relations between the sexes. Such verdicts were first recorded to any extent at the end of the twelfth century by Andreas Capellanus in his treatise *De Amore* with the addition of thirty-one *regulae amoris*. All later collections really go back to this.[9] The judgments by eminent women contained in this work show an insight into the necessities of love and life from which many men and women are still far remote. However lively the experience, they are thoroughly sane in tone, and we catch more than a glimpse of the realization that the individual can only put the ideal into practice in a very restricted sense. The judgments of the courts of love are an attempt to find a rational solution for the conflict which arose in courtly love between the obligation of beautiful form and the real feelings of men and women.

In literature, it is allegory which, by means of personification, best expresses the doctrines of the courts of love. Allegory is that specifically medieval mode of imagination by which typical human situations and kinds of behaviour are depicted with both poetry and common sense. The best and, as regards the *Hypnerotomachia*, most important example is the *Romance of the Rose,* which contains, in the form of fiction, something like a real theory of courtly love.

[9] Cf. Leonardo Olschky, *Die romanischen Literaturen des Mittelalters (Handbuch der Wissenschaft,* Athenaion Verlag, Berlin, 1928), pp. 102 ff. *et passim;* also *The Art of Courtly Love,* translated by John Jay Parry, New York, 1941.

Like the *Hypnerotomachia*, the *Romance of the Rose* is the story of a dream. The author, Guillaume de Lorris (c. 1240), relates how, in his twentieth year, he went wandering one May morning. On his way he came to the Garden of Love, which is enclosed within high walls on which there stand all the enemies of Love—Hatred, Envy, Malice, Avarice, Lust, Sadness, Age, and Sickness. There is a little door in the wall which is opened to the dreamer by the portress, Idleness. In the garden, he finds splendid beings, Pleasure, Joy, Beauty, etc. Cupid is there too, with the Glance of Love bearing his quiver. The dreamer joins in a dance with Wealth, Largesse, Franchise, Courtesy, and so on. Then Cupid leads him on through the garden. He comes to the fountain of Narcissus and sees in it the Rosebud, which now becomes the goal of his longing and aspiration. Cupid shoots five allegorical arrows at him, the dreamer yields and does homage, and his heart is locked with a key. Then Cupid instructs him in the rules of courtly love. A youth, Fair Welcome, offers his services to the dreamer, and the two now try to find their way to the beloved Rosebud. They are attacked by Danger, Calumny, Shame, and Fear—and Fair Welcome takes flight. The Lady Reason now exhorts the dreamer to renounce his love, but he pays no heed to her. He then finds Friend, who instructs him how to win the good graces of Danger. Venus brings Fair Welcome back again, but Calumny betrays him to Jealousy, who now builds a high keep round the Rose, locking Fair Welcome in it too along with an old woman, Vekke.

At this early stage, Guillaume de Lorris died. Jean de Meung finished the story, but in his hands it became crude and obvious. Vekke degenerates into a mere bawd. Hypocrisy is the most potent helper in the conquest of the Rosebud, whose transformation into a full-blown rose is described at the end in a way which leaves no doubt as to the meaning.

In Guillaume de Lorris' part of the *Romance of the Rose* there is a tenderness in the poetry which invests the somewhat dry allegory with charm and gives a hint of a hidden meaning. The second part owes its fame to its alluring salaciousness and to its worldliness. In any case, the influence of the *Romance of the Rose* on the contemporary and later world cannot be overestimated. It was constantly read in the Romance countries, especially in Italy, and an Italian translation, *Fiori,* has been ascribed to Dante by a number of scholars.

In addition to works of this kind, which were, in the medieval sense, doctrinal, we have the exuberant flowering of the French poetry of courtly love, which has never lost its hold on the European imagination. It is in the poetry of the north of France that we hear most clearly the echo of the emotional upheaval caused by the realization that courtly love was guilty. That love, which was the knight's noblest aim, may also be his greatest guilt, from which he can only be redeemed by suffering patiently borne, that love is an inexorable fate and unites the lovers even unto death—all this has been handed down to us in the stories of Arthur and Tristan.[10] The sense of sin impinged upon the realm of the psyche, and gave rise to the mysterious notion of a service detached from the real woman and transferred to a sacred symbol, such as we find in the legends of the Holy Grail.[11]

In Italy, this body of ideas was taken up in a merely superficial sense. A much profounder impression, on the other hand, was made by the love-poetry of the troubadours, which turns on a very different kind of problem. It expresses a deep longing for redemption from the gross compulsion of the senses, which may have been originally only too powerful. For that reason there runs through the love-poetry of

[10] Cf. Jacques Boulanger, *Les Romans de la Table Ronde,* 4 vols., Plon, Paris, 1923; Joseph Bédier, *Le Roman de Tristan et Iseult,* Ed. d'Art, Paris; Sir Thomas Malory, *Morte d'Arthur.*

[11] Cf. A. E. Waite, *The Holy Grail, its Legend and Symbolism,* Rider & Co., London, 1933.

Provence an aspiration towards refinement and nobility which triumphed in two ways. Firstly, we can recognize that aspiration in the growing exclusiveness of courtly love and its restriction to the nobility, lay and spiritual. That is why it is now veiled in mystery and expressed in wilfully obscure and artificial language, which only the man of noble birth and mind can understand. On the other hand, the idea of courtly love is refined by the rule that fruition is difficult or impossible, the beloved woman becoming ever farther removed from the lover by circumstance or inward necessity. In this way the conflict inherent in the love relation is recognized as essential to it, and at the same time spiritualized. True, the real woman is still there, but she becomes more and more the pretext of an erotic and aesthetic exaltation. Thus a situation arises in which we are never sure whether the yearning is addressed to a real human being or to the phantom of an anima.

Yet the love of the troubadours, apart from some individual cases, cannot have been a mere fiction. After all, the singers were dependent on the courts and the women who ruled them. Present reality formed them, filled them, and yet left them suspended in an unresolved tension between desire and spiritualization which found vent in their poetry in the form of longing. The finest example is Bernart de Ventadorn's (1140–1195) *Can vei la lauzeta mover,* a beautiful poem the sense of which is roughly as follows: [12]

"When I see the lark rising on glad wings towards the sun then, overcome with the sweetness in her heart, falling silent back to earth, a great envy fills me and my heart is like to melt with longing.

"Alas! I weened that I knew much of love and knew nothing, for I must love her who will never hear my prayer. She took my heart away, and with it herself and the whole

---

[12] [No verse translation is possible, since it would only distort the very intricate and beautiful form of Bernart's stanzas.—TRANS.]

world, and, having taken herself from me, she left me nought but longing and a heart full of desire.

"Once she showed me to myself in her eyes as in a wondrous mirror, and from that time I belonged no more to myself. Mirror, since I saw myself in thee, the sighs that rise from the depths of my heart have killed me, so that I am lost even as Narcissus the fair was lost in the fountain."

The image of the beloved's eyes as a mirror was a convention of the time. We shall find again, in the *Hypnerotomachia*, the same image, the same feeling, and the fountain of Narcissus.

The Italian Trecento took over from France this strange, sensuous, super-sensuous love-poetry of Provence, for until Dante's time, Italian art and culture were derived entirely from France and were entirely dependent on France. Even in the *dolce stil nuovo*, that style which, we might almost say, went beyond pure art to become a manner of life and thought, it is French seeds which are springing on Italian soil. It inaugurated in Italy an epoch in which woman and the feminine principle took their place in the foreground beside man and the masculine principle, just as they had done in France. In this sense, medieval chivalry and the cult of delicately cultivated women dominated Italy up to the mid-Renaissance. There is, however, one difference: this Italian chivalry was not confined to one social class. In Italy, chivalry and the fascination of women were bound up with personal power and personal culture. Lorenzo the Magnificent was dreaming the dream of chivalry when, in 1475, he held the great tournament in honour of Simonetta which Angelo Poliziano immortalized in the *Stanze per la Giostra*. Even that fierce pagan Sigismondo Malatesta bowed to its decrees when he turned the church of San Francesco di Rimini into a love temple in honour of his idolized wife

Isotta, transforming all the angels into cupids. *Divae Isottae Sacrum*—such is the inscription on the church, and the wealth of intertwined initials of Sigismondo and Isotta bears witness, not to the love of God, but to the eternal triumph of courtly love over the grave and the passing of the beloved. There is an abundance of examples of the kind, down to the famous Vittoria Colonna, who was the high lady of many a great man. These were the contemporaries of our author, and their dream of love, like his, points back to the poets of Tuscany who called themselves *fedeli d'amore*.

The *fedeli d'amore* (i.e. the group of poets to which Dante belonged as a young man) were the first to define the Italian conception of courtly love so clearly that we may really speak of a theory. In his book, *Die romanischen Literaturen des Mittelalters,* Olschky says:

"[The doctrine of courtly love] reflects in poetry the two trends of the Italian culture of the age, the rational and didactic, which had risen to pre-eminence in the schools under Dominican leadership, and the spiritual and mystic, which owed its rise and conquests to the Franciscan movement. These currents of thought and feeling conflicted as little as the orders themselves, which worked side by side and were complementary to each other. . . . While the rational school was founded on Aristotle and Thomas Aquinas, the other drew on Neoplatonic doctrines which had passed into Christian mysticism by way of St. Augustine and the pseudo-Areopagite. Heavenly and earthly love were reconciled in its spirit, as love of the creator and love of the creature are reconciled in the Hymn of St. Francis, for even the beauty of the transitory is a divine emanation, and the contemplation of that beauty is one of the ways by which the soul can be—in the language of the mystics—in-Godded. As earthly beauty is a reflection of the heavenly, earthly love is a stage in the progress of the soul and its object is sacred. True, only noble hearts *(cor gentil)* can attain this love, but on the other hand it justifies the sensual view and presupposes a corporeal being as a condition of the ecstatic vision. Hence the women worshipped by the poets in this fashion certainly appear as ideas, pure intelligences, angelic abstractions, yet it is just in this mystic, Neoplatonic sense that they cannot be regarded as mere figures of the imagination, as allegories and fictions. Their existence as living beings can be postulated from these teachings, even if their image appears in the poems of their worshippers in purely spiritualized form. The sincerity of the *stil nuovo* which Dante praises consists, in contrast to the merely courtly and didactic lyric, in the real experience underlying its spiritualized poetry.

"For that reason, the women always appear in their double nature, earthly and spiritual, and *amore* is both a sensual impression and a mystic goal. Thus we can understand how religious feeling often comes to pervade secular poems. . . . In the spiritualized sphere of the *stil nuovo* the problem of *amour* as we find it in Provence and the *Roman de la Rose* has deepened into a philosophy which gave rise, within the poem, to philosophic speculation and a peculiar dialectic."

The great Florentines, especially Dante, took the troubadours' conception of courtly love far more seriously than the troubadours did themselves. The courtly convention still held good for them, living on the threshold of a new age, yet it held good no longer. What had been, in the eyes of the French poets and nobles, purely outward form, whether as poetry, magnificence, or a collective ideal, and had been put into action in the pageantry of court festivals, appeared even at the beginning of the Italian Renaissance in a much more personal sphere, and strove with growing urgency to turn inward. This inwardness was only achieved in the vision of the greatest and best of the children of reawakening Italy, where Dante, for instance, first took over the French rules of courtly love very literally, only to enlarge them in a quite new, symbolic sense.

As in the French poets, we find in Dante the idea of love as fate, of an *amor* from whose stern dominion no man can escape. Not only he, but Petrarch, Boccaccio, and other poets give a quite concrete suggestion of this in the solemnity of the circumstances attending the first sight of the beloved. It takes place in a church or is, as in the *Vita Nuova*, enframed in a multiple mysticism of numbers. As in the troubadours, the beloved one is wrapped in noble secrecy; she is unattainable or dead, and her name is not divulged. With the Florentines, this has ceased to be a social convention. The experience of love becomes a personal obligation, connected in Dante with spiritual growth and in Petrarch or Boccaccio with artistic achievement. The actual woman who is the object of the experience exists and is as real as she can be, but she exists only as a catalyst which effects a transformation in the substance of the soul or the poet's creation. And as the catalyst does not itself combine with the chemical substance it transforms, the woman who effects the transformation must remain remote and unknown. All the same, she exists.

This is the "double nature" of women and of love of which Olschky speaks. It springs from a strange simultaneity of utter renunciation and the sensual passion which safeguards reality. This tenacious hold on a concrete cause even in spiritual things would seem to be a characteristic of the Southern mind, and sharply distinguishes it from everything Northern. While the German, for instance, must painfully seek the matter into which his spirit may bring forth, and is exposed in doing so to the gravest aberrations, the sensuality and emotionalism of the Italian are simply too pronounced and too highly developed even to present a problem. The result is that the sensuality and the emotionalism of the Southern peoples are apt to grow hollow and superficial, and need a special incentive if they are to acquire depth.

As an example of the Italian romance of courtly love, the *Hypnerotomachia* closely follows its great Italian models. By effecting a profound transformation in the hero of the book, Polia, its heroine, is a sister of Dante's Beatrice. And because at the same time the joys of the senses and the feeling for reality revive and take shape in the mind of the monk Francesco Colonna, it is Boccaccio who provides him with the best model for the form of his story. Yet with all its borrowings, the *Hypnerotomachia* is the record of actual experience.

The genuineness of the experience can be discerned through the borrowed form mainly by the remarkable consistency in the events of the dream. They follow upon each other naturally and by necessity, like the leaves of a plant in growth. This is truly surprising, for the book contains no purely unconscious fantasies or visions. The presentation in the form of a dream goes back to a tradition which had its own specific import. We have seen, for instance, that the *Romance of the Rose* gives instruction in courtly love and life in the form of a dream. We find other works of a didactic character cast into the form of a dream in the *Tesoretto* of Brunetto Latini, who was Dante's teacher. The lady who guides the dreamer is Nature; the book is a code of morals and contains moral exhortations. By giving the opening of his *Divina Commedia* a similar form to that of the *Tesoretto*, Dante gives us to understand that he, dreaming like his teacher, is about to pronounce universal truths. Petrarch's *Trionfi*, one of his last works, is also a dream; sleeping in a spring meadow and guided by his transfigured Laura, he sees the forces which move men—love, chastity, death, fame, and divinity. We find in Boccaccio's *Corbacchio* a dream beginning in exactly the same way as the *Tesoretto* and the

Divina Commedia, which imparts the doctrine of womankind with virulent malice. Thus dreams are works which impart knowledge, doctrine, and truth. The idea that this must be done in the form of a dream would seem to rest on the Thomistic view that man cannot know all things but only a few, and that it requires a divine decree for him to perceive the relation between them. Now according to the most ancient view, dreams are inspirations, and when didactic works are cast in the form of a dream, it is a subtle reminder that the general knowledge they contain has been accorded to the author by divine decree. In this sense, namely as a didactic work, the *Hypnerotomachia* is a dream too. It presents its author's knowledge in narrative form—his knowledge of architecture, classical art and mythology, natural history, and philosophy. It is the product of spacious learning, yet it is, as we would say, popularized. Its great symbolic importance, however, does not rest on this didactic content of the story, but on the sequence of the visions which, on closer study, shows a strict logical continuity that no artifice of the author's could produce. If he arranges and applies these visions in this and no other way, it is because he is obeying an inward voice, such as Dante described in the *Divina Commedia:*

"I am one who, when Love breathes in me, notes it and expounds it after whatever manner he dictates." [13]

There is a further point. When our author was writing, it was far easier for a secret meaning to creep into a didactic work than it would be today. It was but a thin curtain which at that time separated consciousness from the unconscious. The various fields of knowledge interpenetrated, thought was tinged with religion, science with poetry. In the same way, heart was linked to head, and the background of things lay close to the foreground. That is why we sense the symbolism of the *Hypnerotomachia,* even though it was not

---

[13] *Purgatorio,* Canto 23.

meant as a symbolic work. We should be doing it an injustice in overlooking its symbolic character, just because it is an involuntary growth and therefore is the pure and genuine expression of the soul. On the other hand, it is all the more important to discover as definitely as possible what may have belonged to the consciousness of the age, so that at any rate some rough distinction may be drawn between its foreground and the background which projects into it.

We have already discussed two of these "foreground regions," humanism and the tradition of courtly love. It only remains for us to briefly consider the third, alchemy.

We know from alchemical treatises that there were many kinds of alchemy. To some, it meant the crucible of the gold maker, and a means by which fools and mountebanks might gain wealth and prestige. To others, alchemy was the secret way of a rebirth, it was the Great Work in which the adept was involved, in action and in suffering. As he put forward all his powers in his struggle with matter, it became the mirror of his unconscious, and his work the moving symbol of the change and liberation of his self.[14] Apart from these two extremes, however, alchemy was also that branch of science out of which medicine and, later, chemistry grew. Further, at the time of the *Hypnerotomachia,* it offered a means of expression, or a figurative language, in which all educated men could express with ease everything they knew about the psyche. When we reflect how few men of that age really became masters of alchemy, yet how familiar and interesting the world of alchemy was to most cultivated people, we may perhaps find the closest analogy to the subject in the psychology of our day, which is a science, yet may at times degenerate into jargon. Just as we speak today

[14] Cf. C. G. Jung, *Psychology and Alchemy.*

of complexes, projections, and functions, and, approaching a strange and disturbing potentiality, neutralize by naming it, men of that day spoke of chaos, red mercury, of elements and operations, knowing, without in the least understanding, what was behind it all. It was the right thing for educated people to dabble in alchemy or in astrology, which was the same thing. It was a scientific pursuit, but there was about it something of the fascination arising from the secret of the psyche, which was, for the men of that time, enclosed within the alchemist's symbolism. Like psychology today, it was the most disputed of sciences. In some it led to a salutary inner crisis, others it misled into abuses, aberrations, and the jargon of the charlatan.

As regards alchemy in Italy, we may say that there is evidence to show that it made its appearance and was practised there very early, perhaps as early as the eleventh century. Jakob Burckhardt attributes the early disappearance of alchemy in Italy to its early rise—as if it had been like a disease which had its course to run. It is certain that, from the fourteenth century onward, alchemy was in bad odour in Italy. Dante, for instance, relegates the alchemist to the lowest circle of Hell.[15] But that is not the whole story, for the public rejection of alchemy was an act of prudence towards the church and by no means excluded private practice. The literature of the Quattrocento would in itself suffice to prove how actively the Italians were interested in alchemy at the time, for it abounds in alchemical expressions and figures of speech. One example is Boccaccio's romances, in which the figurative language of alchemy re-echoes remarkably often.

The industrious monk who wrote the *Hypnerotomachia* had obviously practised alchemy as a science and taken it

[15] For other condemnatory or contemptuous judgments, cf. O. Lippmann, *Entstehung und Ausbreitung der Alchemie,* Springer, Berlin, 1919.

seriously. The book displays a remarkable knowledge of the subject, not only as regards its fundamental symbolism, but also in the form of an extensive lore of plants, herbs, and stones. Further, it is planned out in stages not unlike the famous *Turba Philosophorum*.[16] That is why, as we have seen, its author was claimed as a fellow labourer in the field by the later French alchemists. Nor were they alone in doing so. Even the Italian alchemist, Giovanni Battista Nazari, drew largely on the *Hypnerotomachia* in his little work *Della tramutatione metallica*,[17] especially in the *sogno terzo*.

Hence in our author's book, scientific alchemy plays a large part. It is certainly not the leading part, but by the fascination which alchemy exercised outside of its purely scientific aspect, it might, more than any other science, lead a man of the Renaissance to his profoundest experience, namely to the secret of classical antiquity. Besides, alchemy has preserved a classical mode of thought in its conception of matter as possessing life or soul. It is mainly from this point of view that the alchemy in the *Hypnerotomachia* is important and leads up to its central experience. But as the book proceeds, we can see the alchemical symbolism, which was so clear and significant at the beginning, growing steadily thinner and more superficial, and even degenerating into jargon, while an aspect of classical antiquity unknown to the author, and at first concealed behind it, steadily gains in force.

The antique fulness of life, however, which attracts the liveliest interest in this work of a humanist, forms at the same time the dark background, charged with emotion and surmise, from which everything in it springs. In the *Hypnerotomachia*, classical antiquity appears, as it were, in twofold

---

[16] In *Artis Ariferae etc.*, Basilea, 1593, vol. prim.
[17] Brescia, appreso Marchetti frat. 1572.

guise. Firstly, it is that classical culture which, as has already been described, was the goal of the humanist's aspiration and longing, but secondly, and more mysteriously, it was the experience of the religious life of the ancients as revealed in the old mystery cults. This second, secret aspect of the ancient world, however, forms no part of the foreground phenomena which the dreaming Poliphilo of the *Hypnerotomachia* describes in images. It is the symbol of the living process of growth which had been set going, obscurely and incomprehensibly, in the men of his time and had made of the Renaissance the beginning of a new era.

We must not, however, anticipate in this introductory chapter the element of the ancient mysteries which comes to complete, as a region of liberation and a fourth, the three foreground regions of humanism, courtly love, and alchemy. In company with our author we must find our way towards it, and discover it as he did himself, as an elixir of life for himself and his age.

The following summary of the *Hypnerotomachia* must of necessity be strictly limited to essentials, for its world of images is so profuse that any attempt to grasp them all would be to embark on the infinite. We must therefore sacrifice a host of illuminating and charming details which actually give the book its peculiar character and make of it a veritable labyrinth of inventions and allusions.[18] Even the architectural side can only be taken into account in so far as it enters into the illustrations, for it is mainly through the illustrations

[18] For those who are interested in the actual text, there is Claudius Popelin's extremely scholarly translation, which has already been referred to. It would appear to be absolutely satisfactory. Popelin's translation comprises 800 pages of letterpress. It is literal, if perhaps a little too elegant. There are also illuminating notes explaining the countless scientific, literary, and mythological allusions, most of which are incomprehensible to the modern reader. In this connection, it might

that the architectural element comes into the foreground.[19]

Further, it will not be possible to leave the discussion and summary of the contents to the end. In the way characteristic of ordinary dreams, Poliphilo's dream follows on in an unbroken stream; indeed the profusion of images swells into a flood which at times threatens to drown the reader. The writer himself attempted to reduce them to some kind of order by a division into chapters, but he was too helpless under the impact of the psychic events to master them completely. Hence his chapter divisions are often meaningless, and cut across the thread of coherence. We cannot therefore follow him at this point, but must try to master the wealth of action by dividing the *Hypnerotomachia* into sections which correspond to its organic structure. This division arises to a certain extent spontaneously from the march of events in the dream, which proceed from sphere to sphere, each sphere being marked by a cardinal symbol. The reader will find these, the most important images of the *Hypnerotomachia,* in the section headings of the present volume, which thus give a survey of the most important dream symbols in sequence.[20] The synopsis of the contents of each section is followed by a very brief commentary. Further, as far as possible these synopses are given in the words of the original, or at any rate an attempt has been made to render their prevailing mood.

The language in which the *Hypnerotomachia* is written

be well to point out that the present study does not set out to be a work of philosophical or literary learning. It is strictly confined to the psychological interpretation yielded by a close and exceedingly careful examination of the original text. For that reason a considerable number of special studies of Poliphilo's Dream have not been taken into account.

[19] According to Popelin, the numerous woodcuts in the book are in all probability the work of a goldsmith of the Bolognese school. Cf. Jos. Poppelreuter, *Der anonyme Meister des Poliphilo,* Strassburg, 1904, which puts forward the school of Mantegna with Venetian influence. The illustrations in the present volume are but a fraction of those contained in the original edition of 1499.

[20] For a synopsis of the events of the dream as a whole, see Contents.

is a highly personal form of a north Italian dialect,[21] so interspersed with Latinisms and even with Greek words that it results in an extremely idiosyncratic style which is an organic part of the work. This style itself shows that the author has attempted to express wonderful and very exceptional matters. Only the title of the book is in Latin, apart from the word coined of Greek elements described above. The title runs:

POLIPHILI HYPNEROTOMACHIA. UBI HUMANA OMNIA NON NISI SOMNIUM ESSE OSTENDIT, ATQUE OBITER PLURIMA SCITU SANE QUAM DIGNA COMMEMORAT

(This is the *Hypnerotomachia* of Poliphilo, which teaches that all things human are but a dream, and in which many things are set forth which it is salutary and meet to know)[22]

[21] Cf. C. Popelin, *La Songe de Poliphile*, Introduction, pp. 172 ff.
[22] See title-page to the original edition, which is reproduced in the present volume on page xvii.

PART I

SECTION I

The Ruined City

(His thoughts full of the divine Polia, Poliphilo falls asleep and dreams that he is lost in a wild, dark forest. By prayer, he finds his way out. He is startled by a wolf in a palm-grove. He comes to a ruined city of the ancient world. Poliphilo enters a porch and finds himself in darkness. His way back is cut off by a triple-tongued dragon. He roams about in gloomy vaults. Under a lamp he sees three golden statues. He finds the opening which leads out of the gloomy vaults.)

(Chapter 1) A prey to the turmoil in his mind, Poliphilo lies tossing on his couch till nearly dawn. He is alone save for his faithful companion, sleeplessness. Finally, his thoughts turn to the divine Polia. He summons up her image, which lives in him, fills him utterly and is graven on his heart. The thought of Polia brings him repose and sleep, and Poliphilo's love-dream begins:

He dreams that he is standing in a spreading plain. The scene is beautiful, yet he feels uneasy, for there is neither man nor beast in sight. He wanders on and on, and suddenly finds himself in the midst of a wild, dark forest (Fig. 1). This can be none other than the Harz (*Hercynia silva*), which, as he knows, is swarming with beasts of prey. Poliphilo hurries to find a way out of the forest, but he cannot, and in his fear he begins to run, faster and ever faster. Again and again he stumbles, thorns scratch his face and hands, and he is hampered by his long gown, which catches on every bush.

(Chapter 2) Faint and trembling from his long search for

Fig. 1. Poliphilo in the Forest

the way, he at last begins to pray. He calls for help on Diespiter,[1] in whom alone he trusts. He prays—and the forest vanishes. But this relief only serves to make Poliphilo aware of his raging thirst. He seeks for water, and finds a brook which is soon swollen into a river by tributaries from the neighbouring mountains. He is on the point of drinking when he hears in the distance a melodious sound, so sweet that everything else is blotted from his mind. He follows it, hurrying hither and thither, for the sound flits from place to place.

Overcome by the heat, and again tortured by thirst, he sinks down under an oak, despairing of his fate. Finally, he submits to it. He thinks over all his wanderings, and in doing so, falls asleep under the tree. Thus his first sleep is fol-

[1] This is an analogy to the initiatory prayers customary in alchemical literature.

lowed by a second, in which the action moves on to another plane.[2]

(Chapter 3) The second sleep bears Poliphilo into a pleasanter region, springing green with trees, bushes, and healing herbs. Near the middle of the plain he finds a grove of palms of the kind that was so precious to the ancient Egyptians.

Suddenly a wolf dashes out of the grove, so hideous to look upon that Poliphilo's hair stands on end (Fig. 2). He tries to scream, but his tongue cleaves to the roof of his mouth. Yet hardly does the wolf catch sight of Poliphilo when it flees back into the grove. Poliphilo is reassured, and now sees great ruins of the ancient world spread out before him in hilly country. They lie enclosed between rocky heights, above which a shining obelisk towers (Fig. 3). Round about, there lie fallen statues overgrown with fresh verdure, with lizards rustling among them.

Awe-struck, Poliphilo approaches the largest building, which occupies the whole space between the rocky heights. Above its broad front there rises a wonderful step-pyramid, 3000 paces in circumference and 1410 steps high. It is surmounted by a cube with sides four paces long which serves as a plinth to the obelisk. The obelisk is crowned by a winged nymph of gilt copper. There is a profusion of curls on the nymph's forehead, but the back of her head is bald.

The entire plinth of the pyramid is hewn out of the virgin rock. It is entered by a huge porch surmounted by a great head of Medusa, whose open jaws form the entrance to the pyramid. The interior of the pyramid is light, and accessible in all its parts, so that the dreamer can mount up to the obelisk with perfect ease. Poliphilo at once goes up through the jaws of the Medusa, though a feeling of giddiness troubles

---

[2] The principal literary parallels to this opening are to be seen in Boccaccio's *Corbaccio* and Dante's *Divina Commedia*. Dante too falls asleep twice at the beginning of his journey; the second time is during the crossing of the Acheron.

Fig. 2. Poliphilo and the Wolf

him. And now something strange happens; he hardly dares to look down from above, for everything below, at that distance, looks indistinct.

At the foot of the obelisk, Poliphilo discovers an inscription saying that it is dedicated to the sun. There too he finds the name of the architect of the whole; it is Lychas the Libyan.

(Chapter 4) Poliphilo slowly redescends from the obelisk and gazes at the magnificent statues lying round the pyramid. The plinth of the pyramid with the great porch is covered with decorative reliefs. Among them there are figures of maidens who remind Poliphilo so vividly of his beloved Polia that he sighs in sadness. In front of this splendid building there is a space surrounded by double colonnades in which Poliphilo finds the following symbolic figures:

First there is a winged horse of copper which little chil-

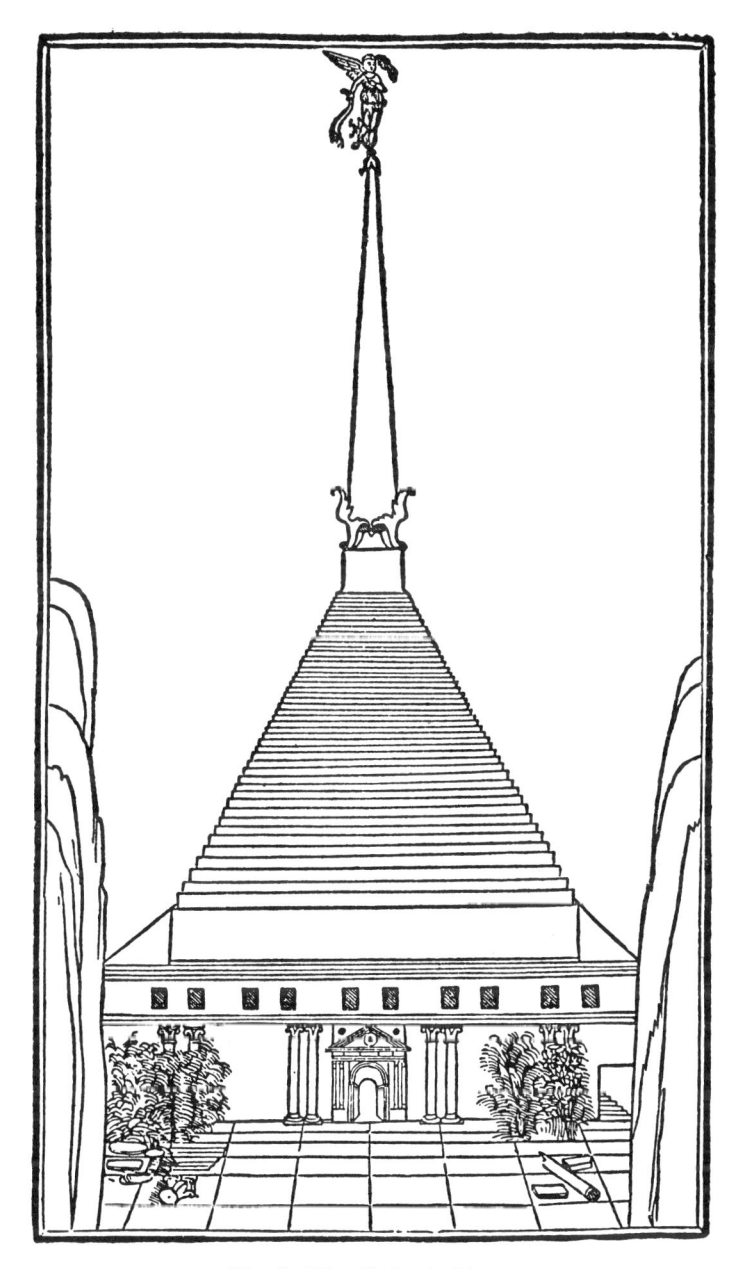

Fig. 3. The Ruined City

Fig. 4. Relief on the Plinth of the Winged Horse

dren are struggling in vain to mount. On the horse's forehead there is inscribed the word "Generations." There are two reliefs on its pedestal, one showing human beings with double faces looking forward and backward; they form a circle by crossing their arms in such a way that the men hold the men's hands, the women the women's (Fig. 4). The title of this relief is "Time." The other relief shows youths and maidens picking flowers, and bears the title "Loss."

The second thing that Poliphilo sees is a bronze colossus. Terrifying groans issue from it, but Poliphilo realizes that it is only the wind blowing through the figure. The colossus represents a hideous middle-aged man lying on the ground, with only his head slightly raised above it. The figure is hollow, it can be entered, and Poliphilo finds in it models of all the organs, nerves, diseases, and remedies for them noted exactly in three languages. When he reaches the heart, the thought of Polia returns. He calls upon her, groaning aloud, the colossus reverberates horribly, and Poliphilo flees in terror.

Beside this colossus there lies a second, the figure of a woman, but only the forehead and a small part of the head can be seen. The rest is buried in the earth.

The third thing to be seen near the horse is a lustrous black elephant bearing a small obelisk on its back (Fig. 5). The inscriptions on it run "The brain is in the head" and "Work and Diligence. The elephant too is hollow, and Poliphilo enters it. In its hind quarters a light is burning, under which the crowned figure of a black man stands on a sarcophagus bearing the inscription: "I would have been naked had the beast not covered me. Seek and thou shalt find. Leave me in peace." In the elephant's head there is a second light with a female figure under it pointing behind her, with the inscription: "Whosoever thou mayst be, take of this treasure as much as thou willst. Yet I warn thee, take from the head and touch not the body." The sight of these two figures fills Poliphilo with awe, and he goes away deep in thought.

From the very outset, he has been fascinated by the great porch in the base of the pyramid. He now hastens to look at it, and for a long time remains lost in the harmony of its proportions. Then he proceeds to describe in detail the scenes depicted on it. (Chapter 5) These cannot be given here in full; they are all mythological in nature and reminiscent of Ovid's *Metamorphoses*. The porch is surmounted by an inscription which runs:

Diis Veneri, filio Amori, Bacchus et Ceres de propriis (s. substantiis) Matri pientissimae.[3]

---

[3] "To the pious Mother Venus and her son Amor, Bacchus and Ceres have given of their own substance." The inscription is given in two languages, the first being Greek. To simplify matters in this volume, in bilingual inscriptions only the Latin version is given.

Fig. 5. The Black Elephant

Through the porch a vista of deep and vast vaults opens before Poliphilo's eyes. Can it be that the altar with the flame dedicated to Venus is in those depths? Poliphilo asks, and at once enters. A white mouse runs across his path, but he pays no heed to it, for he is enthralled by another sight. The smooth walls of the interior of the porch contain black mirrors of polished stone, in which Poliphilo sees his own reflection from both sides, right and left. Though startled by this unexpected sight of his own image, he goes on to the inner end of the porch, where all the sculptured decorations come to an end. It is now so dark that he does not venture farther, and is just turning back when, to his horror, he sees that he is being followed by a frightful, triple-tongued dragon whose scaly tail rattles along the floor. It beats its wings and gnashes its huge teeth. Poliphilo's way is cut off. Trembling, his hair on end, he plunges into the darkness (Fig. 6).

In the echoing stone vaults he roams about blindly, maddened by the darkness and in desperate fear of the dragon. Is he to die here, losing with his life his beloved Polia? Ah! bitter, double loss! But suddenly he begins to pray, calling on all the gods, and his prayer is at once answered. He sees a faint light and hurries towards it. Yet what he finds is not a way out of the dark vaults, but an altar faintly illuminated by glimmering light in the twilight halls of rock. Three golden statues are enthroned on the altar. There, in the holy gloom, Poliphilo pronounces a prayer before the altar. It would seem that his prayer is answered, for he descries in the distance a little opening which seems to lead from the depths into the open air. The mere sight of this opening revives his spirits, his thoughts of death vanish, love reawakens in his heart, and he even hopes that he may find again what seemed for ever lost to him.

As he hurries towards it, he sees that the little opening is a wide and very ancient exit. Poliphilo rushes through it

Fig. 6. Poliphilo Flees from the Triple-Tongued Dragon

into the open air, hurrying on and ever on because he is still possessed by his dread of the dragon.

COMMENTARY TO SECTION I

The story begins with a description of Poliphilo beset by warring thoughts and tormented by sleeplessness. Not one of us in our own day but has met with human beings in this painful state. It is the commonest thing in the world, yet it might be very significant, as Poliphilo's example will show. We are prone to say of people in this condition that they are suffering from overwork or nervous strain—what they need is relaxation. Most likely, but from what? In Poliphilo's case it would seem to be the intellect that is tormenting him. A storm has broken out in his mind that he cannot quell by thinking, for it is obviously a storm of conflicting thoughts, and there is nothing to tell him which to accept and which to reject. In other words, Poliphilo is in a state of mental conflict. For a man of learning whose supreme value is in the functioning of his reason, such torment is grievous indeed. For the moment, however, there seems to be no issue to the conflict. Poliphilo is in an impasse and can find no way out. We are not told the nature of the conflict. We only learn that it is the image of Polia that brings release. She is the woman whom Poliphilo loves. Thus he is released from his intellectual conflict by moving into the totally different sphere of feeling, where everything is of one kind, flows from one source, and makes for one goal. Here the conflict of irreconcilable thoughts comes to an end, and the tension in the overwrought consciousness is relaxed. Here, by the intermediary of feeling, the link with the unconscious, which has clearly been lost, is restored. Our story expresses this by the transition from sleeplessness to sleep.

Polia is presented from the outset as a familiar figure. Poliphilo simply calls her the Divine Lady whose image is graven on his heart. This one short sentence is an obvious allusion to the tradition of courtly love discussed in the introduction to the present volume. Polia is the noble lady whom Poliphilo loves and longs for as one unattainable.[4]

The word Polia may be an allusion to the name of Hippolita, which was possibly that of the actual woman the writer loved. But beyond this possibly personal origin, the word contains the most manifold suggestions. πολός means

---

[4] At this early stage, Polia is also referred to as an "idea" in the Platonic sense. But as it becomes clear later that the Platonism of the Renaissance had only a superficial appeal to our author, the Platonic aspect of his work will be left to a brief discussion in Part II.

white, shining, like sea-surf; it also means white-haired and is used to express age. Applied to the actual woman Poliphilo loves, the name "white, shining" would seem to be an allusion to the transfiguration of her required by convention. Further, if we reflect that this story is also a humanistic treatise, this white-haired, aged woman becomes a personification of classical antiquity. On the other hand, if we try to find its meaning in terms of alchemy, Polia is a "white woman," one of the most frequent symbols in the alchemical treatises, where, in conjunction with that of the "red man," it stands for the feminine principle of that archetypal duality which effects transformation and is itself transformed.[5] The astronomical aspect of this shining white feminine image is Luna, the queen of night, and Polia reveals herself in this function by bestowing sleep. Further, the name Polia contains a hint of an origin in the sea-foam, like that of Aphrodite. Thus both moon and water are component elements in the image of Polia.

All these things are facets of the one figure of a beloved woman, which draws to itself all the vital forces of the man as in a great meditation.

All things proceed from the One through the meditation on the One—so runs one of the most frequently quoted precepts of the *Tabula Smaragdina*.[6] The One from which all things proceed is, for Poliphilo as for Dante, the Beloved. From this standpoint, the love of these Italians is—to use an Indian term—a yantra, i.e. an instrument of devotion and introspection. The attitude they take up towards it recalls the beautiful story of the Indian lover related by

[5] Cf. the Beja in the *Visio Arislei* in C. G. Jung, *Psychology and Alchemy*.

[6] J. Ruska, *Tabula Smaragdina* (Heidelberg, 1926), p. 2: "And as all things proceed from the One by the meditation on the One; from this One all things proceeded by being created in the likeness of the One."

Heinrich Zimmer in his *Weisheit Indiens* (Wittich Verlag, Darmstadt, 1938):

One night, a Prince, hastening to his beloved, stumbles over a yogi in prayer, who shouts at him in rage. "I implore your pardon," says the Prince, "I am hurrying on my way to a woman who holds all my senses captive. My heart sees her alone, therefore I am blind to all that is outside me. But how comes it that thou canst mark what is passing outside of thee when thou art lost in the contemplation of God?" The yogi had no answer to give him, but the Prince became a saint. Bidding farewell to his beloved, he said: "Thou hast been more than my great delight. Thou hast been my teacher, for it is thou who taught my soul to love God." [7]

This is exactly what is meant when the image of Polia brings repose and sleep to Poliphilo at the beginning of the book. Contemplating her image in the spirit, he sinks into meditation.

The goal of meditation is higher knowledge, wider in sight, which can release man from the clash of his opposites. We may certainly infer that this is meant from the fact that the beginning of the dream so closely follows both the *Divina Commedia* and the *Tesoretto,* which are the great didactic poems of the Italian masters. As in the *Divina Commedia,* the basic assumption operative in it is that the world is the correspondent to the individual human being and that outward events mirror the soul. Hence, like the *Divina Commedia,* the *Hypnerotomachia* has from the very beginning a double meaning, outward (macrocosmic) and inward (microcosmic).

The arid plain, the dark forest, in which the dreamer wanders, are not only the images of the desolate, confusing world in which man is involved; they are at the same time the image of the sadness and darkness of the soul. That it should be the Harz, a German forest, that is named would

---

[7] Abridged.

seem to derive from humanistic ideas. The humanists, Petrarch among them, rediscovered the ancient conception of barbarism. For the Italians of that age, it was the Germans who were the barbarians. The invasions of the Germanic tribes which had struck into the vital nerve of the country and paralysed it for centuries were still a living memory. The north of Italy was still full of German nobles. The disproportionate number of foreigners was branded by the humanists as the abomination of desolation, and they called upon their own genius to rebel against it. Indeed, the humanists were as a whole great patriots. It is this range of ideas which is alluded to in the image of the Harz forest, which at the same time bodies forth the desolation and barbarism of the man estranged from himself, the melancholy which terrifies him until, by meditation, the wilderness is made to blossom with a life as yet unknown, symbolized by the images of the brook, the sound, and the tree. The symbols of running water and the sound mean, firstly and quite simply, that by meditation something within that very melancholy is being set in motion,[8] both in the lower, more emotional sphere of the human being as in the higher, spiritual sphere. The tree indicates that this is a natural growth which has come about without any action on his part and even without his knowledge. That, however, is as yet beyond the dreamer's comprehension; all he can do is to surrender to it. The self-surrender of the great scholar to the unknown, however, is a feat which at once bears fruit.

The dreamer falls into a second, deeper sleep. This suggests a deepening meditation, promising a deeper insight, which now appears in the dream as the second, more beautiful and fertile plain. This entrance into a second plain is an image of a change of level and also marks a turning-point. In meditation, the attention turns away from consciousness

[8] That melancholy is beneficial or even healing was a view with which even the ancients were familiar—it emerges also from Dürer's beautiful engraving.

to the depths of the unconscious, which brings fresh life to a consciousness devastated by conflict.

The grove of palms of the kind so precious to the ancient Egyptians points to the fact that the unconscious contains ancient wisdom, which is, like sweet dates, a food that can sustain life. The medicinal herbs round about give the dreamer, as he hesitates, the promise of eventual healing. He needs this solace and encouragement, for the first tangible image from the unconscious that presents itself is the grisly wolf.

To the age of Poliphilo, the wolf was the symbol of greed and ravening lust. It is in this significance that it appears at the beginning of the *Divina Commedia* and is cursed even in the *Purgatorio:*

> *Accursed be thou, hoary wolf,*
> *Seizing more prey than any other beast,*
> *For thy ravening which knows no end.*

These are the words which Dante uses of the wolf when he is already approaching Paradise and recalls for the last time the raging desire that once nearly cost him his immortal bliss.

To the Dominican author of our book, the wolf had a still more special meaning. *Domini canes*—faithful sheepdogs of the Good Shepherd—such was the name given to these monks, while the heretics in whom the devil dwelt were called wolves in contrast. In the heretics, the Dominicans were, so to speak, fighting the devil himself. Thus if the image of a wolf appears at this point, it means first and foremost that a heresy, or even the devil himself, may be threatening the Dominican. But this heresy is also a raging desire. It is all the sinful lust of the world.

That a wolf should appear and vanish at this moment in the *Hypnerotomachia* is a kind of symbolic pointer to some fierce and evil lust in the dreamer. Then, as Poliphilo goes on his way, we learn what the object of that lust is.

The sequence of images in dreams and visions always reveals a definite connection between the unconscious contents that are being raised into consciousness. This connection, however, can only be inferred by long reflection. In our story, what follows immediately upon the image of the wolf is the great vision of the ruined city. It would therefore appear that the object of the lust is what that image stands for. Poliphilo calls the ruins he sees before him the remains of an antique city. They are, he tells us, ancient buildings, surrounded by colonnades, in which some columns still stand in their classical splendour.[9] Now as we know, the humanists flung themselves upon the remains of the classical world with an avidity we can hardly imagine today. The scattered remains of the antique world were to them the loveliest and most desirable of things. Nor does Poliphilo weary of describing his delight at the sight of the ruined city. But when he proceeds to describe the splendours spread out before him, we begin to wonder whether they really are the remains of a classical city. A step-pyramid of gigantic proportions soars upward, an obelisk points to heaven, while above it, the figure of a nymph leads the eye still farther upward. This is an extremely pronounced vertical which was never born of the classical spirit; no such thing even

---

[9] The sculptures and buildings described in the book are always accompanied by peculiar hieroglyphic reliefs. These are emblems, some single, some placed side by side, each with an appropriate motto. Poliphilo describes these hieroglyphics as a kind of aphorism, and in each case gives a careful description of the scene depicted and the aphorism. Further, the reliefs themselves are symbolic in character, since they anticipate future events in brief form while indicating the right attitude to be taken towards them, as many dreams do. It is for that reason that these hieroglyphic reliefs would repay the special study which space forbids here.

existed in the ancient world. That is why classical forms fail the author in his description. He has to call in the aid of Egyptian elements in order to reach the bright height he is aiming at. Yet he *calls* this daring construction of fantasy a classical building. He means it seriously, and therefore we must accept it as such while recognizing that the ruined city is not a picture of true classical antiquity but a symbol of what classical antiquity meant to the humanist of our dream —what he hoped from it and projected into it. It is the wealth of hidden meaning, of desires and projections, which, in spite of the author's protestations, makes the ruined city unclassical, and hence confusing to the reader.

Above all, however, we are struck by the way this huge pile soars. It is here that we can most clearly recognize the alien, unclassical element that has invaded the description. This steep rise to heaven does not correspond to the classical, but to the medieval Christian mind, the most outstanding characteristic of which was the upward and forward movement. Just as, for the medieval mind, all man's thought turned on God, man's whole will was directed towards immortal bliss. The earth lay in darkness; light only came with the approach to heaven. This is the superb vertical familiar to us in the Gothic cathedrals as the expression of a system of learning, knowledge, and ideas which are all oriented to the other world.

That spirit, however, is the spirit of our dreamer too. In spite of all the changes of time, he is a Christian, therefore he cannot but see the spirit of antiquity from the standpoint of the spirit that generations have implanted in him. It appears to him as a summit, yet not a summit as classical antiquity knew it, but of the kind familiar to him as a Christian. Hence the spirit of classical antiquity appears to him simply as his own Christian, heaven-soaring spirit. All he sees in it is a means to a still greater, still loftier, still more intense spiritualization than the Middle Ages could give him with their highly developed philosophical mode of thought.

What he expects from his plunge into classical antiquity is still more clarity, still more light than he has already. That is why he hurries up through the pyramid to a peak—we might almost say, an extreme—from which everything below him looks indistinct.

This is a situation which closely resembles the intellectual pride of a large number of men in our own day. It is a situation in which conscious knowledge is credited with the power to master every problem and in which men live only in their heads and above their heads. The true value of such a situation is characterized by various images connected with the pyramid. First comes the head of Medusa which forms the entrance. It is a symbol of the petrifaction which threatens any man who identifies himself with the light of the intellect. For whoever looks upon the head of Medusa is turned to stone. The second symbol is the nymph who only has hair on her forehead while the back of her head is bald. Such a nymph decidedly lacks charm. The fore part of the head is the seat of consciousness and though there is a rich growth here, apparent spiritualization stands revealed as mere identification with consciousness and a mere half of things, in which the connection with the unconscious—since there is nothing behind—is entirely lacking. The third and most important symbol in this connection is the reference to the builder of the huge pile, whom Poliphilo names Lychas the Libyan.

λύκος means wolf, λύχνος a candelabra. These two words seem to have been fused in the name of the builder and to give it a double meaning. If the wolf, the symbol of lust, has built the pyramid, it means that it is the lust of power and universal knowledge which has reared these dizzy heights. The avidity of the humanist has led this man of the early Renaissance to an extreme, to an overalertness of consciousness which can do no more than attempt to satisfy insatiable intellectual desires. On the other hand, the idea of the candelabra and the name of the Libyan point to a more mysterious light than that of consciousness. If the author says "Libyan," he certainly means that the African who built the pyramid and the obelisk was an Egyptian. But the Egyptians were the first masters of alchemy. Hermes Trismegistus, a Hellenistic variant of the Egyptian Thoth, is said to have been the father of alchemy; it is he, for instance, who speaks to the adepts in the *Corpus Hermeticum*.[10] He is the symbol of a spirit which embraces the opposites of light and darkness, which, leading from the heights to the depths and back to the heights again, mediates between consciousness and the unconscious.[11] Here, in the light, he appears as light, but, in accordance with his changeful being, only as a light that turns. The sense of every extreme is that it provokes a crisis, and by the mere fact that it is untenable, sets going the movement to its opposite pole. Poliphilo realizes this too, for he cannot remain on these dizzy heights.

The figures that Poliphilo sees in the ruined city after the harsh light of this climax must all be regarded as stations of his descent. True, this is not put into words for the reason given in the introduction to the present work. The man of the early Renaissance had already lost his bearings. Unlike Dante, who knew the depths into which he had to descend to the very floor of Hell, our dreamer simply sees his descent as a progress. And in a deeper sense he is right. For after the too lofty heights, the turn to the depths conforms to vital growth.

The descent leads the wanderer into the unknown region of those contents of the human psyche which either have

[10] V. W. Scott, *Hermetica*, Vol. 4, Oxford, 1924.

[11] This is expressed, for instance, in the second verse of the *Tabula Smaragdina:* "What is below is like unto that which is above, and what is above is like unto that which is below, that the marvel of the One thing may be fulfilled." J. Ruska, op. cit.

become estranged from his consciousness or cannot possibly be known to him yet by experience, and which therefore appear to him in the image of the object of his longing, the ancient world. The fascination of every projection resides in the fact that it offers to man, in an external object, a life that is not dreamt of in his philosophy.

The first figure that Poliphilo encounters on his progress is the winged horse on its lavishly decorated pedestal. The inscription on it is "Generations," and it is this which will give us the clue to the understanding of the figure. In itself, the horse incorporates speed and endurance; in the present context it probably means the inexorable march of time. The children climbing up and falling down are images of the generations of men succeeding each other in time. What is represented here is the cycle of growth and decay in which the son, when he dies, hands on to his son the life he has received from his father, like a drop of water in a wave. In the ever-rolling stream of time, man is no more than part of creation, which is eternally renewing itself, yet remains eternally the same. A child of nature, he remains, like an animal or a plant, unconscious and childlike to the end. The children on the winged horse are, as it were, a hieroglyph representing natural, primitive humanity. In the text, Poliphilo notes that the winged horse recalled to him the horse of Meius Sejus, which brought misfortune to all its riders. Thus, almost casually, he hints at the hopeless sadness of all life bound to time and nature.

The same theme is further elaborated in the two reliefs decorating the pedestal of the winged horse. These two reliefs give an impressive picture of what is common to men and women in the world of purely natural existence, and of their condition in that state. On the relief on one side, youths and maidens are gathering flowers, and the word which belongs to them is Loss. That means that in youth, men and women share the experience of joy and sorrow. Laughter and tears—so much they have in common. But what is the meaning of this shared delight and its bitterness? Seen from a higher standpoint, it is merely loss. The other relief, in which men and women, standing in a circle, join hands (Fig. 4), on the contrary, is a picture of adult life. True, they are together and form a whole (= the circle), but they neither see nor touch each other. What they have in common is only the double, forward and backward, look of their two faces, which shows them their common world and common background. Yet they remain strangers to each other and are only bound in a negative way by the conflict of the sexes. Thus these two reliefs bring home the sadness of the limits set to the relationship between the sexes; they did not only exist in the age of Poliphilo, but are present wherever men remain mere creatures of nature, formed as human beings only by the collective consciousness of their time and by the collective unconscious. As long as man does not exist as an individual, he has no real "thou," and remains, in life and death, an anonymous particle of the mass.

Thus in his encounter with the winged horse, Poliphilo descends into the realm of purely natural existence. It is what a very intellectual man, living entirely with his head, is only too prone to forget—that he too is primitive, collective, a particle of a mass just like everybody else. And every human being is commonplace, transitory, negligible. But what does such a man know about himself? What is he when he is isolated from the mass?

This question is, to a certain extent, answered by the next figure Poliphilo encounters. This is the hideous bronze colossus lying on the ground like a sick man with groans issuing from its mouth. This colossus is an anatomical figure of *Homo sapiens,* that is, of corporeal man. We can see that in a certain direction the humanist of our dream knows a great deal about the corporeal man which, after all, he is himself. He knows all the organs, nerves, veins in his body, and so is familiar with them as a man of learning. But apart from his scientific interest, this corporeality clearly seems hideous in his eyes in a way which almost recalls Nietzsche's "ugliest man." The realization of the distasteful ugliness of corporeal man is characteristic not only of the author of the *Hypnerotomachia,* but of the whole Renaissance. As humanism awoke to the spontaneous appreciation of all things, the Christian view of the corruption of all things by sin faded away, to be replaced by a strong feeling for human nakedness—on the one hand in the form of wilful eroticism, but on the other in a cruel observation of unvarnished reality. The idealization of the human body, which was necessary for that very reason, was coupled with the consciousness of the all-too-human in its dirt, its deformity, and its utter lack of charm. In his *Corbacchio,* Boccaccio, who has described so many lovely nymphs and heroic youths, has illustrated this totally different way of looking at things with unsurpassed realism. The woman shown to him by a Red Cloak (i.e. a devil) is a vessel of filth and abomination. Even the obscene was exploited by the Renaissance with a somewhat distasteful emphasis,[12] which simply goes to prove that natural things were not really taken naturally, but with a double response—attraction and repulsion.

Poliphilo's corporeal man, however, is also represented as a poor, sick creature, and we can to a certain extent infer from the picture the cause of his sufferings. Beside him there lies a female colossus, so buried in the earth that only a small part of the head is visible. Thus what the man lacks is woman. Lying there in his helplessness, he looks like some Adam before the creation of Eve—a half lacking its complement. This can be interpreted in a double sense, for woman is for man a double thing—reality and image. The actual

[12] For instance, by Pietro Aretino (1492–1556).

woman is necessary to man as his complement, since she leads him into all those spheres of life to which his nature as a man gives him no key. But as an image she incorporates his soul, which is feminine in contrast to his masculine mind.[13] The feminine image of the man's soul contains everything which he represses for fear of appearing "womanish"—everything connected with that sphere of emotion, feeling, and relationship to others which is naturally alien to him. Thus if in our story the woman is buried in the earth, the meaning is that the man is lonely and soulless—that is his infirmity. From this standpoint, the image of the metal colossus which only gives forth sound when the wind blows through it recalls St. Paul's saying: "Though I speak with the tongues of men and of angels, and have not charity, I am become as sounding brass, or a tinkling cymbal" (1 Cor. XIII. 1.)

It is disconcerting enough to find a description of such a kind in the book of a lover, but it is just when a man loves that his soullessness becomes a problem. There is, however, this to be said. When Poliphilo reaches the heart inside the colossus, the recollection of his beloved Polia comes over him, and he groans in longing for her. And his groans reverberate so dismally in the cavity of the colossus that he flees in terror. We must now ask what this signifies. Is Poliphilo afraid of the echo which love finds in corporeal man? Is he taking flight from the problem it raises?

There are plenty of men who imagine that they can master even love with their heads. They think that love is a simple thing—primarily erotic, and beyond that rational or even philosophical. It is the women who complicate matters. But what if love stirs the depths? And what if it echoes horribly in the body? In that case the man must try to comprehend

---

[13] See C. G. Jung, "The Relation of the Ego to the Unconscious," in *Two Essays on Analytical Psychology,* translated by H. G. and C. F. Baynes, Baillière, London, 1928.

the corporeal man in himself as well as the spiritual if love, and with it he himself, are not to be desecrated.

Since this is as yet beyond Poliphilo's power, he turns still farther downward and encounters an animal; the richly caparisoned, gleaming black elephant with the obelisk on its back might be an embodiment of animal nature, that is, of the very thing which seems to him so hideous. If this is the case, however, we are dealing with a special kind of animal nature.

Poliphilo presents the elephant as the opposite belonging to and complementary to the pyramid. The pyramid was all light, the elephant is all darkness. But each, in its kind, is the biggest that exists. Both are characterized by an obelisk, and the obelisks in the *Hypnerotomachia* always stand for a kind of exclamation mark. Wherever an obelisk appears, the place is important. Thus the pyramid and the elephant are both important; the one represents the greatest light and a summit, the other the greatest darkness and a depth. While the pyramid points the way to heaven, the elephant, being its opposite, points the way to earth. Both ways lie open. Thus Poliphilo, having passed through the bright pyramid, also enters the elephant from the back of the pedestal, and again by steps in a significant arrangement.

We can infer from the fact that the elephant is here placed in contrast to Poliphilo's much admired pyramid that he has little liking for the kind of animal nature here symbolized. It has the character of a "grievous necessity." And yet it is presented in the figure of an elephant, and thus stresses certain definite characteristics which show what the symbol really means to the dreamer. Firstly, the strange inscriptions "The brain is in the head" and "Work and Diligence" emphasize the qualities of wisdom and ability. Further, in Poliphilo's day the elephant was, in a very general way, the representative of a number of definite qualities which appeared, among other things, in the fables in which it had figured, along with all the other animals, since ancient times. A summary of them can be found in the *Mundus Symbolicus* of Philippus Picinellus,[14] which, though it is a work of the seventeenth century, unites all the old familiar motives in the conventional description of animals. We find there that the qualities of the elephant are all supremely praiseworthy. He is wise, magnanimous, gentle, fearless, pure, and devout. Among lambs he places his feet with care so as not to injure them. In battle, he is a noble if dangerous enemy. When he feeds, he first tosses the grass up to heaven with his trunk, and thus becomes a symbol of religious feeling. Further, since, in dying, he kills the serpent which has stung him, he is a symbol of Christ, who overcame the wicked adversary by His death. But above all, the elephant loves water and worships the moon. He cannot swim, and so, his way through deep water being barred, he has humility enough to walk round it. Before he worships the moon, he bathes in a spring. Indeed, his love for the orb of night is so great that, when the new moon appears after the days of moonless darkness, he pronounces prayer after prayer to make up for lost time.[15]

Thus the symbol of the elephant brings home to the wanderer in our dream the wisdom and purity of an "animal nature" which is so strong and has so great a power of suffering that it may be compared with the exalted figure of the Saviour. And it is important for the lover to know that there is a connection between this "animal" and water and the moon, which are, for Poliphilo, embodied in Polia. The elephant who worships the moon is also a symbol of true love.

Interpreting the elephant on the psychological plane, we

[14] Coloniae Agrippinae Sumptibus Thomae et Ebrici Theodori von Cöllen, 1715.
[15] Picinellus, op. cit., V, XIX, pp. 237 ff.

can see it as an image of the inferior function,[16] that is, of that form of psychic activity which, as the individual developed, remained backward and therefore unconscious, and now forms the link with the unconscious. When the first, outward development of the human being has reached full term, it is this inferior function which becomes important and even redeeming, since it opens the way to the unconscious by which a second, inward development is made possible. To the man who is primarily conscious of his mind, his inferiority, and with it the unconscious, first makes its

[16] Cf. C. G. Jung, *Psychological Types*, Definitions, under "Inferior Function."

Since symbols of the psychic functions constantly appear in the *Hypnerotomachia*, the following brief summary may help to make them clear. Under the psychic functions of orientation we understand definite forms of psychic activity which remain constant in changing circumstances and from which consciousness derives its character. C. G. Jung distinguishes four of them, namely, thought and feeling (valuation) as rational functions, and intuition and sensation as irrational functions. In the course of the development of every individual, two functions at least achieve a more or less permanent form in which he apprehends reality and in which he expresses himself. Thus quite apart from his attitude to life, they determine his type of consciousness, making him, for instance, a thinker who has also a command of ideas (intuitions) of his own, or a man of feeling with a reliable sense of reality (sensation), etc. The psychic function which remains most backward in the course of development is denoted the *inferior* function. It can never be quite assimilated to consciousness. Just because it remains largely unconscious, it may present a problem as life goes on, for it contains everything that "disagrees with" the conscious personality, that disturbs or even thwarts it. Thus, for instance, feelings are the most alien of things to a man whose main approach to reality lies in thought. They are either so inferior or so generalized that he quite loses his bearings in them. He cannot apply them to life as he would like to, and if he has to come to terms with them, he encounters on the one hand painful, on the other suprapersonal contents of the unconscious which his consciousness cannot master. The importance of the inferior function resides in the fact that it indissolubly links consciousness to the unconscious in a way which is both dangerous and life-giving. It is in this sense that symbols of the inferior function continually recur in the *Hypnerotomachia*, and it is here that the book offers particularly instructive material.

appearance in the animal sphere, and it is there that he first experiences all the values that he cannot discover with his mind. That is why Poliphilo's inferior function appears as an animal characterized by peculiar qualities. We can see that this actually opens the way to the unconscious by the mysterious figures inside it, the black king and the nymph who points the way, and is not disfigured like the nymph on the pyramid. The black king and the nymph are contents of the unconscious that Poliphilo sees, but cannot understand. The words they pronounce are cryptic and oracular. Like the figures themselves, they point to the fascination of the unconscious that Poliphilo here encounters like a prince of fairyland.

The entire descent of Poliphilo from the summit of the pyramid to the mysterious elephant gives the impression that a future way is being anticipated and a programme presented in images. The whole has a provisional character, for what Poliphilo sees in the ruined city are mere simulacra of life. Everything lies motionless and he cannot yet achieve life. Thus what we have here is a first approach to the contents of his psyche which he feels but faintly within him. Possibilities exist, he is given directions and instruction, but nothing is put into action. Poliphilo has a long way to go before he finds life in the gift which is shown under the symbol of the elephant. And we ask—what will this gift look like when it comes to life? We do not know yet. We only know that something which looks like an elephant at the first approach is potentially there, and as such, it has a certain power. It is so charged with deep meaning that it attracts Poliphilo, and so leads him on.

He hastens to the portal which, as we have seen, has fascinated him from the outset. In this way he proceeds from the former depth to the verge of another, which no figures animate, for it is hewn out of the virgin rock. He enters a region where nothing blooms; we might call it the darkness of the mineral kingdom. The portal is crowned by a very strange inscription which also introduces a significantly new note: "Bacchus and Ceres have given of their own substance to the pious Mother Venus and her son Amor." So runs the inscription (see p. 39). For the first time we encounter the names of the divinities ruling the service of courtly love, Venus and Cupid. They stand there as the rulers to whom sacrifice is made—even of a man's own substance. The sacrifice itself is probably all that we have just seen—the descent into the collective commonplace, the body, "animal nature." This sacrifice, the entrance into nature, is made to the rulers of courtly love; it is offered up to love. Hence the path to the depths is not meaningless; it has a goal.

Here the dream gives a superb lesson to the man who is unfolding the inexorable sequence of his visions before our eyes. The humanist craving for antiquity, the lover holding fast to a figure of light—both are told that the way of fulfilment takes its beginning in a sacrifice and in the deepest depths of nature.

Under the portal, Poliphilo finds a last image; he sees himself to right and left in two black mirrors. He thus recognizes that he has two sides which constitute opposites. In ancient times the right and left sides were always felt as opposites, a special meaning being given to the left side because it was connected with the left hand. Sinister = left meant not only clumsy, awkward, but also repulsive and ominous. The left side is dark; evil dwells there. Poliphilo sees in two mirrors that he is light and dark; he is confronted with the ambiguity which is the portion of all mortals, and cannot be eluded even by one who is struggling towards the heights.

Then Poliphilo sees nothing more. The splendid visions which have spun their magic round him disappear, and what stretches before him is an endless, gloomy vault. This absolute darkness, of which nothing is known and nothing can be told, is the unconscious. No wonder that Poliphilo's first thought is to turn back as soon as may be. Many a man of our day does the same thing by turning his back on the unconscious, imagining that if he sees no more and knows no more, there is nothing there but a terrifying void. But for him who reaches this threshold, the way back is cut off, and Poliphilo is caught. His fate is no longer in his own hands. The inexorability of the process which has set in with his dream journey is incorporated in the triple-tongued dragon, the sight of which is so horrible that it drives Poliphilo into the darkness.

As a reptile, the dragon belongs to the subhuman realm of cold-blooded creatures. As a fabulous monster, it seems to man dangerous, unfamiliar, unnatural, and utterly alien. It is venomous, cold as metal, yet it spits fire, and this unites the opposites in itself. It is also an antediluvian creature for the monk who wrote our story, perhaps the incorporation of Leviathan or Lucifer the fallen angel. In this creature, Satan himself, the wicked adversary, appears and drives the dreamer into hell.

To the conscious human being, the unconscious, at the first approach, actually looks like hell, indeed the only feeling it arouses in him is that of primeval dread of threatening danger. Poliphilo feels this dread in the highest degree, and he is particularly terrified, he tells us, by the foul smoke issuing from the dragon's mouth. This deadly smoke is the symbol of the venomous, blinding danger of the unconscious which threatens to annihilate human consciousness if the human being cannot overcome it by entering into the unconscious. But if he enters, perdition turns to salvation. It was alchemy which perceived this double significance of perdition and salvation best of all. There the dragon is the menacing mystery of Mercury, the destroyer and helper, as he first appears in the phial and forces the adept to complete his work lest he perish with it.[17]

Poliphilo too succumbs to this compulsion. As though he were himself a captive in a dark phial, he wanders about in the gloomy vaults and can find no issue. This is Poliphilo's hell—how different it is from Dante's! In his descent into the deepest depths, Dante is never alone. At all times he is surrounded by thousands of figures. And those thousands are never alone among themselves in the various spheres. They see and hear each other, though what they see and hear only adds to their wretchedness. But Poliphilo hears and sees nothing; his pains of hell are his utter solitude. His situation recalls Mephistopheles' description in Part II of *Faust* of the way to the realm of the Mothers (Act I, Dark Gallery):

> *No way! Into the untrodden,*
> *Not to be trodden; into the unwished for,*
> *Not to be prayed for. Art ready?*
> *Here are no locks, no bolts that thou canst loose,*
> *Echoing solitudes shall steal thy peace.*
> *Knowst thou the wilderness, the solitary place? . . .*
> *Nought shalt thou see in that eternal void,*
> *Nor shall thy halting step make any sound,*
> *Nor shalt thou find a solid ground for rest.*

Complete solitude is the first condition of individuation. The man who has never really separated himself from the mass remains part of it.[18] Whatever his situation, he can

---

[17] Cf. C. G. Jung, *Psychology and Alchemy*.

[18] Cf. in C. G. Jung, *Psychology and Alchemy*, the Commentary to 3 (hypnagogic impression), Part II, Chap. II. In a general way, the sequence of dreams dealt with in that work offers striking analogies to Poliphilo's sequence of images, which lie in the very nature of unconscious processes. For that matter, we might recall the great part played in primitive initiation rites by separation (isolation in sweating huts, solitude in the bush, creeping through a cave). A very fine example of the isolation of a future medicine man can be found in John G. Neihardt, *Black Elk Speaks*, William Morrow & Co., New York, 1932.

always appeal to what "is done," to what "was done" in older times. Such appeals have no meaning for the solitary. Even Poliphilo, the type of the man of learning, is utterly ignorant when he is first thrown back upon himself. What has happened to him is exactly the opposite of all he desired. He had expected supreme awareness from the discovery of antiquity, and now the clash with it has cast him into primordial chaos and rendered him utterly unconscious.

Under the deadly oppression of his desperate plight, something begins to stir in him, some recent experience that has accompanied him into his solitude. What helps him is the piety of the elephant, or, we might say, a religious instinct. He calls on all the gods that be, and in the prayer there lies the realization that there may be some higher court of appeal concealed in the hell of unconsciousness, and that he is submitting himself to it, though unconsciously. Poliphilo's prayer in the deep vaults signifies a change of attitude, the subjection of the conscious to the unconscious and the acceptance of the unconscious in the teeth of his despair and fear and ignorance.

This change of attitude at once takes effect. In the gross darkness, Poliphilo sees something. It is as though the unconscious were being activated by his acceptance of it. What Poliphilo sees in the awe-inspiring darkness (*venerande tenebre*) is three golden statues on an altar. Thus Poliphilo finds supreme value, namely gold, and a venerable trinity where, in Dante's hell, Satan is enthroned in ice. That the gods of the underworld should not be regarded as Satanic and that they should be worshipped equally with the gods of light is the first classical conception that is borne in upon Poliphilo. Further, we might recall here that Poliphilo described his dragon as triple-tongued. Thus there is a secret identity between it and the three golden statues, for the number three belongs to both. We might anticipate by saying that the hidden unity underlying the various forms in which symbols of transformation appear in the *Hypnerotomachia* can be demonstrated throughout the book. The base upon which the whole development reposes can be discerned from the beginning, and in the beginning everything is potentially present. This might be put in another way. Everything is the same, yet not the same. The varying forms of the figures do not signify a difference of essence, but a difference of experience. It is important to note here that the "triple-formed" or Mercury is first experienced in its negative, archetypal aspect as Satan, and only reveals its positive, divine qualities on deeper penetration.

It shows how completely and freely the monk Colonna submitted to the guidance of his imagination that he should feel divinity even in this place and worship the holy in the horror of the depths. This is the first intimation that the unconscious contains divine, supreme values, and may act as a guide to the seeker. It is true that this realization is as yet provisional and weak (the vault is, after all, illuminated only by a glimmering lamp); it is a mere intuition of an underworld trinity which appears as a light in the depths corresponding to the outer light. The mere appearance of the glimmering light is enough to help Poliphilo on. To him, the light is primarily a path which he is now to take under the compulsion of the dragon. Nothing further can be said about the three golden statues here, for the author does not describe them in detail. What really matters is that they exist. The seeker has made a first discovery; it certainly stands opposed to all the values familiar to him in the past, and so he cannot understand it, but all the same, it guides him on like a star in the depths. Alchemy gives to the first discovery in chaos the name of *prima materia*. We encounter it here under the figure of the three golden statues, but it is a mere hint, a first flash.

If we briefly recapitulate this opening of the *Hypnerotomachia,* comparing it with that of the *Divina Commedia,* what chiefly strikes us is the difference in their basic pattern. Dante sees his world of hell ordered in strata, rather like strata in rock, and his whole valuation is based on the relative height or depth of these strata. In Poliphilo's account, on the other hand, the feeling for height and depth, as we have seen, is very vague. The prevailing idea underlying the structure of the ruined city is that of the mean between two opposites. This comes out quite clearly in the diagrammatic representation of the city (Fig. 3). Further, Poliphilo explicitly states that the city lies outspread between rocky heights, which are symbols of the opposites. True, the seeker first aims too high, namely at the pyramid, in his search for the mean. But when he descends, he again endeavours to find the mean between the opposites, and finds it in the portal under the pyramid. Thus in a certain sense he takes the middle way, so that when, in the end, he arrives in front of the three golden statues, the fact that they are in the depths does not affect his valuation of them—he does not even notice it.

Psychically, the Renaissance is already far remote from medieval Christianity. Hence in its main features, the *Hypnerotomachia* might better be compared with Goethe's *Faust* than with the *Divina Commedia*. Just as, at first, Poliphilo stands on the pyramid in his ragged old cowl, we first see Faust standing, prematurely aged, on a peak of knowledge. Thus both, at the beginning, stand too high. A petrified system of knowledge has oppressed both and made them precocious. Both Poliphilo and Faust then fall victim to a sacrilegious lust of knowledge, only to be overthrown by a *mysterium tremendum,* which appears to Poliphilo in the guise of a triple-tongued dragon and to Faust as the Earth Spirit. It is the chthonic powers which overcome both. And both would go down to death if a new path were not revealed to them in a symbol of transformation. For Faust, this symbol is the resurrection of the Redeemer, for Poliphilo, the gold in the image of the three golden statues —the supreme value and goal of the alchemical process.

SECTION II

The Realm of Queen Eleuterilida[1]

(Poliphilo finds himself in a fertile plain. He meets five lovely maidens. They take him to the bath-house to bathe. Then to the court of Queen Eleuterilida. Banquet with the Queen and her ladies. The Queen appoints two of her attendants to be Poliphilo's guides and directs him to his next goal. The Queen's gardens and maze. The last garden and the golden obelisk. Poliphilo arrives at the three portals of Queen Telosia. He has to choose between them, and chooses the portal of Mater Amoris. His companions leave him. He is fooled by Dame Love-Potion.)

When Poliphilo has made his way out of the gloomy vaults, his story continues thus:

The beauty of the region into which he escapes soothes his fear. After a while, he even ventures to look back, and sees that what was a ruined city on the side of the gloomy vaults is here a wooded mountain slope. The opening through which he has escaped, and which must lie directly opposite to the splendid porch under the pyramid, is here a rocky defile, primevally ancient and almost overgrown with luxuriant trees.

Poliphilo wanders on, longing for the sight of a human face. He arrives at a bridge spanning a river which divides into two brooks to right and left. Its lush banks are swarming with all kinds of water-fowl. On the far side of the bridge there is a fertile plain planted with fruit-trees. Above the tree-tops there rises a high-pitched roof which the wanderer hastens to reach.

What he finds is a charming octagonal building with a fountain set in one side representing a recumbent nymph from whose breasts two little streams of water flow, cold to the right and warm to the left (Fig. 7). These streams mingle

---

[1] Throughout the present volume, proper names are usually given in the form of the original text.

ΠΑΝΤΩΝ ΤΟΚΑΔΙ

Fig. 7. The Nymph Fountain

Fig. 8. The Five Sense Maidens

on the ground to form a brook which keeps the whole region fertile. On the frieze of the fountain Poliphilo discovers the inscription:

ΠΑΝΤΩΝ ΤΟΚΑΔΙ

(To her who brings forth all things)

Here, at last, he can quench his thirst. Suddenly he hears a noise and is startled. But there is no need for fear, for it is no danger which approaches him, but five lovely maidens singing to the sound of a lute (Fig. 8). Poliphilo proceeds to give a minute description of their magnificent garments. When the maidens catch sight of him, they stand still and whisper together, while his blood freezes in his veins, for the adventures he has been through have left him very timorous.

Suddenly the boldest of the five asks him: "Who art thou?" And as Poliphilo, in his terror, makes no reply, she calms his fears with gentle words. Then he speaks, saying: "I am an unhappy lover, for I know neither where my beloved is nor where I am myself." Then he tells the maidens the story of his adventures, and they bid him thank God that he has escaped from dangers that few can overcome. He has nothing to fear, they say. He is in the land of eternal gaiety and fruitfulness, the realm of Queen Eleuterilida, and it is to her that the nymphs mean to take him, for a human being will be something quite new in her experience.

(Chapter 8) But first the maidens take him back to the little octagonal building he has already seen. It is the bathhouse, and they had been on their way to bathe. As they walk together, they tell him their names. They are: Aphea, Osphrasia, Orasia, Akoe, and Geusia—that is, Touch, Smell, Sight, Hearing, and Taste. In their company, Poliphilo can inspect the bath-house at his leisure and he gives a detailed description of it, both interior and exterior. The bath is invitingly full of warm water. The maidens disrobe, quite unconcerned, put on golden bathing caps, and enter the water. And Poliphilo must needs do the same, though he feels like a crow among white doves, and is abashed. As the maidens bathe, they question him again as to his name, and at last he tells them that he is Poliphilo, and that the name means "Lover of Polia." Then they cross-examine him on the degree of his love for Polia, and nothing but the most precise information will satisfy them.

Corresponding to the nymph fountain on the outer wall, there is a little fountain on the inner wall with a Pissing Manikin which, by an ingenious device, can be made to squirt water into the bather's face. The maidens play the trick on Poliphilo, and rejoice in his consternation. But that is not the only trick they have in store for him. After bathing, everybody is perfumed, and when Poliphilo's turn comes, the mischievous maidens anoint him with a balm which fills him with overwhelming lasciviousness and turns Poliphilo the crow into a very ass. His companions laugh uproariously. But in the end, Lady Taste remembers that there is a little herb which will serve as an antidote, and then, in perfect amity, they all make their way towards Queen Eleuterilida's palace.

The kindly reader will hardly expect a reproduction of Poliphilo's minute descriptions of the Queen's gardens and palace. They are entirely baroque in feeling; the trees are sculptured like stone, and the stone of the palace seems to have dissolved into creepers and verdure.

(Chapter 9) The palace is surrounded by three hedges, the outer wall taking the place of the fourth. Three interior courtyards give access to the innermost, square court. This has a chequered floor and its roof is formed of creepers and honeysuckle made of gold and precious stones. The seven compartments of the main wall bear the names of the seven planets. Where the sun stands, the Queen sits on her golden throne surrounded by her ladies. Above her throne there is the figure of a beautiful youth with golden curls, borne on the wings of an eagle.

Queen Eleuterilida welcomes the weary wanderer most graciously (Fig. 9). She too marvels at the happy fate which has brought him hither. She knows what hardships he has had to overcome. But she bids him restore himself at her court, and enjoy her splendours along with the others. He is permitted to sit down with her ladies, and he calls it a mere chance that his seat should happen to be by the wall with the planets and directly under Mercury. In his dirty, ragged clouts he cuts a pitiable figure among the richly dressed ladies, but now he can even forget that, for the banquet goes on for hours. A superb feast is wonderfully served to music. The dishes are brought in on golden carriages, shaped with art, precious perfumes accompany the

Fig. 9. At the Court of Queen Eleuterilida

dessert and the only shadow on Poliphilo's contentment is that, in spite of the wine and food, he cannot cease thinking of Polia.

(Chapter 10) The banquet is followed by a magnificent ballet, then Queen Eleuterilida summons Poliphilo to her side and addresses him in well chosen words.

He has now, she tells him, been able to rest and restore himself at her court. He has enjoyed the delights of her realm, and there are none like them in the world. But now he must fare forth in search of his love. If he is to do so, he must first find the three portals of Queen Telosia (i.e.

aim or goal). On each portal there is an inscription telling him what it signifies, and everything will depend on his choosing the right one. To help him on his way, Eleuterilida gives him the ring with the stone Anchite set in it (this is the miraculous stone of the ancients, possibly the diamond; the derivation of the word in unknown). Further, two of her maidens will accompany him, namely Logistica, or Reason, and Thelemia, or Will. Poliphilo must follow their instructions, for they know the way and will guide him to the portals, which he will be able to open by means of the ring. The ladies will lead him to Queen Telosia, without whose favour nothing can be attained. She is Eleuterilida's sister, but there is no likeness between them, for she lives in strictest seclusion and deludes those who seek her by constantly changing her shape. The man who sees her doubts, even despairs, and does not know her. But that is just what she wants. All the same, Poliphilo must be of a good courage, since Logistica and Thelemia, Reason and Will, are to be his companions.

Poliphilo does not know how to thank the good Queen. As he goes away, he turns back again and again to look at the splendid hall where he has enjoyed such delights. And now he sees the inscription above it:

Ο ΤΗΣ ΦΥΣΕΩΣ ΟΛΒΟΣ
(The Wealth of Nature)

Logistica and Thelemia now proceed to show him four sights which are new to him in the Queen's realm. Firstly, there is to the left an enclosed garden as big as the whole palace, which is a faithful copy of nature in gold and glass, complete down to a faint artificial perfume.

Close beside it there is a maze; its winding path is a river which must be traversed in boats. Logistica explains the maze to Poliphilo as they look down upon it from above. He who enters it can never come out again; he is forever captive. Above the entrance there is an inscription: "Worldly fame is like the drops of water in rain." There sits the portress, Fate, distributing her lots blindly. The entrance past, the journey on the water is delicious, but alas! the nearer they come to the middle, the wilder grows the river and the more desolate its banks. Nor will any sighs or tears save a man from that ineluctable middle, the lair of a dreadful dragon which will one day devour everyone who enters the maze. This dragon is called "The wolf of the gods who knows no compassion." There is a touch of the macabre in this description; it is bathed in the poetry of mortality.

Then Poliphilo is shown another garden on the right-hand side of Eleuterilida's realm. This too is artificial, and is made of pearls and silk. In its centre there is an arbour where Poliphilo sits down with Thelemia. She takes up her lyre and plays a splendid and enchanting air on it.

But now Logistica grows impatient. She draws Poliphilo away, for she, in her turn, has something to show him that will please his mind rather than his eyes. It is another garden with the following construction in its centre. First there is a chalcedony cube with the word "Inscrutable" on it. On this cube there lies a flat red cylinder with the following devices in its circumference: firstly, a sun, symbolizing the ineffable divine light, secondly, a rudder, symbolizing the indivisible guidance of God, and thirdly, a lamp, symbolizing the incomprehensibility of love. On the cylinder there stands a black, triangular prism ornamented with the figures of nymphs holding cornucopias, while the whole is crowned by the three-sided golden obelisk. Three circles on its sides signify past, present, and future, and above them there are three Greek characters, omicron, omega, and nu (Fig. 10). We may assume that they are intended to form the words ὁ ὤν (He who is). Logistica explains to Poliphilo that the divine harmony is contained in these three figures, which are dedicated to the infinite Three-in-One. The cube is sacred because it is born of unity, the circle because it has neither beginning nor end. But now Logistica's explanation

Fig. 10. The Golden Obelisk on the Cube, Cylinder, and Triangular Prism

becomes somewhat confused. She cannot really interpret the black prism and the golden obelisk. In the end she merely adds that man cannot clearly recognize past, present, and future at one and the same time, and it is for that reason that the three characters—omicron, omega, and nu—have been wisely added.

Poliphilo, however, pays no great heed to the failure of logic to which Reason clearly succumbs at this point. The work of art before him seems a thousand times more beautiful than anything he has ever seen. Lost in awe, he contemplates the golden obelisk which rises, mysterious, upright, firm, indestructible, amidst the garden's flowers and grasses.

Yet he must tear himself away again, for now it is time to set forth in search of the three portals of Queen Telosia. The way once more leads across a river towards a stony, desolate region where the three portals are hewn in the rock (Fig. 11). With his ring, Poliphilo first opens the door to the left, on which the inscription "The Glory of God" stands in four languages. It opens. Out of a smoke-blackened hut there steps a venerable old widow with poverty-stricken attendants, who raises a lean arm up to the rainy sky. Poliphilo at once realizes that this is no place for him, though this annoys Reason profoundly. Together with Will he then opens the portal to the right, which bears the inscription "Worldly Fame." A fierce-eyed matron steps out. She carries a sword, a palm, and a crown, and her retinue is composed of viragoes. It all looks too laborious to Poliphilo. Reason realizes this, yet she strives to keep him here. She even sings in the attempt to convince him, but without avail. Therefore Will decides that they might as well open the third portal and see what is behind it.

No sooner said than done. The inscription above the middle portal, again in four languages, runs: "Mother of Love" (Mater Amoris). It opens, and the voluptuous Dame Love-Potion steps out with her flighty train. Poliphilo is delighted. Logistica, who is deeply shocked, urges him not

Fig. 11. The Three Portals of Queen Telosia

to remain here. If he knew, she says, how repulsive Dame Love-Potion is seen from the back, if he knew how quickly her lovely maidens would abandon him, he would certainly hurry away. But Poliphilo does not heed her. He has already made up his mind to stay. This so enrages Logistica that she breaks Thelemia's lyre and runs away. But Thelemia approves. She tells Poliphilo that he is right, for here the desire of his heart will be fulfilled. Poliphilo imagines that she is speaking of Polia, for his heart knows no other desire or thought. But now Thelemia has to leave Poliphilo, the attendants of Dame Love-Potion caress him till he is aflame with desire (Fig. 12). But suddenly they have all vanished, and Poliphilo finds himself alone with his frenzy in a wide plain. As Queen Eleuterilida foretold, Poliphilo has not seen Telosia (the goal) in the three portals. It is by his own will that he has chosen his further path, though he is utterly blind to the meaning of his own actions.

COMMENTARY TO SECTION II

The change of mood through which we have passed with Poliphilo is extreme. From the deathly gloom of the deep vaults we have issued into a blooming landscape and can rejoice in his account of the pleasures of life. Poliphilo now states explicitly that the two slopes on the nearer and farther side of the deep vault belong to one and the same mountain. What was, on the other side of the mountain, the ruined city is here simply forest, primeval rock, and a green valley, that is, nature. Thus what we have here is a pair of opposites which we can describe in a general way as spirit and nature or—applied to the dreamer's personality—as church and world. The transition from the one opposite to the other is represented by the archetypal image of the river-crossing. The Poliphilo who reaches the other side of the river has

Fig. 12. Dame Love-Potion and Her Train

ceased to be a cleric in his outlook and has become a natural man and a worldling. What is the nature, and what the world, to which he has found his way back?

We have seen that Poliphilo, as a humanist, turns towards classical antiquity. That is the goal of his longing, it is in that direction that his being moves. In the ruined city, he first imagined he had found it as a higher illumination, but all he attained was the night suffused with the faint radiance of alien divinity, which was all that antiquity actually signified to him for the time being. Surrendering to that night, he passes through a death, he dies to his former life and is no longer identified with his conscious prejudices. And now he enters upon the wealth of a life according to nature, expressed by the images of the fruitful landscape in which he finds himself. He discovers nature—but is it the nature of the ancients? He discovers a world—but is it the ancient world?

As we have already seen in the symbolism of the ruined city, the wanderer does not at first find things as they actually are, but as his own nature imagines them to be, as he desires them, or as they appear in the light of his projections. Over the classical antiquity which now draws him on, his own nature hangs like a veil, or like a mist, and this is the region through which he wanders first.

Emerging from the deep vaults, he first finds himself on a wild, wooded, rocky mountain side in all probability a symbol of the fact that nature in this man has lain untouched and untended. From this moment on, it is the longing for the sight of a human face that lends wings to his feet. Thus it is the burning desire to overcome his isolation which causes him to find the way to his own nature, which has been formed by countless generations of human beings like himself. For human nature is not like that of a wild animal, hence the nature of Poliphilo the man, once he has found his way into it, is symbolized by a cultivated landscape.

There the first thing he finds is the nymph fountain, where he can at last quench his thirst. The water which flows from the breasts of the nymph, and is sacred to the mother of all things, is patently some special kind of liquid. In his description of it, the author makes open use of the symbolic language of alchemy. The "Virgin's Milk" (*lac virginis*) is a well known alchemical symbol, sometimes for the *prima materia* of the process, sometimes for the purifying substance occurring in it, which is used with much the same meaning as dew.[2] What both symbols mean is the "divine water" of

[2] See John Read, *Prelude to Chemistry*, Bell & Sons, London, 1919, p. 157, footnote, pp. 205-6, etc.

alchemy, that is, the one (cool, damp) form of that mysterious primordial substance on which the whole work turns, and which is called mercury by the alchemists. In its watery form, mercury is primevally female and all-nourishing, that is why the allusion to the "mother of all things" is appropriate to the nymph fountain. Transposing this symbolism into our own language, we might say that it is intended to give an impression of the animating action of the unconscious, which is as delightful as a cool drink to the thirsty and as wonderful as the pure milk of a virgin.

In the present context, the image of the nymph fountain is precursory in kind, not unlike the images of the brook and the sound at the beginning of Poliphilo's journey. It shows that something is on the move and welling up from the depths, but now, in contrast to the beginning, Poliphilo can grasp. What he grasps is shown in the following images:

Five lovely maidens appear and announce themselves as the five senses. Here we have the record of an observation which could be made very widely today. Men like Poliphilo, whose energies are harnessed to their differentiated functions, and who attempt to put into action only what appears to them and their age as the best and highest, may, in their passion for perfection, very well lose touch with their plain five senses. In both the literal and the figurative sense, they cannot smell or feel, they are blind and deaf. They repress the life of their senses to such a degree that they have to establish a connection with the unconscious before they can attain the natural perceptions of a child or a peasant. If the subject is a man, his anima[3] becomes the bearer of his five senses and reanimates them in him when, as here, she appears in the form of five lovely maidens, fascinating and a trifle dangerous because they are unknown to him. Fur-

[3] For the conception of the anima, see below, p. 111.

ther, a particular effort is required to regain possession of the senses once estranged. It takes, so to speak, a ritual, which is represented in the *Hypnerotomachia* by the symbol of the bath.

The bath-house and the bath are again alchemical symbols which are to be found with great frequency in the literature and its illustrations, and appear in the most manifold variants. Sometimes the bathers merely sit in a wash-tub and have water poured over them. Sometimes the process is symbolized by the washing of clothes.[4] The water which purifies the bathers is the "divine water" or "virgin's milk." This is represented in the *Hypnerotomachia* by the fact that the water-supply in the bath-house comes from the nymph fountain. But that is not the whole story. There is yet another fountain in the bath-house itself, namely the Pissing Manikin. Thus the water of the bath is a blend of two waters, the one female, the other male, in origin. *Lac virginis* is sweet and mild, *urina puerorum* on the other hand acid and unpleasant. The two must be regarded as the opposite forms of appearance of the one mercury, which is thus contained whole in the bath water.

The symbolism of the union of the waters finds its parallel in the union of Poliphilo with the five maidens in the bath. But this union takes place in a peculiar setting. The bathhouse, as described in the *Hypnerotomachia*, is the first description in the book of the alchemical vessel. The symbolism of the vessel shows that the union is as close as the fusion of two chemicals in a new substance. Hence a trans-

[4] Cf. John Read, op. cit. Fig. 23, Two Washerwomen from the *Viridarium Chymicum* (Stolcius, 1624); Fig. 26, The Bath of Saturn, from *Liber Mutus* (La Rochelle, 1677); Fig. 28, The Washing of Latona, from *Scrutinium Chymicum* (Michael Mayer, 1687). C. G. Jung, *Psychology and Alchemy*, Fig. 56, The Fountain of Youth, from *Codex de Sphaera* (Florence, Cod. Estensis Lat. 209); Fig. 57, Imperial Bath, Codex 1474 (Biblioteca Angelica, Rome), etc.

formation takes place, but it cannot be a final operation, for the vessel is not hermetically sealed (the water escapes to the outside through the nymph fountain). Nor has the vessel as yet the proper spherical form. It is described by Poliphilo as octagonal, hence it is divided into twice four regular parts, so that the bath-house may be denoted as a mandala.[5]

The bath-house is a sacred precinct, a mid-point in which the goal of life is figured as that of a centred whole. The symbolism of the union and transformation in the sacred place shows us a man in the making. In the bath-house, Poliphilo becomes the natural man with five senses which he always was, though without knowing it. To be natural is the first wholeness he achieves. The dignity of human nature

---

[5] The notion "mandala" is used here as it is used in analytical psychology, i.e. as a technical term for a definite range of symbols whose chief characteristics are symmetry and a central point.
Cf. C. G. Jung, *Psychology and Alchemy* (trans. R. F. C. Hull):
"The term 'mandala' was chosen because this word denotes the ritual or magic circle used in Lamaism and also in Tantric yoga as a *yantra* or aid to contemplation. The eastern mandalas used in ceremonial are figures fixed by tradition: they may be drawn or painted and, in certain special ceremonies, they are even represented plastically. . . .
"The mandalas used in ceremonial are of great significance because their centre usually contains one of the highest religious figures. . . .
"It is not without importance for us to appreciate the high value set upon the mandala, for it accords very well with the paramount significance of individual mandala symbols which are characterized by the same qualities of a—so to speak—'metaphysical' nature. Unless everything deceives us, they mean nothing less than a psychic centre of the personality not to be identified with the 'ego.'"
Further: "All that can be ascertained at present about the symbolism of the mandala is that it portrays an autonomous psychic fact, characterized by a phenomenology which is always repeating itself and is everywhere the same. It seems to be a sort of nuclear atom about whose innermost structure and ultimate meaning we know nothing. We can also regard it as the real—i.e. effective—*reflection* of a conscious attitude which can state neither its aim nor its purpose and, because of this refusal, projects its activity entirely upon the virtual centre of the mandala." (Projection is thought of here as a spontaneous phenom-

is restored to him as an indispensable step to the attainment of his goal.

The only psychic content which the man finds on his way back to his own nature at this point in the book is again courtly love. Poliphilo presents himself to the five maidens as a lover—his only name is Lover of Polia—and the cross-examination on his love to which the five maidens subject him is simply and solely a renewed meditation on the One as bodied forth in the Beloved. It is a fresh meditation, for it is performed by the human being restored to his condition as a natural man. But alas! the lover turns out to be no "spiritual wooer," for sensuality awakens with nature and grows heated. The details given with so much humour in

---

enon, and not as an intentional putting into. Projection is not a phenomenon of the will.) "The compelling force necessary for this projection always lies in some situation where the individual no longer knows how to help himself in any other way."

Cf. also C. G. Jung, *Two Essays on Analytical Psychology:*

(p. 265) "I have called this middle point the self. Intellectually the self is nothing but a psychological concept, a construction that serves to express an undiscernible essence, and which in itself we cannot grasp, since, as its definition implies, it transcends our powers of comprehension. It might just as well be called 'the god in us.' The beginnings of our whole psychic life seem to be inextricably rooted in this point, and all our highest and deepest purposes seem to be striving towards it . . ."

(p. 268) "The self could be represented as a kind of compensation for the conflict between the inner and the outer worlds. This formulation would not be at all unsuitable, since the self has somewhat the character of a result or an achieved goal, something that has come into being only very gradually, and has become part of our experience at the cost of great effort. Thus the self is also the goal of life, because it is the most complete expression of that fateful combination we call individuality. And not only is it the goal for the single man, but also for a whole group, in which one is needed to complete the picture of the other."

The whole subject is of such cardinal importance that it must be put and kept before the reader's mind with the utmost clarity, so that we may realize, as the dream proceeds, the extent to which the construction or mandala of the self "comes into being very gradually and at the cost of great effort."

the text show why a man striving after spirituality is so apt to repress his natural side. There are times when it puts him into extremely awkward predicaments. But nature herself provides the cure. Poliphilo tells us that Lady Taste knows of a herb to cure his sad condition, which means that the gift of good taste is also proper to natural man.

Restored to nature and enriched by the experience of his sensual self, Poliphilo enters the realm of Queen Eleuterilida. The Queen's name characterizes this realm as the region of liberation. Later, we find its other aspect set forth in the inscription over the royal hall: "The Wealth of Nature." But as Poliphilo relates what he saw and experienced in the Queen's realm, the latter seems to us neither free nor natural nor—not to put too fine a point on it—classical. True, the realm of Queen Eleuterilida is full of splendours and delights, but they are governed by a firmly established style and subject to a very rigid etiquette. We are presented with a world of perfectly definite forms which must not be transgressed. Further, the splendours of the Queen's hall are extremely artificial. Even from the literary standpoint, Poliphilo's account here takes on a definite style. It is allegorical in the medieval sense, somewhat after the manner of the *Romance of the Rose*. In both, moreover, we have a stately picture of the pleasures of life in their medieval form. We see the medieval ideal of an accumulation of splendour, precious materials, jewels, and gold, the delight in ostentation and the game of allegory, the pleasure in endless eating and drinking in ceremonial forms. If we were to look for a time and place in the actual world which really put the magnificence of Queen Eleuterilida into practice, we should probably find it at the court of the dukes of Burgundy, where, for a brief efflorescence, this ceremonial, this precious artificiality of life was displayed.[6] Thus the court of Queen

[6] Cf. J. Huizinga, *The Decline of the Middle Ages*.

Eleuterilida is the reflection of a refined secular culture, and it is in that culture that we now find Poliphilo enveloped. For the spiritual man that Poliphilo was, the wealth of worldly culture also means freedom, for it is precisely the cultural form that he needs if he is going to live out his natural side. Now this culture is incorporated in women and maidens only. Queen Eleuterilida's court is a wholly matriarchal domain; that is not surprising, for Poliphilo's way, from the moment he enters the gloomy vaults, lies in the unconscious, which has in the man, by way of compensation, a predominantly female, maternal character. Since the domain of the Queen represents the medieval world, we further realize that the path to the unconscious is at the same time a path into the historical past, a regression,[7] the medieval world first appearing to the man of the Renaissance as the maternal womb from which his own age sprang. Here Poliphilo finds cultural values which can enrich and complete his newly awakened nature. These values are represented in the story by the gifts of Queen Eleuterilida.

The first gift is the ring with the miraculous stone Anchite, which might be regarded as an alchemical symbol for wholeness, perfection, and eternal duration. This contains a hint that man might be made whole and sound by a treasure which lies hidden in his own nature. To Poliphilo himself, the gift of the ring means above all an increase of strength, for he is told that the ring will open the door to his unknown goal. Thus the gift of the ring probably symbolizes the fact that a notion of wholeness, which was known to the Middle Ages, is being constellated in Poliphilo and that that very constellation is giving him greater strength to overcome obstacles.

Further, Queen Eleuterilida gives Poliphilo Reason and Will to be his companions. In the medieval view, Reason

[7] Cf. C. G. Jung, *Psychology and Alchemy*, Part II, Chap. 2, Dreams 4 and 21 and in particular Commentary

and Will were the supreme psychic forces of man, and the only ones that the soul possessed independently of the body. Reason and Will are the faculties which raise man above his instinctive nature and can lead him to knowledge. In their company, Poliphilo leaves Queen Eleuterilida's court and contemplates it from the outside with the eyes of knowledge. The impressions he now receives from it are quite different from those made on him when he was merely indulging himself in the Middle Ages. In the two gardens of gold and glass and of silk, he sees the artificiality of civilization, which forms the seductive and insignificant husk of every temporal culture. But then Reason leads him to the maze, the sight of which gives him true insight.

The maze represents the dance of life, which begins in gaiety and ends in grief, and in which the transformation of sensual man is only achieved in the death of the body. In the interior of the maze we again find the wolf, denoted this time as the messenger of the gods who knows no compassion. In the text, the wolf of the maze is also designated as a dragon. This is an allusion to the identity of the two powers we first encountered separately in the ruined city. Thus wolf and dragon are one; they are the alchemical Mercury, which here appears as the death of the body, as the rattling skeleton which, with frightful fantasies, startled medieval man away from the pleasures of life. The sight of the wolf in the heart of the maze signifies that *memento mori* which, for instance, is the true theme of *Everyman*, where death, with its dreadful menace, confronts the medieval appetite for pleasure.

Poliphilo, who, on his way to the past, has reached the Middle Ages, has discovered the boundless sensuality of the Middle Ages in himself. It lives in his exuberant account of the delights of Queen Eleuterilida's court. With his senses and his sensuality, the appetite for pleasure has awakened in him too. He too is an Everyman, that is why the foreboding of old age and death comes over him in the maze, which is the counterpart of the medieval dance of death. The compelling thought of death is the dragon which compels him not to succumb to the temptations of the world, but to seek what may redeem him from them.

It is as a symbol of the principle of redemption and as the antithesis of the maze that we find, in the last garden of Queen Fleuterilida, the golden obelisk resting on the prism, the circle, and the cube. The obelisk and the precious material out of which it is fashioned emphasize the importance of the figure, which, being the last in the Queen's realm, obviously contains its most secret and profound element—the supreme value to be found in the region. The whole erection is a configuration of purely alchemical significance, and probably the most interesting alchemical symbol in the book. The superimposition of the parts would suggest a progress in stages such as characterizes the Great Work. This progress always represents a history of creation too, which culminates in the making of the philosopher's stone. We can see this very clearly, for instance, in an illustration (Fig. 13) preceding the first chapter of Thomas Norton's *Ordinall* in the edition of the *Musaeum Hermeticum Reformatum*.[8] The emblem is built up in a very similar way to our figure.

At the bottom there is a cube denoted as chaos and the darkness of the abyss; above it there arches a heavenly sphere. As a cube, chaos is conceived as female, and the heavenly sphere is the male opposite belonging to it. This figure has much the same meaning as the first verses of Genesis, where the spirit of God moved on the face of the waters. The cube and the sphere are, in a sense, the parents from which a first creation proceeds. This is shown in the next figure, namely

---

[8] Francofurti MDCXXVIII, p. 441; John Read, op. cit., p. 86, gives a similar figure from Manget, *Bibliotheca Chemica Curiosa*, 1702, with the title "Man, Alchemy and the Cosmos."

Fig. 13. Cosmic Emblem of the Alchemical *Opus* (from *Musaeum Hermeticum Reformatum,* Francofurti MDCXXVIII)

a triangle which is formed of the four smaller triangles of the elements. It is conceived entirely in the alchemical spirit, for in alchemy the four elements contain in themselves the whole of creation. In its turn, a circle proceeds from the triangle of the elements. The circle stands in the centre of the whole figure and is denoted *Homo*. This must be taken in a gnostic sense. It is an Adam Kadmon or Anthropos who, as in the gnostic myths, is at the same time the first man and the Saviour. The circle denoted *Homo* is an emblem of the philosopher's stone. It represents a second, higher creation in which the whole Work is perfected, the dross of the first creation purged away, and, with wholeness, the mid-point between height and depth discovered.[9]

In the same way as in this illustration from the *Musaeum Hermeticum* there is, at the bottom of the figure in the *Hypnerotomachia,* a cube which, in view of its "inscrutability," may be compared to the abyss in the other picture. It is characterized by its whiteness as the female *prima materia* (Luna) of the alchemical process and hence as the mother. The red cylinder is, by its colour, the male (Sol), which corresponds to the father. Exactly as in the emblem from the *Musaeum,* a triangular figure rises from this father and mother. Yet there is nothing to associate the black prism with the four elements. It is characterized only by its blackness. From it there rises the golden obelisk which would correspond to the central point designated as *Homo* in the *Musaeum.*

To understand these last two figures, the black prism and the obelisk, we might turn to another alchemical emblem. It occurs in a treatise ascribed to St. Thomas Aquinas and is reproduced in Jung's *Psychology and Alchemy*.[10] The

---

[9] The illustration in the *Musaeum* contains, in addition, a supreme, supraterrestrial sphere which bears the inscription *Mundus archetypus* and forms the bright, upper counterpart to the chaos beneath. There is no parallel to this in the illustration here reproduced.

[10] Fig. 88

two parents there appear in the semblance of two fountains (silver = Luna; gold = Sol), with two creatures proceeding from them, a dragon and a maiden, both of which signify the same thing, namely, Mercury. The dragon is the first, dark form in which Mercury appears, the maiden signifies his perfection.[11]

The black prism of the *Hypnerotomachia* can be equated without difficulty to the dragon in this picture. We have already seen that in Poliphilo's dream, the number three corresponded to the dragon image and its variants. Thus in the treatise of pseudo-Thomas and in the *Hypnerotomachia,* the first created thing that proceeds from the primeval parents is the first form in which Mercury appears. In our book, the gold of the obelisk then arises as a second, higher creation. In gold, the goal of the alchemical process is attained when that process is regarded as the transmutation of metals. Gold has the same symbolic significance as the philosophers' stone. Thus the golden obelisk offers an analogy to the maiden in the illustration of pseudo-Thomas. The fact that the obelisk in the *Hypnerotomachia,* like the prism on which it stands, is three-sided shows that the two figures are conceived as identical.

Thus the alchemical configuration with the golden obelisk in the *Hypnerotomachia* is an abstract representation of a mother, a father, and a twofold son, dark at his origin and growing bright. But the whole figure is of stone, as if the writer wished to proclaim the ancient wisdom of alchemy—everything is the stone, from beginning to end, through all transmutations. It is always the One which, in the process, grows out of the darkness of chaos into perfection.[12]

[11] The maiden might just as well be represented by the youth denoted as the Young King. The perfected stone is represented both as male and female, and sometimes as hermaphroditic.

[12] The conception of the One from which all proceeds and to which all returns is most beautifully represented in the emblem of the Uroboros; see John Read, op. cit., p. 117.

As Reason now explains to Poliphilo, the figure in the last garden of Queen Eleuterilida is dedicated to the Trinity. If we reflect for a moment, we shall come to the conclusion that this is a somewhat unusual trinity. As a representation of father, mother, and son, the figure might perhaps be denoted as a triad, such as occurs in alchemy when, instead of two substances, three (salt, sulphur, and mercury) are employed as the basic materials for the making of the stone. Since all three are forms of appearance of the One, we might speak of their "identity of essence." In this case the cube would correspond to the salt, the cylinder to the sulphur, and the black prism to the mercury, from which the obelisk would proceed as a symbol of the stone. But that would take no account of the fact that the black prism in itself represents a preliminary form of the stone. Thus the only kind of trinity that could be meant would be one in which the third element is represented in twofold guise, dark and light. Poliphilo's trinity would, in that case, have a somewhat ambiguous meaning.[13]

From the standpoint of the figure pure and simple, however, it would be possible to take quite a different view, for, as we see it, the figure consists not of three, but of four parts. The cube, cylinder, prism, and obelisk form an alchemical quaternity, which is characterized by the four colours, white, red, black, and yellow, and by the union of the square, circle, and triangle.[14] Yet, as we saw above, two of the four are at the same time one. The ideas of trinity and quaternity are so inextricably interwoven in this figure that we can hardly wonder if Poliphilo's Reason is some-

---

[13] Gnostic parallels might be quoted to throw light on this symbolism (cf. Irenaeus, *Against the Heresies*, I, 15, 1, *et passim*), more especially those which survived in the heretical systems till late in the Middle Ages and in which the Demiurge, or Lucifer, is represented as *primogenitus*. (Cf. Charles Schmidt, *Histoire et doctrine de la secte des Cathares, ou Albigeois*, Paris, 1848.)

[14] For the notion of quaternity, cf. C. G. Jung, *Psychology and Religion*, Yale University Press, Oxford University Press, 1938.

what baffled by it.[15] Reason would prefer to give the figure a trinitarian, that is, a Christian, interpretation. It would suit her very well to see only three here, for, according to Christian reason, the only fourth to the three is the devil. Since the triangular prism is another symbol for the triple-tongued dragon, darkness and venom are, in point of fact, contained in the figure too. The same idea is again expressed in the figure of the obelisk, which is a sun-symbol, and contains the attribute of depth by reason of its three-sidedness. Like the figure as a whole, the obelisk too is both light and dark.

Looked at from this standpoint, the figure in the last garden of Queen Eleuterilida is a reconciling symbol, in which not only light and dark, but also unity, duality, trinity, and quaternity are contained. The whole emphasis rests on the fourth, the golden obelisk which, by its form, also comprises the trinity and the opposites of light and dark. From this standpoint, namely as a "special" fourth which is the compensation for all that has gone before, the symbol of the golden obelisk is a development of the symbol of the elephant which we found in the ruined city. It points to a development in so far as what was found after and under the ruined city in the form of the three golden statues is here combined with the symbol of the fourth. This time the trinity of the underworld forms part of the fourth, elevating it and turning it into gold. We have attempted to interpret the elephant as a symbol of the undeveloped potentiality of man still imprisoned in the unconscious, i.e. the inferior function. This again finds expression in the golden obelisk, but now it is supreme value because it contains the hidden divinity. This divine principle is here named ὁ ὤν (He who is). Thus what we have here is a "divine harmony" in which past, present, and future are simultaneously con-

---

[15] For the problem of the three and the four, see C. G. Jung, "Zur Psychologie der Trinitätsidee," *Eranos Year Book,* 1940-1.

tained, a supratemporal entity which transcends human understanding. All these things form part of the intricate and mysterious symbol of the Self which, just because it transcends human understanding, can only be stammeringly described as a whole in which all opposites are contained.

The alchemical emblem before us is the first fully developed mandala in the *Hypnerotomachia,* far more so than the image of the bath-house, which was not quite sealed and not completely centred. Its harmonious order represents simultaneously a process of transformation and changeless duration, for in it everything is always the One. As a symbol of individuation and the Self, the alchemical figure is a promise of release from mortality. But the dreamer is not yet contained in this mandala. He has not yet reached the goal, and who knows if he will ever reach it? He can, however, at least see the goal, and that in itself brings joy.

It is highly significant that an alchemical emblem should stand at this precise point in the *Hypnerotomachia.* It makes us realize that alchemy holds that key-position in the book which was discussed in the introductory chapter to the present volume. It was alchemy which actually redeemed medieval man from the frenzy of sensuality in which he lived by teaching him that there is a living soul in nature as well as matter and that growth and decay can be understood as a process of transformation. By this means, matter was not only redeemed, but made accessible to the scientific and devout contemplation which Poliphilo embodies as he stands in ecstasy in front of the golden obelisk.

Poliphilo, however, must not linger here—indeed, he cannot, for he has another goal. Queen Eleuterilida has given him not only three gifts, but a task, which is to find the three portals of Queen Telosia. The search for a hidden goal, as a task imposed by Queen Eleuterilida, would here appear to be a cultural challenge the response to which arises in the inner and not in the outer world of man. This challenge is first presented as an action of the will, as a choice. Here the story apparently follows the conceptions of medieval philosophy, since the choice, as an act of the will, is placed side by side with knowledge, an act of the reason. And the lover's will chooses love as the supreme concupiscent passion, as St. Thomas Aquinas puts it. Since these philosophical allusions are clear in Poliphilo's narrative, his manner of thought appears to be entirely medieval. But he at once shows the absurdity of such an interpretation by making a choice which completely contradicts the medieval theory of will and love. For according to Aquinas, love is the supreme passion because it leads to good, and the will is also oriented towards the good, that is, towards God. But Poliphilo chooses neither God nor the good.

As a monk and a devout Christian, he would have to choose the left-hand portal of Queen Telosia, the Glory of God, and that is the decision his reason requires. In that case he would return to his starting-point, where there was no conflict and no grave decision to take—and no hope either. Poliphilo cannot find his way back to the ideal of a life lived in the blessedness of God, that is why another ideal is shown to him in the right-hand portal. This right-hand portal, Worldly Fame, signifies the virtues of the militant Christian. The man who cannot be satisfied with monastic seclusion also chooses the good in the Christian sense if he takes up the struggle for the faith against the infidels and the enemies of the church. The two portals, the Glory of God and Worldly Fame, stand here to right and left as symbols of the two great institutions of the clergy and chivalry, whose omnipotent and supreme representatives were for so many centuries the Pope and the Emperor. They incorporated the forces which fought against each other in the Christian era like hostile brothers, which hated each other, yet worked together as the fundamental and manifest opposites within Christendom. Poliphilo now finds himself confronted by these great opposites as symbolized by the right- and left-hand portals of Queen Telosia. Whichever he chooses, he will remain within the Christian community. He would seem to have become estranged from the clergy by his humanistic labours and his courtly love, but now he might return to the world as a militant Christian. Is it possible that this juncture in Poliphilo's dream reflects the secret desire of a monk who is beset by doubt? Is he longing for an open breach with a life that he believes he can no longer live? It would almost seem as if we were confronted here with the problem of the living lie which may well arise in the course of a man's development when he feels that he has outgrown the frame that was once spacious enough for him. What he would like to do is to burst his fetters and endeavour to give expression to his transformation by revolting against all his former life. Then, at any rate, he would be an honest man. Reason would side with such honesty and after some hesitation she is ready to enter Worldly Fame side by side with Poliphilo. But Poliphilo cannot choose the honourable breach with the past either. The harsh Christian either-or has no charms for the natural man he has just regained. That is why he obeys his nature and chooses the only thing alive in him, courtly love, the un-reasonable middle between the opposites, though it promises him no glory. For Dame Love-Potion, who approaches him from the portal of Mater Amoris, is a courtesan pure and simple, that is, a sinful being forbidden to the Christian, religious or layman.

Further, when Poliphilo makes his choice, he is no longer a Christian. His decision lies in quite a different direction. As he has already done in the ruined city, he takes the "middle way," indifferent whether Reason accompanies him or not. He once more chooses the middle between the opposites. And once more, like the portal in the ruined city, the entrance to the middle way stands under the sway of

Venus, for Venus is the mother of love. Thus once again we encounter the classical goddess as the predominant symbol at a critical moment, and she embodies not only love, but classical human nature in all its exuberance. By yielding to the guidance of his own nature and his love, Poliphilo also enters into possession of that nature which he has longed for.

Another question arises however. Does Poliphilo really know what love is? Apparently not, if we are to judge from the dream-symbol, for the realm of Mater Amoris appears to him in the old familiar guise of sensuality which, in the figure of Dame Love-Potion, approaches him like one of the beautiful "ladies that were enchantresses" in the Arthurian cycle, only to fool him with old desires. The dreamer, however, knows all about sexuality and sensuality—he has learned a great deal from the five lovely maidens in the bath-house. And while sensual delight still attracts him, in the dream itself it is valued as a temporary aberration. The attraction subsides as quickly as it arose, and Poliphilo once more stands alone in a wide plain, as he did at the beginning of his dream journey. Yet there is a difference, for now the scales have fallen from his eyes. He stands in a void, everything has been blotted out, and Poliphilo stands there as he really is, a man who has not yet discovered what there is in him. The humanist's dream, courtly love, and the meditation on the One in the figure of his beloved have taken him away from everything he ever knew and led him to the threshold of a *vita nuova,* as yet not understood and utterly unknown.

The only thing he knows about the new life is that it stands under the rule of Venus. Hence it looks as if Poliphilo, on that journey through the past which has stripped him of all his Christian principles, has reached the frontier of the domain of classical human nature. But it is as empty and desolate as a newly created earth that living figures have not peopled.

Up to the point we have just discussed, we might again draw a rough comparison between the march of events in the realm of Queen Eleuterilida and Goethe's *Faust*. Like Poliphilo, what Faust discovers first after his experience of death is a natural world which belongs to the past, the medieval, everyday world of the plain citizen, his father's world, which looks peaceful and kindly enough even though he can no longer quite form part of it. But it is in that very setting that Faust too, in and with Mephistopheles, discovers the life of the senses. His contract with Mephistopheles sets him on the path to an unknown goal which estranges him from his former life and leads him first into a witches' kitchen, where his potion is brewed too. There, too, he is granted the sight of Helen, the image of his aspiration, and this figure, which is related to Venus, also points back to the classical world.

As we proceed to relate what happens further in the *Hypnerotomachia*, we shall see whether Poliphilo is granted a vision of the same significance after his encounter with Dame Love-Potion.

SECTION III

The Triumphal Chariots

(Poliphilo is alone. Through an arcade of verdure he sees a group of youths and maidens. A nymph bearing a torch comes to be his guide. Poliphilo is enamoured of the nymph. She leads him to four triumphal chariots on which the place of the hero is taken by Europa, Leda, Danaë, and a vase containing a vine. At the fountain of Narcissus. Can the nymph be Polia? She leads Poliphilo to the fifth chariot, that of Vertumnus and Pomona, and to the altar of Priapus. Then past Pan and Silvanus to the seashore. The Temple of Venus Physizoa and its construction.)

(Chapter 11) Poliphilo now stands alone in the wide plain, not knowing whether he is awake or asleep. At last, raising his eyes, he sees in front of him a leafy arcade quite overgrown with jasmine. He is only too glad to hide in the green gloom and think over all that has happened to him. Then Polia once more captivates his thoughts, for Queen Eleuterilida has promised that he will find her again. Polia! he sighs, and his sighs re-echo in the green arcade. Passing through it, he sees in the distance a group of youths and maidens. As he watches them, a figure leaves the group and a nymph carrying a flaming torch comes towards him. Her hair is a profusion of golden ringlets, she has laughing eyes and a dimple in her chin. She is as white as snow and as red as blood, and her graceful figure is draped in a splendour of jewels and silk.

For a moment, Poliphilo thinks she is his Polia, but her dress and her surroundings tell him that she cannot be. (Chapter 12) The nymph approaches. With every step she takes, the sight of her entrances his senses until he is nearly distracted with the conflict of her many charms. He cannot but lay his heart at her feet on the spot. But oh! if only he knew whether she is Polia or not! Now she is quite close and, stretching out an arm as white as paper on which there lies a tracery of pink veins, she says in the sweetest voice: "Come hither to me, Poliphilo, and have no fear."

He is thunder-struck. How can she know his name? Without a word, aglow with love, he gives her his hand and allows her to lead him (Fig. 14).

Full of treachery and danger, like the Trojan horse, the love of this nymph has made its way into his heart—her eyes have scorched him as lightning scorches an oak. She walks by his side like an old friend, yet he does not dare to raise his eyes to her lofty beauty, which must surely be reserved to some god.[1] (Chapter 13) Poliphilo sighs as the dreadful fires of love rage within him, yet, realizing the pitifulness of his human condition, he speaks no word. But the queenly nymph can read his heart. She turns her heavenly eyes on him, saying: "Poliphilo, know that true love hath no eyes for the outward shape of things. Therefore let not thy garments daunt thy noble spirit, which perchance is worthy of this sacred spot. Cast all fear from thy mind, that thou mayst contemplate in freedom the realm which Queen Venus prepareth for those she hath crowned."

This lovely admonition completes Poliphilo's enchantment, and the nymph herself seems worth more than all Queen Eleuterilida's treasures put together. He is caught in her toils, he is utterly enslaved, yet he cannot understand himself. Poliphilo, he says to himself, how comes it that thou canst so soon forget that first, close bond of love which united thee to the beloved Polia? How canst thou serve another? He struggles to regain his self-command and turn his thoughts to Polia, but his efforts are unavailing because the nymph so strangely resembles his Polia. It is a delicious torment to him to think that he might have to abandon his Polia for the sake of this nymph, that he must renounce his first love to serve this stranger, and he weeps bitterly at the

[1] This description closely follows Boccaccio's *Ameto*.

Fig. 14. Poliphilo Led by the Nymph

thought. But then he says to himself: this nymph may yet be Polia herself who will not reveal herself to me. Lost in the thoughts which hurry to and fro between the nymph and Polia, he walks on, hand in hand with his lovely guide.

In this fashion the two arrive at the right-hand side of the plain where a lovely spot is enclosed by fruit-trees. Here a great crowd of youths and nymphs comes towards him. With music, play, and mutual caresses, they dance along beside four triumphal chariots which approach in their midst.

(Chapter 14) Here Poliphilo interrupts his story to say: "I know that nought is hard to the gods. They can perform all things, and do what they please, at every place and with every creature. Therefore they are called almighty. Do not, therefore, wonder at the strange, bewildering, nay divine things of which I now have to tell. Art, which learns from nature, essays as best she may to imitate the works of nature. But that divine work which cometh into being without effort, by the breath of genius, she may not copy. Therefore let us not inquire too deeply into these matters but, in all peace of mind and with due reflection, confess that that which seemeth impossible to us is possible to the heavenly gods."

After such an exordium, we may expect a description of incomprehensible creations such as are brought forth by the gods themselves. These are the four triumphal chariots which Poliphilo now proceeds to describe. They are made of gold, silver, and the most splendid precious stones, and are richly adorned with carving. Each chariot is the representation of one of Jove's loves and serves at the same time to glorify Cupid. Each is surrounded by a host of lovely, richly adorned nymphs, singing and dancing to the sound of horns and shawms in a way most wonderful to behold and hear.

The first chariot is drawn by centaurs. It presents scenes from the rape of Europa by the divine bull, and shows Cupid wounding gods and men.

The second chariot presents the story of Leda and the swan. The image of Cupid figures on it as lord of the imagination and fate of the cosmos. This chariot is drawn by elephants.

The third chariot represents Danaë receiving the shower of gold with the sweetness and bitterness of Cupid beside her. This chariot is drawn by unicorns.

These three chariots are alike in that the three women beloved of the god are represented in life-size with the divine lover in his disguise taking the place of the hero.

This is not the case with the fourth chariot, which now follows (Figs. 15 and 16). Here the earthly beloved, Semele, and Jove in the form of a cloud are only seen in the reliefs

Figs. 15 and 16.

on the sides of the chariot, while a vase with a vine growing out of it is enthroned on the chariot in the place of the hero. The vase itself is ornamented with two significant pictures: firstly, Jove himself, with sword and thunderbolt, transforming seven nymphs into trees, secondly, a youthful Bacchus with a maiden's face, his head encoiled by two snakes, one white and one black. Cupid appears on this chariot too, but this time he is himself wounded by Psyche's lamp. The chariot is drawn by panthers, while a host of nymphs, fauns, and satyrs, naked or clad in skins, swarm round it, crying "Evoe!" in harsh voices. Behind it comes Silenus, riding on an ass, then comes a shaggy sacrificial goat. The whole is a noisy bacchanal, a turbulent yet solemn and ancient religious rite. In the rear of the rout there strides a ferocious virago, shaking a winnowing-fan over her head

The Fourth Triumphal Chariot

with demented laughter. This last procession startles Poliphilo. It seems less lovely than the others. But there is worse to come.

(Chapter 15) For the present, however, Poliphilo watches very intently the youths and maidens who form, as it were, an outward shell to the four processions. A large number of them carry flaming torches, like his nymph. And now it turns out that this is a place of the blessed, the place of everlasting spring, everlasting day, and everlasting ripeness. These are the Elysian Fields, peopled by gods, demigods, and heroes, and by all the heroines of antiquity who loved, made poems, or sang. The nymph tells Poliphilo their names and shows him too a crowd of young maidens led with divine gestures by three holy matrons. As she does so, she speaks, and her voice is moved: "My Poliphilo, know that no mortal woman entereth here whose torch hath not been lit by deep love and great toil. And there is also need of the safe guidance of these three matrons." Then she proceeds with a sigh: "For the sake of thy love, I must needs offer up and extinguish my torch in the holy temple."

These mysterious words strike Poliphilo to the heart. My Poliphilo, the nymph has said—may she yet be Polia? The thought turns him pale with sweet alarm, but the cunning nymph quickly turns his mind from herself by leading him out of the Elysian Fields and farther on.

(Chapter 16) By a lovely path the two reach that crystal-clear spring in which Narcissus saw his own reflection. All round this fountain, a swarm of lovers, all young, youths and nymphs, take their delight in the sports of love two by two. The nymphs raise their garments to bathe their feet in the clear spring, baring their legs up to the knees. This moves Poliphilo to an acute observation—that such a sight would inflame the veriest clod to love. And, to his own growing delight, he watches the pretty couples kissing, caressing, and embracing each other as close as the shells of an oyster. The sight is so delicious that he nearly loses his soul watching it. Is it a dream—is it an enchantment? But when he thinks over all he has seen, he knows that it is a reality which his mind cannot yet quite comprehend. Then he returns to brooding whether the nymph is indeed Polia. And so, in his inmost self, he is once more imprisoned in his conflict. Who is she? Who is he? Shall he desire life or death? Shall he ask her who she is, or must he refrain? He longs to cry—help me, save me, I am in mortal peril. But then there flock in upon his mind countless examples of heroes of antiquity who provoked the wrath of heaven by hubris. This cools his fever, for he has no wish to be presumptuous. Comforted and silent, he is content to *watch* the beloved figure moving before him with the divine beauty that he can at least enjoy incessantly with his eyes.

(Chapter 17) Walking on through groves of fruit-trees,

Fig. 17. The Altar of Priapus

Poliphilo and his nymph reach a region where green meadows are divided into fine, regular squares by green-bordered paths. They find a crowd of people of a kind that are rarely seen together. They are clad like country-folk and, in company with the hamadryads, they accompany a fifth triumphal chariot on which Vertumnus and Pomona are enthroned, adorned with all blossoms and fruit and with the implements of rustic labour. The chariot and its accompanying train circle round a marble altar in the centre of the meadows, which has the four seasons depicted on its four sides.

On this altar there stands a statue of an ithyphallic Priapus holding a scythe under a rude arch of leaves, with burning lamps swaying and rattling in the wind (Fig. 17). The crowd now presses round this altar, laughing, dancing, and leaping. The people have slaughtered an ass and, according to rustic custom, are hurling bottles of asses' blood, milk, and wine at the statue of Priapus, where they break. Then again they carry about the decorated statue of the antique Janus. As they do so, they sing, to the accompaniment of rustic instruments, a medley of hymns and extremely obscene nuptial songs.

This barbaric ceremony astounds Poliphilo as much as all that went before moved him to admiration.

Once again the way leads on, and through the tree-trunks of the forest, Poliphilo sees Pan and Silvanus with nymphs, dryads, nereids, oreads, and singing shepherd-folk celebrating a sacred flower-festival. But his nymph leads him past all these things to the shore of the sea which receives all the rivers of the land they have passed through.

They reach a round temple beautifully situated on the shore (Fig. 18). It is dedicated to Venus Physizoa and is divided into ten parts. Golden mosaics on the wall depict the course of the sun and moon through the zodiac, and the orbits of the fixed stars and the planets, all with explanatory

Fig. 18. The Temple of Venus Physizoa

inscriptions in Greek characters. Thus the walls are like an open treatise on astronomy. The roof of the temple is formed of seven closely entwined vine branches, worked with great art out of a single piece of gilt copper. But the most remarkable thing about the temple is the contrivance for collecting rain water. The pilasters of the outer wall are hollow, the rain water flows through them and on through pipes under the temple into a cistern situated in the middle of its interior. (Here Colonna the architect takes advantage of the opportunity for an excursus on eaves in general.)

As we have already seen, the cistern opens in the centre of the temple—Poliphilo calls it, by the way, a "fateful" cistern—while above it a strange and beautiful lamp hangs down from the summit of the dome. It consists of four external globes and a central one. The four external globes are red, blue, green, and yellow; the central one is white. All are filled with an absolutely pure spirit which is never exhausted.

Corresponding to this globe in the interior, an echoing hollow globe is mounted on the outer summit of the dome, bearing a crescent moon surmounted by an eagle.

Fig. 19
The Central Lamp in the Temple of Venus

To recapitulate this highly intricate symbolism: the circular temple with its ten divisions contains the following superimposed central points: at the bottom the cistern, above it the lamp with a central white globe surrounded by four coloured globes, and above that, on the dome, the crescent moon bearing the eagle.

The central lamp (Fig. 19), swinging between heaven and earth in the temple, is shown quite simply and clearly as a piece of alchemical laboratory apparatus, namely a vessel with Mercury in the guise of a flame in its centre. It is above all this lamp that leads Béroalde de Verville, the French translator of 1600, to claim Poliphilo's dream as an alchemical treatise. He is in so far right as this drawing might be regarded simply and solely as an alchemical credo, for what it means is that Mercury is the centre of all things (ὁ ὤν).

COMMENTARY TO SECTION III

After Poliphilo had passed through the portal of Mater Amoris, his first experience was the distressing and ridiculous affair of Dame Love-Potion and her lustful train. Like a boy, he had identified love with sensual desire, and in doing so, found himself in an aberration as tedious as the desolate plain on which he stands. It is only when the veil of this error has been lifted that he can open his eyes—that is, concentrate on what he sees. He resumes his meditation and at once sees a vision that he calls the jasmine walk.

This walk is, by its form, a cave, just like the gloomy vault behind the great portal in the ruined city. Poliphilo's present situation is analogous to his former one; once again he has passed through a central gate and once more he gazes on the unknown. Like the gloomy vaults under the ruined city, the jasmine walk is a symbol of the unconscious, but now it is no longer dark; it is bright and blooming. Jasmine is a plant which flowers very early, even in winter, before the leaves have had time to unfold. Thus what we have here is a first growth, an early spring.

We must not, however, forget that this spring lies outspread behind the portal of Mater Amoris. Thus it is the realm of Venus which begins to bloom for Poliphilo. Hence the unconscious appears under the symbol of classical nature in springtime bloom, and in this symbol, the dreamer can apprehend some of its contents.

These contents are then seen bodied forth in a crowd of men and women—they are together. This is indeed something new. In the ruined city, as we have seen, there was no image for a real contact between men and women. In the symbol of the colossus, the dreamer was shown a man who is lonely and sick because he lacks his feminine counterpart. And that corresponds to the situation of the courtly lover which was his starting-point, for it consists precisely in the fact that the woman has her being at an exalted height and remains an image of unfulfilled and unfulfillable yearning. The men and women he sees here in each other's company show him in a symbol that matters can be otherwise. There is a way for man to find his feminine complement. That way lies through the jasmine walk, that is, it leads through the awakening of the soul. If man is to acquire the feminine component which makes him whole, he needs the love which wells up from his soul.

It is also notable that the masculine principle makes its appearance here for the first time in an image. This again is quite unprecedented in Poliphilo's dream. Up to this point, he has always been the one man in a flood of femininity. A crowd of female figures, not one of which had any particular relationship to him, had cherished and led him like a child, but now the image of the man too takes visible shape on the stage of his dream, and this must certainly be taken to mean that the spectator has already passed through a development in the course of his journey, and has grown from childhood to manhood.

At the same time, one single, clearly defined figure detaches itself from the throng of women—a nymph carrying a flaming torch approaches Poliphilo. It takes him a whole chapter to describe the enchantment radiating from her person and the beauty and splendour of her garments. Tirelessly he depicts her glory in all its details; a thousand images express what he feels at the sight of her. As a female figure drawn from classical mythology, the nymph in Poliphilo's dream is the first embodiment of nature as it appeared to the ancient world which really touches him. She comes towards him as an elemental spirit, though with a special significance. As daughters of the rivers, the nymphs are children of water like the later Melusinas of the fairy tales, and like them, they carry with them the babbling coolness of the springs. Thus Poliphilo's nymph is a water-spirit, yet at the same time she bears a flame; she contains opposites which cannot otherwise be reconciled. Thus it follows from Poliphilo's account that the opposites meet and mingle in the figure of the nymph; the divine and the merely human, the incomprehensible and the familiar, dread and supreme sweetness are united in her.

This fusion of opposites in the figure and the fascination she exercises leave no room for doubt that the nymph is the first real anima figure in our story.[2] The manner of presentation is so absolutely characteristic that it might be called a classic description of an anima. It is in precisely the way here described that the man is ravished and stirred to the depths by this primeval image rising from the psyche, and it is in precisely this way that it assumes supreme value when he has put away childish things and become a man. From that moment on, the anima takes the lead in his life because, along with her watery darkness, she brings him a new light.

Later, the nymph says of her torch that it can only be lit by great love and great toil. But that love and toil are

[2] For the conception of the anima as the female soul-image of the man, cf. C. G. Jung, *Psychological Types,* Definitions, under "Soul and Soul-Image"; *The Relation of the Ego to the Unconscious,* Part II, Chap. 2; "Über die Archetypen des kollektiven Unbewussten," *Eranos Year Book,* 1934, p. 204 ff.

Poliphilo's. By love, the nymph means the meditation on the One which Poliphilo has practised throughout his journey hitherto; she means his unwavering attachment to the sacred image of the beloved woman. As for the great toil, she means the labour of self-knowledge that Poliphilo also had to take upon himself on his way. He had to discover his common humanity, to recognize that he was not really a supersensual being. To attain such insight means very great toil, for it is precisely against the common condition of man that spiritualized masculinity rebels most fiercely. Yet this toil, together with the warmth of love, has actually produced something like a light, a torch in the hand of the anima, which from now on illuminates the uncertain path.

In addition to all this toil and love, however, the torch could only be lit with the help of those three matrons who were seen in the distance in the Elysian Fields. The classical analogy to these matrons might be seen in the Roman *tres matres* or the triple-formed Hecate. They are mysterious goddesses of the depths, like the Mothers in *Faust*. They are the female aspect of the image we have already encountered in the triple-tongued dragon, the three golden statues, and the triangular black prism in Queen Eleuterilida's garden. They symbolize the maternal, life-giving function of the unconscious, without whose powerful—and dangerous—aid no inward growth is possible. And there echoes too in the image of the three matrons the humble and devout reservation that alchemy makes when setting out on the Great Work with a prayer for God's help. Without some impersonal proviso, love and labour will be in vain, nor must man ascribe success to himself.

The very fact that Poliphilo cannot consciously apprehend what is going on shows that it would not be right for him to do so. Passionately moved as he is, he cannot recognize his anima when she comes to him. That is why he yields to her fascination quite passively; he cannot help himself. This very compulsion, however, is characteristic of the early stages of the man's experience of the anima.

The description of the bewilderment and conflict arising from the transference of the archetype to a real woman is both fascinating and illuminating. Poliphilo's restless puzzlement as to whether the nymph is Polia or not, his fear and trembling, his despondency and tears—all these are the symptoms, depicted with perfect truth to life, of the painful process of the withdrawal of a transference. The nymph, for her part, is quite untroubled by this conflict and the grief it causes Poliphilo. What the situation apparently requires of him is simply further meditation, the unwavering concentration on the One, in whatever form he may apprehend it, and wherever it may be sought and found. If Poliphilo remains faithful to this task, events will also proceed on their undeviating course. Anima, the guide, stands revealed as the vessel which holds illumination. She points the way to fresh and radiant images.

These images are the triumphal chariots which Poliphilo and the nymph now see.[3] The first four belong together and form a whole in the midst of the men and women who surround them. Further, they have one characteristic in common, namely the figure of Cupid, which is represented in one way or another on them all.

As we know, Cupid is the son of the great mother, Venus, but he is a very peculiar kind of son. Originally, Cupid was the embodiment of desire; he springs from the Greek

[3] From the literary point of view, the description follows Petrarch's *Trionfi*. Triumphal progresses were, however, an important medium of expression of the age. A parallel in alchemical literature is offered by Basil Valentine's *Triumphal Chariot of Antimony*.

Himeros-Eros, yet the figure has nothing to do with the old Greek god Eros, who was a god of generation. He must also be distinguished from the cosmogonic Eros of Hesiod and Orphism, as well as from the philosophers' conception of Eros. The Eros-Cupid of the *Hypnerotomachia* arose in very early times, far removed from any cult or theology, as a product of the secular imagination. He is a creation of secular art and poetry, in which he was always depicted, in contrast to the phallic god, as a daemonic child, tameless, bitter-sweet, and akin to fire. In later times Cupid came to incorporate with growing distinctness the fire of love. In accordance with the secular origin of the figure, its development became increasingly personal and legendary. It was in this sense that it was taken over by the Romans, and it was mainly by way of Ovid that the little spirit made its way into the Middle Ages, the Renaissance, and later times.

It seems characteristic that the monk Colonna, in his dream, should seize upon this symbol, which developed on purely secular ground, and hence stands for no religious experience but for the greatest experience the world has to give, namely the love of one human being for another. It is, so to speak, outside of the church door that Cupid, as the son of the great mother, Venus, becomes the spark emitted by the rose. He is the light which has already been represented by the nymph's torch. In the alchemical sense he is the symbol of the "divine fire," whose discovery and maintenance is a fundamental condition of all the stages of the Work. When he flashes up, the alchemical transformation has set in.

The first things to be warmed and illuminated by Cupid in the *Hypnerotomachia* are the four beings represented by the first four chariots. These four beings are simply denoted as the four earthly women beloved of Jove. In a case like this, the readers of the age of humanism needed no more than the names. They were, after all, familiar with ancient myths and legends. They were, moreover, familiar with the century-old method of interpretation which gave to all the important legends of antiquity a definite allegorical or symbolic meaning and in that way drew them into the world of Christian ideas. Hence we must take the chariots with the women beloved of Jove simply on the basis of their allegorical meaning.

The first chariot, with Europa, who bore to Jove Minos and Rhadamanthus, the two judges of the dead, stands for the earth.

The second chariot, with Leda, the mother of Castor and Pollux, signifies air.

Danaë, on the third chariot, as the mother of Perseus, stands for fire (ordinary fire, that is, which must be distinguished from the "divine" alchemical fire).

And now we come to the fourth chariot. Here the description takes on a different tone. The image is more mysterious, yet at the same time much less splendid, and Poliphilo finds it slightly repellent. The vine and the vase point to wine in the mixing-vat; thus the fourth element is no ordinary water. It is the "peculiar sap" which alchemy calls ὕδωρ θεῖον or *vinum ardens*. We must take the alchemical significance of the symbol into account because the figurative language of alchemy is especially clear in the account of the separate parts of the chariot. There is, of course, a reason for this stress on alchemical symbolism. It expresses the fact that while the fourth element is a water, which, like all others, is present everywhere, a power of transformation dwells in it which makes it worthy to be called divine.

In addition to all this, however, a completely new element has crept into the description of the fourth chariot, namely the allusion to an ancient mystery cult. What is going on round the chariot is a bacchanal, a *thiasos*, and since such rites were always celebrated at night, this chariot brings us close to night. Bacchus-Dionysos was not only the lord of wine, but also the god of disembodied spirits and the dead, and his mysteries were linked with death and resurrection.

One of the figures in the train makes it perfectly clear that this is meant—the old maenad with the winnowing-fan. Her wild laughter recalls the Dionysian frenzy, her ferocity the terrors inseparable from the process of transformation of the mysteries, which signified a death and rebirth and whose emblem was the winnowing-fan. The new-born Dionysos (= the symbol of rebirth) was cradled in the winnowing-fan, and the purpose of the Delphic festival of Dionysos was to awaken the divine child in it.

The allusion to the ancient mystery cult at this point is made only in passing. The first four chariots represent in outline simply and solely the four elements. But before describing them, Poliphilo has, so to speak, made a solemn pause and denoted them as incomprehensibly glorious works of the gods. Therefore we must regard the four elements, one of which is so remarkably different from the others, as symbols of psychic facts. They are images of the four functions, one of which, the inferior function, remains, as the symbolism requires, obscure and alien.

To make this clear, it will be best to inquire what application it has to the author of the *Hypnerotomachia*. We know him as a man of highly developed intuitive powers. His supreme gift is intuition, that is why he moves with such ease in the world of dreams. Further, he has the extremely active mind which marks him as a humanistic scholar. But his capacity for feeling has remained backward, for, even when it is genuine, it remains attached to collective ideas. When this man loves, he does not love according to the needs of his own nature but as the general conception of courtly love prescribes. Nevertheless he puts his feeling into action, if only in this form. He is capable of following its dictates consciously and even with deep emotion. What is really inferior is his sense of reality. Sensation, which should enable him to apprehend reality, is his inferior function. Wherever he should apprehend a thing as it really is, he becomes inferior. As we saw first in the bath-house scene with the five sense-maidens, and later at his meeting with Dame Love-Potion, the first stirrings of sensation (as a function) in him are both jejune and barbarous. He blunders his way into the first misunderstanding that presents itself. It has needed a special development for him even to realize his common human condition. All that he knows about his body at first is anatomical terms. Later, it is not until his dream leads him through the realm of Queen Eleuterilida that he learns something of the meaning of worldly culture and civilization. Thus he only comes to know reality by plunging into the unconscious. Sensation is for him the point at which he remains entangled in the unconscious and the past; he feels worthless and weak, while a chaotic savagery stirs in him like the bacchic frenzy of the ancient mysteries. That is why his inferiority is repulsive to him; he dreads it too, for it removes him from his ordinary consciousness and thus awakens in him the fear of madness. Yet the inferior function has a divine aspect too, since, just because it is predominantly unconscious, it can open the way into the unconscious. It is indeed the "divine water" of alchemy, a common thing, yet endowed with powers of transformation.

In the image of the four elements, the four functions are represented in our book as three accompanied by a fourth of a totally different nature, in part divine, in part daemonic. This symbolism is complementary to that of the alchemical figure with the golden obelisk in the last garden of Queen Eleuterilida, but from the standpoint of consciousness. The three are not, on this occasion, mysterious; they are "ordinary," they are symbols of what we have and know, hence of consciousness developed in three directions. The fourth, the symbol of the inferior function, is now neither exalted nor made of gold, for, seen from the standpoint of consciousness, it is alien, chaotic, and obscure. Its meaning becomes clear in the symbol of the vase, the alchemical nature of which is emphasized by the two scenes which figure on its sides. The first is Jove transforming seven nymphs into trees,[4] the second is the youthful Bacchus with the maiden's face and the two serpents, black and white, coiled round his head. The seven nymphs represent the seven stages of the alchemical process, in which transformation is brought about by the action of the divine fire. The maidenly Bacchus represents the goal of the process; he is that hermaphrodite which so often appears in alchemical treatises as the symbol of the philosophers' stone. The white and black serpents with which he is crowned form a twined circle in which light and dark are united. They correspond to the widespread alchemical serpent symbolism which embodies the two forms of appearance of the One[5] on which the whole process is based. As the wearer of the snake-crown, the hermaphroditic Bacchus is also the Twofold One (*Mercurius duplex*), but in its perfection.

Expressed in words, what these two scenes on the vase have to say is roughly this: behold! the regular process of transformation is taking place in this vase. This is where the alchemical process in stages can be accomplished. Here grows the philosophers' stone. Hence the inferior function is equated with the hermetic vessel, and in this way it is brought near to consciousness in the form in which it must be understood and recognized, namely as a sinister darkness which nevertheless possesses supreme value because in it the One can emerge into visibility. Hence this One, which Poliphilo has so long yearned for and contemplated in the figure of his beloved, now appears at a totally different place, namely in that very side of himself which he dreads so much and in which he cannot see clearly. Here, in this unfamiliar region, the picture on the vase tells him, a supreme value lies hid which may yet unfold like a vine and bear fruit.

The symbolism of the three and of the fourth element em-

---

[4] Cf. C. G. Jung, *Psychology and Alchemy*, Fig. 5.

[5] Frequently there are two snakes, one winged and one wingless, which are intertwined or in mutual combat.

bodied in the chariots, however, is as alien to Poliphilo as was the figure with the golden obelisk. Hand in hand with the anima, the dreamer beholds a possibility he cannot yet comprehend. But at least he sees the image clearly, without Reason's attempting to interpret it.

To judge by everything that Poliphilo's visions have to show later, we might not go far wrong in saying that the nymph is a personification of classical antiquity in a general way, since he finds that she has led him unawares full into the antique world. For as soon as he has finished contemplating the four chariots, it turns out that he and the nymph have already arrived in the Elysian Fields. The men and women surrounding the chariots stand revealed as transfigured heroes and heroines whose exalted names the nymph recounts to Poliphilo. But before he has had time to recover from his awed amazement, the sublime scene has vanished. We are standing by the fountain of Narcissus, and the couples playing and love-making there present as suggestive a picture as Boucher or Fragonard could have painted at their best.

The direct juxtaposition of the supreme bliss of the Elysian Fields and the rippling sensuality by the fountain of Narcissus is most remarkable. With incomparable concision, it reflects shady sides of humanism, which was only too prone to strut about in borrowed buskins and to idealize classical antiquity in literature, only to come to grief on its lasciviousness.

The multitude of couples, however, which swarm round the fountain would seem to signify something more. Poliphilo sees nothing but mating and mating couples, because he cannot recognize himself and the nymph as *the* couple, because with his mind he is blindly and obstinately seeking in the illusion of an actual woman and in the conventional situation of courtly love the complement to himself which is already walking by his side as the loveliest of realities. But by falsifying his outward situation and keeping up the fiction of a love relationship which is, in actual fact, quite beyond his reach, he also falsifies his inner situation, and so is swayed between the sham sublimity of an artistic elysium and a senseless sensuality.

The image of the fountain of Narcissus, however, also contains an allusion to the *Romance of the Rose,* whose author first saw his Rosebud in its waters. It is as though the image were calling on Poliphilo to open his eyes and see his own Rosebud, that is, his nymph. But the image of the fountain of Narcissus probably holds a deeper meaning yet. As we know, that legendary youth of ancient times saw only himself in the water. In other words, whoever fails to see the psychic image in the reflecting water of love will only see himself. It is the ever-threatening danger of introspection that it can be abused by egoism, and that the human being who discovers beauty and significance in himself begins to think that he is himself beautiful and significant. There is, of course, a positive idea in the image, namely that of the sight of one's self. Love brings to light what manner of being a man is.

In the obscure and confusing situation figured by the fountain of Narcissus, Poliphilo, as always, finds help in loving meditation, though this time it takes a fresh turn. Poliphilo surrenders utterly to the heart-rending conflict in which he is tossed between his love for Polia and his love for the nymph. For the first time he looks at the nymph moving before him with undivided attention, so that she becomes the sole object of his meditation. Unwittingly, he abandons the idea of the actual woman as his high lady, and transfers his supreme value to the creative imagination as bodied forth in the figure of the nymph and her guidance of him. At this point in the story, though the dreamer does not know it, he has really passed beyond the convention of courtly love, and as Poliphilo journeys on, led by the nymph, a new stage of his development sets in.

The change from the compulsion of fascination to free contemplation is characteristic of the anima experience. It signifies the actual beginning of the man's coming to terms with the anima and the first real participation of consciousness in the events of the inner life, which cannot fail to produce its own reaction.

It is for that reason that the nymph now leads Poliphilo to images which have a quite unprecedented significance.

First we have the triumphal chariot of Vertumnus and Pomona. Vertumnus and Pomona are the first purely Roman divinities to appear in the *Hypnerotomachia*. Vertumnus, the changeful, is the god of the seasons, Pomona is the goddess of fruit. Her chariot, Poliphilo tells us, is "surrounded by people who are not usually seen together," a peculiar statement. Up to the present, Poliphilo's dream, like every other, has brought together every imaginable kind of figure, nor has the dreamer noticed anything unusual in such associations. But now it would seem as if there were, even in this dream, people whose association is quite out of the ordinary. Yet according to the description, the people in question are simply country-folk, peasants, and they are just the kind of people who are often met with in companies in real life. There is a contradiction here in virtue of which these ordinary country-folk are stamped as unusual, special, and significant. Their actions—the celebration of the rites of Priapus—then show us that they are Roman peasants. For all their ordinariness, they bear a significant impress for the dreamer because they are the company of his own dead. They are his ancestors, and for the living man it is certainly unusual and extremely important to see them together. These ancestors, with the chariot, move round an altar on which the seasons are depicted. Hence we have here a clear symbolism of time, but on Roman soil and in the midst of Poliphilo's own dead. On this soil and among these people, the Italian author of the *Hypnerotomachia* is *at home*.

After he has accepted the nymph-anima, his guide, as the object of his contemplation, the first thing she does is to lead him back to his origins in his own people. The Hades which his prophetic eye had seen as the Elysian Fields were not for him. A Colonna does not descend from blest spirits but from the Italian soil which has been made fruitful by all the sweat and toil of those who have laboured upon it. His ancestors are Italian country-folk with nothing special about them at all. They were all "plain" people. This discovery is manifestly unpleasant to the humanist who has always regarded the Roman past as the acme of perfect distinction. What happens to him now is what happens to everyone else in the same situation. We are all prone to idealize our past, in the good or bad sense, for if we descend from heroes, good or evil, we can be something special without exerting ourselves at all.

The way into the past, however, leads Poliphilo yet farther on. The nymph now leads him to the altar in the centre. We must imagine that in following her, Poliphilo is caught up in the circular movement of the procession. The pulse-beat of his own earthly life bears him along, and he is led to the centre by a *circumambulatio,* that is, a ritual procession. The beings moving round the altar are described as being so primitive and undifferentiated that we must also regard the centre as the deepest depth.

There Priapus is enthroned as the reigning divinity. In the earlier editions of the book he is shown quite openly as ithyphallic, hence there is special stress on the male sex. True, Priapus was by origin a Greek daemon, but his cult became so important in Italy, especially among the populace, and was practised up to such late times, that he may be regarded here as an autochthonous deity. He was the guardian of gardens, the god of shepherds, the god who stimulated the forces of physical procreation. That is why the ass, the most prolific of beasts, was sacrificed to him. Further, Priapus was the protector of sexual intercourse in marriage and of marital fertility. It is this aspect of him which is specially emphasized in Colonna's book.

If we examine this symbolism more closely and then try to imagine the man to whom these visions came, we shall not be able to suppress a certain feeling of sympathy for him. True, sexuality, as we have already seen, presents no problem to the dreamer of this dream in so far as it is, so to speak, the only reality he knows in his ignorance of the world. We saw that in the affair with Dame Love-Potion and her train. Thus if sexuality had been the only point at issue here, the appearance of the Priapus symbol would hardly have made Poliphilo so thoughtful. But Priapus does not mean sexuality in love. On the contrary, this symbol stands for the first creative impulse of the adult man to find a natural differentiation from the chaotic promiscuity of the world by founding a family, so that, having been a son, he may become a father. It is the desire to beget a witness to one's own life for future generations, and there is no doubt that this desire is very strong in the Latin races. Now a Renaissance monk could beget as many children as he chose, what he could not do was to become a paterfamilias and tend the fruits of his garden till they reached maturity.

Thus the Poliphilo who stands confronted with his Italian peasant ancestors, to whom he is accountable for the future, must face, in the symbol of the ancient daemonic protector of sexual union, not only the problem of celibacy but also that of his own natural creative power which he cannot put into action in the world outside him. In the wild confusion of his deepest depths, that power still awaits expression.

This, then, is the first result of his encounter with the anima; the place is revealed where life has lain unlived and unfulfilled, a natural creative power is awakened which has never yet been put into action. Here, where there was once mere conflict, an essential problem now stands, that is, a vital task, and that is in itself a great gain. But the solution of the problem can only become clear through the further course of the anima experience.

The five triumphal processions which have just been discussed also contain a mandala symbolism which might be diagrammatically represented as follows:

The first four chariots which symbolize the elements might be grouped thus:

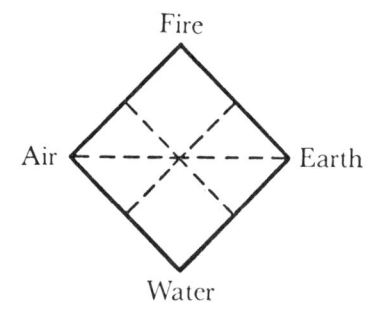

```
        Fire
         ◇
Air ←---✳---→ Earth
         ◇
        Water
```

The train of Vertumnus and Pomona is a *circumambulatio* which can be naturally rendered as a circle. On the other hand, Poliphilo says that the *circumambulatio* takes place in a region divided into paths by regular squares. This would go to prove that the circle belongs to the square of the elements shown above. The seasons are the natural time of elemental space. Hence the following diagram would ensue:

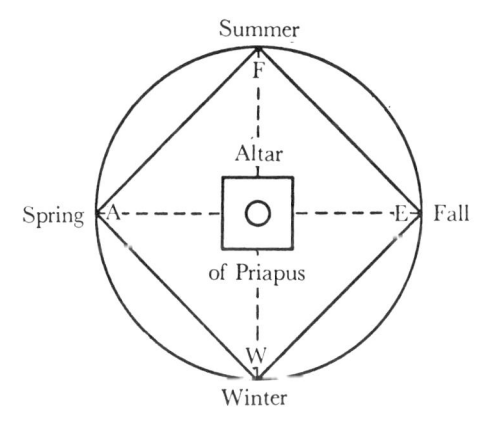

```
         Summer
           F
         Altar
Spring A-----O-----E Fall
       of Priapus
           W
         Winter
```

Here we have a well-developed mandala, the scheme of which follows that current in alchemy. This is justified, since Poliphilo himself emphasizes the alchemical aspect of his triumphal processions. His Priapus is also an alchemical symbol. The scythe he carries is an attribute of Saturn. In the mineral world he is represented by lead, which, by reason of its weight and blackness, so often stands for the *prima materia* of the process. The *prima materia* is the beginning of the Great Work, it is the future philosopher's stone in its first gross form as the worthless and the vile. The combination of the square and the circle which can be deduced from Poliphilo's description of the elements and the seasons, however, is at the same time the symbol of that world-stirring conception of the squaring of the circle which so preoccupied the alchemists at all times.

If we look back over the action of the dream up to this point, and endeavour by its help to interpret the symbols of the altar of Priapus and its sacred precincts, we might say that the alchemical *prima materia* (here embodied in the figure of Priapus) must be taken as the insoluble problem in the life of man. But it turns out that at the very point where fulfilment is denied him, and where he can feel nothing but the oppression of a desperate questioning and longing, the fountainhead of inward life is to be found. To consciousness and ordinary human reason, this is a miracle, and the alchemical symbol for this miracle is the squaring of the circle. It stands for the idea that a method can be found by which the impossible is made possible. The fact that the squaring of the circle is always figured as a mandala further points to the fact that the method or way to the goal which is so difficult of attainment is at the same time the goal itself. The squaring of the circle is a symbol of the Self.[6] In the *prima materia* it appears in its first and lowest form and, according to the *Hypnerotomachia*, this turns out to be sexuality.[7] From this standpoint we can understand a new aspect of Poliphilo's error with regard to the beautiful and disdainful Dame Love-Potion. Like many a man, he imagined that sexuality was a "nothing-but," that it meant simply and solely the crude physical satisfaction of lust. It is only by the intervention of the anima that he can learn to discern in sex too the mysterious stirrings of a creative power which, though rooted in the personal, is in itself impersonal. Since the author of the *Hypnerotomachia* is a monk, what this means for him is the creative principle, which cannot be put into action in marriage. But in other human beings, the same symbol may stand for all those tendencies that cannot be lived out in marriage and the world. In this sense the figures of the *Hypnerotomachia* are universally valid. At the beginning of all things there al-

[6] See C. G. Jung, *Psychology and Alchemy*, Fig. 60.

[7] This description is exactly analogous to Indian Tantrism, where the lowest centre is conceived as being situated in the genital region. The symbol belonging to it shows a phallus entwined by a snake in the middle of a mandala shaped like a four-leaved lotus. The parallel to the snake in our author is the *circumambulatio* round the altar of Priapus by the ancestors.

ways stands the problem of unlived life, of longing and frustration—a problem which, like the *prima materia* of the alchemists, is certainly the commonest thing there is. Yet it is difficult to find, because consciousness, in its pride, hates and despises nothing so much as this all-too-human ordinariness.

At this point in our attempt to interpret Poliphilo's visions, we may seem to have strayed very far. But it is the author himself who lures the reader on. Everything in his book goes to prove that he intentionally concealed far more in it that we can ever grasp in the space at our disposal.

After the rites at the altar of Priapus, Poliphilo's vision continues; he sees Pan and Silvan with shepherds and nymphs celebrating a flower-festival.

Pan might be called the brother of Priapus. He too is daemonic in origin and has a love for country-folk, but he lives, so to speak, in a totally different climate. He has not, like Priapus, settled down into an association with particular localities, but is imagined as a wanderer, a nomad. With his goat's horns and hooves he is half beast, and he is the friend of all nymphs. With the sweet sounds of his flute he bestows sweet dreams, but he can also cause panic terror, nightmare, and epilepsy. Wherever water flows and a tree gives shade, he is there. In his later development he becomes the All (τό πᾶν).

Pan died with the antique world. Legend tells that the steersman Thamus, sailing through the archipelago, heard from an island many voices wailing: "Great Pan is dead."[8] Pan is the symbol of the unconscious psyche of the antique world which manifested itself in the body and in living nature—in the flight of birds, in bleeding entrails, in prophetic dreams, and in the possession of the seers.[9]

[8] Plutarch, *de def. or.*, 17.
[9] Silvan is the Roman variant of Pan.

The image of Pan celebrating the rites is very lightly touched upon in Poliphilo's account, and the nymph-anima does not move towards him and his companions. To plunge into the naked life of nature represented by Pan's flower-festival would be a grave danger to Poliphilo, who stands on the threshold of modern times, for it would submerge him in the unconsciousness of the ancients.

For that reason the nymph leads him still farther back to where the past is neither Greek nor Roman, nor indeed localized in time at all. She leads him to the sea into which all waters flow.

The sea is the symbol of the collective unconscious in which all psychic life is contained in archetypal forms, beyond time and space. "In contrast to the personal psyche, it has contents and modes of behaviour which are, *cum grano salis,* the same everywhere and in all individuals. The collective unconscious is identical in all human beings, and hence forms a universal foundation of the psyche which is suprapersonal in kind and exists in every human being." [10]

Thus if Poliphilo now reaches the sea of the collective unconscious, to which only the anima, the mediator between the personal and the suprapersonal, can lead him, he finds there that archetypal image which has not been formed by his own present and past and is yet of such a kind that he can read in it as in a book the mode of behaviour which would be right for him at the moment.

What he sees he calls the temple of Venus Physizoa, that is, the Venus of living nature. This temple is an alchemical symbol which is just as conventional as the figure with the golden obelisk in the last garden of Queen Eleuterilida. Parallels in plenty could be found in the alchemical treatises. It represents a hermetic vessel ornamented with all those

[10] C. G. Jung, "Über die Archetypen des kollektiven Unbewussten," *Eranos Year Book,* 1934.

marks of singularity which distinguish this important alchemical symbol. The celestial bodies pictured on it make the temple a reflection of the cosmos of the spheres; standing at the ocean's edge and washed round by the waters of heaven, it is situated at the spot where above and below meet. Its division into ten parts points to perfection, for ten is the number of the perfect human being.[11] And all the details in and on the temple allude to the symbolism of the vessel. On the one hand, the cistern, filled with the water of heaven, and the lamp, on the other, with its wonderful central light, are the images of that magic alchemical duality which arises from the four elements (represented by the lamps in four complementary colours surrounding the centre) and becomes one in the vessel. The crescent moon and the eagle on the dome are an allusion to the same union. It is indeed a promising symbol for Poliphilo and his nymph.

At the same time, however, the temple is a shrine of the goddess Venus, hence a symbol of the Mater Amoris whose way Poliphilo chose at the three portals of Queen Telosia. He is now quite near to her and when the close-shut temple door opens to him, he will find rebirth in the mother's embrace.[12]

Further, the temple of Venus Physizoa is an exact reversal of the altar of Priapus. Everything that was there purely male, natural, crude, and unsightly is here female, shapely, and beautifully finished. Nevertheless, the altar of Priapus and the temple are symbols of one and the same thing, namely the magic circle of creative power, which is lived once as a natural instinct "in the coolness of the nights of love wherein thou didst beget," and again in the imagination as the "alien feeling which begot thee," to vary Goethe's incomparable lines. If the male, natural aspect of the creative function appears as darkness because it cannot be put

[11] See C. G. Jung, *Psychology and Alchemy*.
[12] For the alchemical symbolism of the vessel, see C. G. Jung, op. cit.

into action, its female aspect shines in brightest light. Having revealed to Poliphilo his problem, and with it his life-task, the nymph-anima shows him in the symbol of the temple of Venus that the solution must not be sought in external activity, but within him as psychic experience.

But with all that we must not forget that the temple that Poliphilo describes is a Graeco-Roman place of worship dedicated to Venus. True, the altar of Priapus was also a holy place, but it was quite embedded in nature and primitive in kind. The temple of Venus, on the other hand, is a place of religious culture as it developed in the ancient world. It is a place where the divine can manifest itself in a setting created by man. What this means we shall learn when the temple door opens. The proceedings in the temple will show us what is the "living nature" which stands under the protection and divine influence of Venus.

We might briefly point out that the events in the *Hypnerotomachia* which we have just discussed do not run quite parallel to Goethe's *Faust*. Here we see the difference between man at the beginning and man at the end of the modern era. For Goethe, the Priapic experience that he has embodied in Faust's love for Gretchen is a personal matter in which the human beings bear a personal responsibility. Thereby the problem of procreation becomes for Faust a moral problem and his experience turns to tragedy. Poliphilo has no personality of that kind, he is identical with his place in life. Hence his power to beget is not related to a person but to an institution—marriage. And his failure is not a tragedy, but a comedy in Dante's sense, the Divine Comedy which leads the natural man to find his soul.

SECTION IV

In the Temple of Venus Physizoa

(Poliphilo and the nymph are welcomed by the high priestess of the temple and her vestals. The nymph's torch is extinguished in the cistern. "I am Polia." Sacrificial rite and magic apparitions in the chapel. The heavenly feeding. The high priestess blesses Polia and Poliphilo. The nymph sends Poliphilo to visit the Polyandrion, which is dedicated to the triple-bodied Pluto. Cupid approaches. The lovers sail across the sea in Cupid's bark.)

When Poliphilo has studied the temple of Venus Physizoa in all its details, he goes on to relate how the nymph knocks at the temple door, which opens as if of itself. The first thing that Poliphilo sees is two aphorisms which need no interpretation:

> Every man is moved by his desire
> and
> Every man acts according to his own nature

The holy high priestess (*la sacra Antista*)[1] approaches with her seven vestals and leads Poliphilo and the nymph into the temple. She accompanies them to the wonderful cistern, which is filled only by water from heaven. The seven vestals bring a number of objects for the religious rite, a sacred book, a sacrificial knife, sacrificial dishes, holy salt, two veils, two scarlet caps, and a mitre. The illustration shows that one of the vestals is quite a child, and it is she who is to hold the sacred book in the rites which follow.

First the high priestess puts a cap and veil on her own head and on the nymph's. Then she crowns herself with the mitre.

[1] She is subsequently called Priestess, Sibyl, Hierophant, or Monitrice.

Fig. 20. The Torch Is Extinguished

Thereupon she lifts the golden lid of the cistern, throws salt into the water, and pronounces a prayer in Etruscan. The nymph's torch is then lowered towards the water, and the high priestess asks: "My child, what is thy desire?" The nymph replies: "I pray for grace for this man, and desire to go with him to the realm of the Divine Mother, and there to drink of her fountain."

The high priestess then asks Poliphilo: "And thou, my son, what is thy desire?" And he replies: "I pray not only for the grace of the Great Mother, but more especially that this nymph, whom I believe, yet do not know, to be Polia, should let me languish no longer in the pains of love."

Poliphilo is now instructed to lower the nymph's torch into the water, saying as he does so: "As the fresh water extinguisheth this torch, so may love inflame her cold heart" (Fig. 20). The high priestess then draws water from the cistern and gives it to the nymph alone to drink. She then prays with the seven vestals, and now the nymph turns to Poliphilo and reveals herself to him.

"*I* am Polia," she says, "who was lured away from the service of the chaste Diana by thy great love, and who am now conquered. I confess that it is but just to reward thy constancy by my affection. Therefore I am now ready to put an end to thy sighs and pains, to quench the fire in thy heart with my tears, to belong to thee alone and to die for thee if need be." And as a sign, she gives Poliphilo the first kiss. Her words are so gracious, her kiss so sweet, that Poliphilo is bereft of speech like one smitten with epilepsy, and dissolves in tears. The hearts of the priestess and her vestals are so touched by the sight that they all shed a few small tears too.

But that is not the end of the ceremony. The priestess says to Polia: "Let us complete the inward sacrifices which follow upon this holy beginning." All the women now enter a round chapel attached to the temple. Though without windows, its interior is bright, and its dome is formed out of a single stone. Poliphilo remains humbly standing on the threshold.

In the middle of the chapel there is an altar of jasper, also hewn out of a single block, though not with the hammer nor the chisel, but by an art unknown to man. On this altar there lies a golden dish adorned with carbuncles and diamonds, in which a flame is burning. Polia kneels down before the altar. She prays to the Graces to intercede with Mother Venus to reveal herself in her divinity.

(Chapter 18) Then she kills two doves with the sacrificial knife, collects their blood in a vessel, and casts the bodies into the golden altar dish, where they burn to ashes. Meanwhile the seven vestals move round the altar in a ritual dance, chanting the while. When the doves have burned to ashes, smoke rises, and while all the women, with the exception of the high priestess, prostrate themselves, Poliphilo sees from the threshold a little spirit, a messenger of the gods (*spiritulo theosphato*), rising from the smoke. In his hands he carries a myrtle wreath and an arrow, and his golden curls are crowned with a diamond circlet. On glittering wings he soars upward like a sunbeam, or like a lightning flash composed of water, fire, cloud, and wind. He flies three times round the altar, then vanishes, dissolved in smoke.

Polia is now told to collect the rest of the ashes in a sieve with a switch, then to shake them through the sieve on to the seven steps of the altar. In these ashes she has then to make certain sacred signs contained in the sacred book. The high priestess in her turn makes certain signs in the ashes, and this fills Poliphilo with such dread that his hair stands on end, for he fears that Polia may be torn from him by this potent magic. But the dreadful signs are only destined to exorcize and expel all spirits hostile to love. Thereupon the ashes are carried into the temple and emptied into the cistern. The women return to the chapel and the high priestess addresses a great prayer of intercession for the lovers to the goddess Venus.

The high priestess then strews roses and sea-shells on the altar and sprinkles them with sea-water (Fig. 21). Two male swans are sacrificed and their blood mingled with that of the doves. The swans in their turn are burnt in the altar flame and their ashes emptied away into an opening under the altar. Then Polia and the high priestess each dip a finger in the mixture of blood and again write mysterious signs with it. They wash their hands with water, and now the blood that was on their hands is mingled with the water that was on their hands and poured into the altar dish. This rite is performed by the high priestess, then all cast themselves to the ground. For now a mighty whirlwind, an earthquake, and thunder arise with great smoke, as if a thunder-storm were raging in a sealed cave.

Poliphilo's terror may be imagined. But hardly has the worst of the thunder rumbled away when he opens his eyes

Fig. 21. The Sacrifice of Roses and Sea-Shells

again. Then he sees, growing out of the smoke on the altar, a rose-bush which spreads over the whole chapel. The bush is covered with red roses and round, rosy fruit.

The high priestess and Polia rise and summon Poliphilo into the chapel. The priestess plucks three of the miraculous fruits from the bush; one she eats herself, the other two she gives to the lovers (Fig. 22). Hardly has Poliphilo tasted the fruit when he feels strangely refreshed, and his love is inspired with new life and strength. After the divine feeding, the rose-bush vanishes, and the high priestess now dismisses Polia and Poliphilo with her blessing. She tells them that they have received purification and blessing from her. They are now to proceed on their way, obey her commandments, and keep her teachings in their hearts. But since the priestess has given the two no explicit commandments or

Fig. 22. The Heavenly Feeding

instructions, we have to assume that the wonderful proceedings we have just witnessed are themselves her teachings.

Hand in hand, Polia and Poliphilo wander on along the seashore. She, his guide, leads him to a great place filled with ruins of the antique world. Once this was a great seaport, and countless multitudes flocked to it yearly. The place surrounded a temple called the Polyandrion, which was dedicated to the triple-formed Pluto, the god of the shades (Fig. 23).

Polyandrion means graveyard, hence the temple is a place of tombs. The nymph goes on to say that many men and women lie buried here, all of whom had met a wretched end through unhappy love. Old, sacred rose-bushes, whose

Fig. 23. The Polyandrion

blossoms once served to extinguish the sacrificial fire, still bloom among the tombs.

The lovers now sit down on the seashore to contemplate the ruins, or rather, Poliphilo gazes at Polia, not at the graves. As he does so, the flame of love in his heart glows ever more fiercely, till he can hardly bear it.

(Chapter 19) It is such great anguish for Poliphilo to see his beloved so near without possessing her that he feels as if he could cast aside all restraint and prudence and overcome her with herculean force, like the huntsman his quarry. But Polia, in her wisdom, sees her lover's fierce trouble, and to distract him, she says that she knows what pleasure he takes in things of the antique world. He is to go and look at the temple; there he will find many things to his taste. Meanwhile she will await the arrival of her lord Cupid, who will soon come to lead them to his mother, Venus. Obediently, Poliphilo rises and goes.

The symbolism of the place of tombs is so lavish that only the outstanding points can be touched on here. The first thing Poliphilo sees is a great obelisk, red in colour and covered with all manner of reliefs and hieroglyphics. Then, in the middle of the sacred precinct, he finds a little temple borne on six columns, with the centre of its dome open like a chimney (Fig. 24). In the middle of the floor there is a grating through which the space below can be seen. Poliphilo goes down and finds there, in dreadful darkness, a smoke-blackened altar which combines the shapes of a coffin and a fireplace. When his eyes have grown accustomed to the darkness, he can read the inscription on it, which runs:

> INTERNOPLOTONITRICORPORI
> ET CARAEOXORIPROSERPINAE
> TRICIPITIQ. CERBERO

(Sacred to the triple-bodied Pluto, he who is within, to his beloved spouse, Proserpine, and the three-headed Cerberus)

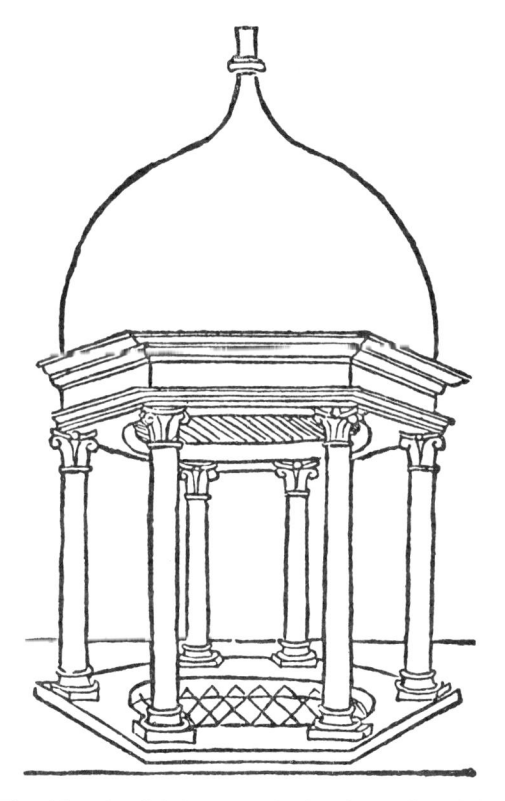

Fig. 24. The Little Temple in the Polyandrion

Not far from the little temple there is an open vault with a great mosaic in its roofing. This represents a Hell with an abyss yawning between rocky precipices, in which two seas, one of fire and one frozen dark, clash together with a horrible noise. Here Cerberus and the Erinyes keep watch over the hapless souls which writhe in the fire or suffer the torments of the ice. A stony path leads up from the depths to a bridge, and to this bridge the wretched creatures hurry, seeking coolness from the heat and warmth from the ice. But hardly have they reached it when it bursts asunder, hurling them all back to their predestined element—the burning back to the flames and the freezing back to the ice. A legend over the mosaic tells that those who have loved too ardently are condemned to eternal flames in this place, while those are plunged into ice who were lukewarm, and have offered unfeeling resistance to love.

Then Poliphilo comes to a multitude of graves where hapless lovers lie buried, together or alone. (One tombstone after another is reproduced in the book, and their inscriptions are given in full. The humanist in Colonna betrays himself in the zealous prolixity with which he indulges in the new fashion for epitaphs.)

Finally, Poliphilo arrives in front of a mosaic representing the rape of Proserpine, and as he studies it, he is visited suddenly by a terrible thought. What if his Polia, like another Proserpine, were to be torn from him while he is wasting his time among these old stones? A dreadful fear overcomes him. As he once fled in despair from the dragon in the first ruined city, he now flees from the frightful thought of a separation from Polia, over graves and stones, through bush and briar, and out of the graveyard. Prostrate with exhaustion, drenched with tears and sweat, he stumbles unawares into the lap of Polia, who embraces him tenderly and asks him the reason for his disarray. When he tells her everything, she smiles. She wipes his sweat away, kisses him, and tells him that her lord, Cupid, will soon be with them. Meanwhile he must be patient and reflect that suffering often leads to the supreme good. These gracious words restore Poliphilo to himself. Though he still looks like a corpse which has already crumbled into dust and ashes and needs to be put together again, he knows that he is saved. Restored to calm, he once more plunges into the contemplation of Polia, and is so lost in it that he cannot understand why she suddenly stands up, makes obeisance, and kneels. But without questioning, he does likewise.

Then he sees Cupid, the little god, approaching from the sea, glittering and lustrous in a golden bark. In the divine voice that can awaken the dead, quell storms, and pacify the ocean's rage, Cupid invites Polia and Poliphilo into the bark. His mother, Venus, has lent a gracious ear to the prayers and sacrifices of the lovers, and is ready to grant them their desire. Under Cupid's protection, they are to be taken to the island of Cythera, where the goddess dwells. Without a word, Polia obeys, and enters the miraculous bark. Poliphilo follows her. Lovely nymphs, their robes tucked up, row the bark out to sea, where Cupid spreads his own peacock-blue wings for sails, and calls on Zephyr to blow. And so the bark speeds across the ocean, and soon the land has sunk on the horizon.

The air is clear, the ocean calm, and the water like crystal, so that they can see down to the ocean bed. But now all the sea-gods rise to do homage to the Lord of Love. Nereus approaches first with the lovely Chloris, then dark-bearded Neptune comes with his trident, on a chariot drawn by whales. Tritons surround him, loudly blowing their conch-shells. The countless host of the Nereids ride by on dolphins. And old Father Oceanus himself comes too with his spouse Amphitrite and all his beautiful daughters. Proteus the changeful rises, borne by sea-horses. Strange monsters, sea-horses, and sea-men swim, dive, and leap through the waters, till the white foam splashes high into the air. Swans sing sweet melodies and form an outer circle to the whole.

Poliphilo, contemplating in turn his lord and his lady, feels like some victorious emperor, for here his Polia can no longer escape him. It seems to him a miraculous thing that the fire of the divine Boy can penetrate the ocean and warm cold Neptune, then rise to burn even the great Jove himself. "Oh, lovely bird," he says to himself, "even so hast thou built thy nest in my heart," and, looking into Polia's eyes, he goes on: "Oh, sweetest of mirrors, how hast thou changed my heart into a quiver for Cupid's arrows. Oh, lovely twain, I am your prey. Share it between you. No greater happiness could befall me."

COMMENTARY TO SECTION IV

The part of the *Hypnerotomachia* just narrated is a veritable living labyrinth, for in it a host of images and ideas are wound into an almost inextricable coil.

We might begin by saying that the whole sequence of events could be interpreted in alchemical terms. That aspect of the section, however, can only be taken into account here in so far as it is indispensable to the understanding of the action.

The vaulted temple precincts in which the high priestess holds sway with her seven vestals expresses the harmony of primordial entities which often figure in the alchemical tracts as the metals in the mountain of the planet fruits on the tree. They are symbolic of the rich and orderly wholeness which is constellated at the very moment the human being, distracted in chaos, is utterly drained. The mysterious self-opening of the temple door probably signifies that if the method of approach is correct, this wholeness can be made accessible or the human being can be united with it.

In the description of the temple's interior, the alchemical vessel symbolism is broadened and deepened. Seen from within, the actual temple proves to be an outer shell in which, as it were, the circular chapel is contained as the next stratum. This in its turn encloses the richly decorated altar with the gold sacrificial dish as the innermost centre. The representation of four parts each contained within the other shows [2] the hermetic vessel as a quaternity corresponding to the four triumphal chariots as symbols of the four elements, the fourth being once more marked as a thing

---

[2] Cf. C. G. Jung, *Psychology and Alchemy*, Figs. 119 and 120. For the symbolism of the temple and the rites performed in it, cf. C. G. Jung, "Bemerkungen zu den Visionen des Zosimos," *Eranos Year Book*, 1937.

apart. This time it represents the supreme value, since it is of gold. As a sacrificial vessel it is at the same time a κρατήρ, that is, the place of transformation. In all probability this means that wholeness can only become attainable through the alchemical Work of progressive transformation, to which the archetypal opposites, man and woman, are now subjected.

The place of transformation is also a place of baptism. The exterior shape of the temple itself vividly recalls an Italian baptistery, with the cistern as the font. It is the nymph who is to be baptized there and to receive the name of Polia. It is as one being baptized that she is given the holy water to drink—the ὕδωρ θεῖον enters into the female substance. Thus the first stage of the alchemical Work is a "treatment" of the female substance.

The baptism by water in the temple is followed by a double baptism by fire in the chapel, in which, both times, an animal substance is rendered volatile, i.e. is spiritualized. The two doves, as birds sacred to Venus, are a symbol of the female substance from which the spirit is released and flies forth. The latter is represented as a winged genius, and if we are told that it flies round the altar three times, that is in all probability in order to associate with it the number three and hence to characterize it as a form of mercury. The winged genius is analogous to the alchemical phoenix; it is the volatile Mercury or *spiritus mercurialis,* one of the first forms in which the stone appears.

Since the two swans which are then sacrificed are explicitly denoted as male in the text, we can see in them a symbol of the male substance which is united with the earth after it has been burnt. There is no direct union of the male and female substances, but their blood, i.e. their essence, is drawn off, mingled, and hence united. From that union there proceeds a subtle body (the spectral rose-bush), which then bears the healing fruit and this signifies the alchemical elixir of life.

What we have here is a symbolic representation in alchemical terms of the processes to which the two originally impure substances are subjected up to the *conjunctio* of their essences and the appearance of the elixir. For Poliphilo the lover, however, this is as yet no more than an anticipation, a first instruction by means of images, and its aim is obviously to guide his desire into the right path. The image of mating that he saw by the fountain of Narcissus is, as it were, corrected by the much more mysterious picture of a "chymic marriage." Cast out of the chaos of the world, Poliphilo suddenly finds himself part of an all-embracing wholeness where he has no longer to act but to be acted upon, and where the union of love also means the transformation of his own being. The instruction by means of images is in itself life-giving too. This is represented in the symbol of the healing fruit brought forth by the spectral rose-bush.

In the temple, the high priestess takes her place between Poliphilo and Polia as the third principal actor. She functions as the bond of union without which the lovers can never be united. When she betroths them, they are themselves drawn into the alchemical process in order that the work of transformation may be fulfilled upon them. In the *chemical* sense, Poliphilo and Polia would have to be taken as symbols of sulphur and salt, while the high priestess corresponds to the mercury which unites the opposites. From the philosophical standpoint, the high priestess is a symbol of the psyche (as representative of Venus), the mediator between body and spirit. Under the image of the betrothal a provisional *conjunctio* of the alchemical couple takes place, which is, however, followed by a fresh separation, the male principal, Poliphilo, like the swans, being sunk in the earth symbolized by the Polyandrion. In Pluto, who is associated with the number three, we have another form under which Mercury appears. In Pluto's realm the male substance is subjected to his action. The meaning of this becomes manifest in the image of the red obelisk, for that points to the future *rubedo*, the goal of the alchemical process.

In the little temple of the Polyandrion we see an alchemist's laboratory with a chimney and fireplace. Then, in the mosaic of Hell, we catch a glimpse of the alchemist's cauldron, in which the opposites seethe. This mosaic and the tombs which follow are symbols of the extremely important alchemical process of the *putrefactio* or *solutio,* the dissolution in death which precedes the new life.

Finally yet another symbol of the hermetic vessel appears —the bark of the God of Love in which the male and female substances are united anew under the benevolent action of fire and water ($=$ Cupid and the ocean). The *sublimatio* begins—the peacock wings of the god indicate that the "peacock's tail is appearing in the vessel," a current alchemical designation of the first manifestation of renewal.

So much for the alchemical signification of the strange action in this section of the *Hypnerotomachia*. As already pointed out, we need not go into it farther since an interpretation from another standpoint will appear later.

Nor need we discuss in detail the fact that, from the temple of Venus Physizoa to the place of tombs and Cupid's bark, we have sacred precincts which are of a pronounced mandala character. Each time, the soil is sacred or the building very precious. Every "magic circle" is subject to a divine figure and closed to the outer world. Poliphilo cannot enter when and how he will, and everything that happens there bears the impress of the numinous; it fills him with horror or bliss. In particular, the Polyandrion is the exact counterpart of the temple of Venus, the place of tombs corresponding to the temple itself, for as the latter is an image of the cosmos of the spheres, the former, with its tombs and the mosaic of Hell, is a picture of the underworld. The little temple of Pluto on its six columns corresponds to the chapel in the temple of Venus. The upper room of the temple with the grating in the floor corresponds to the altar in the chapel, the smoke-blackened furnace below it to the sacrificial dish on the altar in the chapel. The whole plan of the chapel in the temple of Venus Physizoa is oriented upward, that of the temple of Pluto downward. And just as the chapel is bright, with gold in its inmost heart, the temple is dark, and the centre of its interior (= the fireplace) is black. But in the symbol of Cupid's bark, the opposites of light and dark, above and below, are abolished. It stands in the middle between the light breezes and the many-peopled sea. Hence, as Poliphilo sails away in the bark, he is led along a middle path, as he has already been in the ruined city and in front of the three portals of Queen Telosia.

It is further interesting at this point to compare Poliphilo's story with Dante's. In the mosaic in the place of tombs, we have a picture of Hell which is imagined somewhat after the manner of Dante. Further, the words in which Poliphilo describes the sin of those who are punished by cold and heat are Dante's own. When Virgil speaks to Dante of the aberrations of love, he defines them, just as Poliphilo does, as love which is either too hot or too cold. Yet if only love is there, these aberrations seem slight. They are punished, not by hell but in purgatory, and do not stand in the way of eternal bliss. But for Poliphilo, there is only one hell and that is the hell of love. To this man, whose whole path in life is determined by love, love too ardent or love too cool is the one absolutely unforgivable sin. Nor is the picture of hell manifested in vain. His lust for Polia, which he likens to the violent desire of the huntsman for his quarry, shows that his love is too ardent. On the other hand, his rambles among the tombs, his lingering over their epitaphs, show the coolness of his feeling. Here he relapses into a humanistic intellectualism which merely makes use of what another age has created in order to indulge, coldly if brilliantly, in an intellectual game of its own. With that, the afflatus of classical antiquity is almost stifled in him, and his new-found life threatens to sink into Pluto's depths like another Proserpine. In reality, however, the walk through the place of tombs with its monuments signifies a fresh meditation on love in all its aspects. The graves of the hapless lovers bring before his eyes the tragedy that the loss of the beloved means. It is a strangely stern lesson, almost a threat, but the man to whom it is addressed takes it in slowly. In the end, it flashes upon him that he might lose Polia, and as he realizes how unbearable, even fatal, such a loss would be, he fully knows, for the first time, how much she means to him. The thought of losing her gives him his first insight into her true value. And only then does he once more cast aside his humanistic vanity. Fearless of the thorny path of love and the wounds it inflicts, he hurries back to Polia and surrenders utterly to her.

Poliphilo's triple-bodied Pluto might be compared to Dante's Satan in that the latter is also threefold. The comparison would be possible if Pluto were described as a devil, but that is by no means the case. It is only in the ruined city at the beginning of the dream—that is, when Poliphilo is still spellbound by a rigid consciousness—that the trinity of the underworld, in the symbol of the dragon, takes on a purely infernal aspect. The dark image is now present too in the shape of Cerberus, but it is subordinated to Pluto, and through him the depths are characterized, not as hell, but as the underworld of antiquity. What, however, does the image of the underworld mean in this connection? In our attempt to find the answer to this question we must go farther afield, for the emergence of this symbol in the story opens up an entirely new perspective.

The images in the preceding section are almost inextricably interwoven with ideas from the rebirth mysteries of the classical world. This can be seen if only by the fact that the shape of the temple of Venus Physizoa not only represents an alchemical vessel, but, with its outer precincts and inner sanctuary, corresponds in construction to the ancient mystery temples. At this point, the account really has two perfectly distinct meanings. But the allusions to the ancient mysteries are most clear in Poliphilo's walk through the place of tombs, which turns out in the end to be a katabasis, that is, a descent to the underworld of exactly the same kind as we find, for instance, in the *Metamorphoses* of Apuleius. The katabasis was the critical moment in a number of ancient mystery cults. To the neophyte, as to Poliphilo, it brought growing dread and terror, together with a sense of death without which there was no hope of the ultimate transformation and the blissful sight of the light.[3]

We should not be far wrong in saying that the Great Work of the alchemists and the classical rite of initiation signify one and the same thing. Both signify a process in which the mortal is transformed, perfected, and made immortal. In both, the goal is reached by strenuous practical action. In the present case, however, it is the difference, not the likeness, which would appear to be important, but that difference is not quite obvious.

If Poliphilo suddenly recalls the ancient mysteries at this point, it means, first and foremost, that what is at issue here is not matter; it is Poliphilo himself who is being transformed. And the Great Work of the alchemists is based on the same conception. The true alchemists were perfectly well aware that the alchemical transmutation had to do with man. But that knowledge, which they could impart to nobody, cut them off from other men. The masters of alchemy

---

[3] For the whole present discussion, cf. Paul Foucart, *Les Mystères d'Eleusis*, Aug. Picard, Paris, 1914; Franz Cumont, *Die orientalischen Religionen im römischen Heidentum*, Teubner, Leipzig, 1931; R. Reitzenstein, *Die hellenistischen Mysterienreligionen*, Teubner, Leipzig, 1920.

were themselves a mystery, access to which could only be found by some miracle. The idea of segregation plays a very great part in alchemy. In the ancient mysteries, on the other hand, it is only the rite that is a secret which must not be revealed. It was perfectly natural and uninteresting for a man to be a neophyte. It was not about himself he had to keep silence, but about what had happened to him. Thus the segregation in this case is only a question of degree, and the whole weight, the whole value, resides in what happens.

From this point of view, the late classical mystery cults were closely akin to Catholicism, and that kinship comes out very clearly in a number of details in the foregoing section. Christianity and paganism are intermingled in the very names that Poliphilo gives to the priestess of the temple of Venus. As *Antista,* she has the title of an early Christian bishop, as *Hierophanta,* she bears the name of the high priestess of an ancient rite of initiation. To complete the fusion, moreover, she wears a bishop's mitre. Thus the ceremonies in the temple of Venus bear a certain resemblance to the Catholic mass. This will be discussed in detail later.

The blend of Catholic conceptions with those of the ancient mystery cults takes us back to the first beginnings of Christianity, which owes a good deal to late classical ideas of redemption. By leading us down to the threshold of the secret religious feeling of the ancient world, Poliphilo also takes us to the roots of the Christian tree of life, which strike deep into pagan soil. And with that we can also comprehend the origins to which both the Renaissance and Reformation turned for their rebirth of faith. In reaching back to the roots of Christianity, the Reformation rediscovered the individual human being's access to his God. What the Renaissance, on the other hand, found at that root was pagan nature, the female principle incorporated in the great goddess of the mysteries, whose dark radiance outshines all the other gods. This way back is beautifully expressed in Poliphilo's visions.

This must not, of course, be taken to mean that Poliphilo singles out and, so to speak, reconstructs a definite mystery cult. What was dormant in him, and now rises to the surface, is a medley not unlike that of late Roman paganism. Yet Poliphilo knows that the goddess of his temple bears the name of Venus, he sees ritual actions performed by women, and that points clearly to the mystery of a mother-goddess.

The Roman Venus-Aphrodite, whose name Poliphilo gives to the supreme ruler of his *Hypnerotomachia,* had no mystery cult associated with her. The ancient Roman Venus was a goddess of fertility who took gardens and love under her wing and was the embodiment of the gracious in nature and in man's manner of life. She was usually worshipped in company with Ceres. The Hellenization of the cult of Venus then spread from the famous shrine of Aphrodite on Mount Eryx in Sicily, bringing a notable change with it. It is characteristic that this Aphrodite Erucina made her entry into Rome at about the same time as the Magna Mater Deum Idea, that is, at the time of the Punic Wars, when Rome obviously had to call in aid all the female depths of earth in her effort to repulse the invaders. For her part, the Sicilian Aphrodite Erucina had taken the place of a Phoenician Astarte and had retained from her origin a definitely earthly atmosphere. Thus it was an Aphrodite Pandemos (the goddess of the masses still enslaved by their senses) who conquered Rome. Even there her name was coupled with that of Mars. She was mainly worshipped by women of easy virtue, to such a point, indeed, that her festival was also called *dies meretricum.* At the same time Aphrodite was important as the ancestress of the Roman patricians since she was the beloved of Anchises and the mother of Aeneas. It was for that reason that Julius Caesar tried to make an honest woman of her; for reasons of state, he introduced the cult of Venus Genitrix as that of a reverend, divine matron. But efforts of this kind lasted only as long as the Julian dynasty, and in spite of them the Roman Venus-Aphrodite retained her earthbound character to a considerable degree. It was as the goddess of sensual desire that she was handed down by literature to the Middle Ages.

Thus we can discern the three figures blended in hers, the ancient garden-goddess Venus, Aphrodite-Pandemos, and Astarte, and the development proceeds still farther. On her triumphal progress through the Roman Empire, the late Egyptian goddess Isis was also merged in this Venus-Aphrodite. For centuries, the mystery cult of Isis in Rome had a markedly equivocal character. That is why the government made repeated attempts to suppress it. The sanctuaries of Isis were more than once destroyed and burnt down as a result of public scandals. In his *Golden Ass*, Apuleius hits the mark by placing his mystery at the end of an indecorous story. Plutarch, in his essay on Isis and Osiris (Cap. 78), says: "The garments of Isis are of many colours, for the significance of Isis is related to matter, which can turn into anything and take in anything, light and dark, day and night, water and fire, life and death, beginning and end." This matter is the "living nature" which also gives Poliphilo's Venus her name.

It is, however, beautiful to see how purification proceeds from this same equivocal mingling of matter. In spite of their offensive elements, the mysteries of Isis remained free of orgies, frenzy, and drunkenness.

The cult and the mysteries of the great goddess Isis go back to Ptolemaeus Soter, who was ruler of Egypt after the death of Alexander. He consciously Hellenized this cult, its language was Greek, and the mysteries followed the Eleusinian tradition. In this way, very ancient mystery elements entered the late classical age, and the early Greek and Egyptian tradition took on fresh and widespread life and activity. For that matter, the Eleusinian mysteries themselves were very famous and attracted large numbers of worshippers in the latter days of Rome, and we can actually catch an echo of the secret cult of the mother and daughter, Demeter and Kore, in the *Hypnerotomachia*.[4]

The human soul is extremely retentive of memories of the past. That is why Poliphilo can rightly call his high priestess *Monitrice,* which means not only she who admonishes but also she who remembers.[5] She might be called the personification of man's memory of the past. We can see how well that memory functions by the accuracy with which intrinsic elements of the ancient mystery cults are reproduced in the action. In what follows, these are briefly summarized, though without details of their application in the various cults, since in this connection only the basic facts are important.

Firstly, in the temple of Venus, a mystery element can be seen in the very language which accompanies the sacrificial action. In early times, as here, formulae and prayers, rigidly prescribed, very ancient and only partly understood, were used in this way. Poliphilo once states explicitly that the high priestess pronounced a prayer in Etruscan, which was for the Italian in his own country the most ancient of languages. It was unnecessary for the neophyte to understand this language, for it did not enter his mind but went straight to the foundation of his being.

Another mystery element is the elaborate sacrifice in which every detail is charged with meaning. Actually speaking, man only brings the material objects to the sacrifice; what happens to them there is beyond the range of his power. The will of the god is manifested in an utterly unpredictable fashion. That is why the sacrifice must be watched and interpreted with the utmost accuracy. In the temple of Venus

---

[4] For the figure of the goddess, see Franz Cumont, op. cit.; W. H. Roscher, op. cit., Vol. II, Sect. 1, pp. 360-548; A. Wallis Budge, *The Gods of the Egyptians,* Methuen, London, 1904, Vol. II, pp. 186-240.

[5] Psychologically speaking, she represents an archetype, i.e. an image of primordial human experience deposited in the collective psyche.

Physizoa, the unpredictable and the significant are combined in this way with the sacrifice. It is described not only as a human action, but also as a manifestation of the god, before which not only the neophytes but indeed the high priestess prostrate themselves.

A third mystery element is the sacred food as an intrinsic factor in the initiation. The underlying idea is that this food is the gift of the divinity, who is contained in it as the mother is contained in the child. This interpretation is confirmed in various mysteries where the neophyte takes the sacred food from the place in which the divinity is believed to be present. Thus for Poliphilo also, the sacred food grows straight out of the altar and, like an antique neophyte, he feels wonderfully strengthened and sustained by it.

Yet another mystery element is the indirect teaching. The teaching must be indirect because the secret cannot be divulged and is not to be comprehended in words. Hence the neophyte is taught by the priest's action and in images. It is the emotional upheaval caused by what he sees and hears that completes his transformation.

Further, we must not leave out of account the significance of fire and water in the ancient mystery cults. In the cult of Isis, for instance, holy water was always understood to be Nile water, and since Osiris is the Nile, the water was Osiris himself. That is why the water was the water of purification in a higher sense. In the libation, water was united with the sacred fire, as happens in the *Hypnerotomachia* also when the priestess pours the mixture of blood and water on to the altar flame. In Eleusis, the cistern (the virgin's fountain) was a place of peculiar import, because Demeter first appeared to human eyes there. Fire is familiar to the two sorceresses skilled in healing, Demeter and Isis. Both attempted to bestow immortality on a child placed in fire. The torch is an ancient attribute of Demeter, and it passed from her to Isis.

All these elements—the peculiar language, the sacrifice,

the sacred food, the indirect teaching, the significance of water and fire—are now elements of the Catholic cultus also. The baptism of Polia by the side of the cistern, when salt is thrown into the water and a light plunged into it, is clearly reminiscent of Christian rites. On the other hand, the little girl who takes precedence among the temple vestals may again be regarded as a mystery element. We read of an "altar child" at Eleusis who clearly played a similar part there.[6]

The manner in which Poliphilo sees and describes the essence of the Catholic cultus along with its primitive pagan origins is heretical, and he needs the somnambulistic certainty of the visionary if he is not to be startled and overwhelmed by the heresy. But his profound absorption keeps him at that root where there is as yet no conflict between Christian and pagan. The point at which he stands opposed to Christian doctrine, however, is plain to see.

For in the ancient mysteries of the great female divinities, as in Poliphilo's dream, the attention, in contradistinction to the Catholic cultus, is always directed downward. Transformation and the ultimate eternal bliss dwell in the depths under the earth. According to the doctrines of the mysteries, those depths are the home of the ruler and spouse of the goddess, who receives the neophyte with his terrors and his consoling mildness. And Poliphilo, on his walk through the place of tombs, finds a male divinity of the kind beside Proserpine, the underworld counterpart of Venus. He calls him the triple-formed Pluto and sets the triple-headed Cerberus by his side. The threefold body of this Pluto may again be taken as an echo of the Isis mysteries.

The male divinity of the Hellenized Isis mysteries was that Serapis whose cult also goes back to Ptolemy Soter,[7]

[6] Paul Foucart, op. cit., p. 277.

[7] See Franz Cumont, op. cit., Chap. IV and pp. 192 ff.; A. Wallis Budge, op. cit., Vol. II, pp. 195 ff.

who, as Plutarch tells us, brought him from Asia to Egypt "with the help of Providence." The god derives from the old Babylonian Ea, who also appears under the name of Ea Sar Apsi. Ea, the lord of the depths of the waters and father of Marduk, was a god of healing. As Oannes, he rose from the sea to teach men. In Asia Minor, where Ptolemy took him over, the god was changed by Greek and Semitic influences. As god and ruler, he was merged in the Semitic Bel and the Greek Zeus, as lord of the depths, with Hades. Thus the Ptolemaic Serapis had three natures: he was at one and the same time Helios, Zeus, and Hades. Serapis fulfilled Egyptian needs in that he could without difficulty be merged in the figure of Osiris-Apis, that is, the dead bull which was the soul of Osiris. Like Osiris, Serapis was a god of the dead (as shown by the attribute of Cerberus) as well as a god of fertility and a healer. The triple nature of Serapis was, in the later, more refined age of the Ptolemies, no longer represented by three conjoined forms, as Hecate was, for instance. Yet it was always perceptible, for there was added to his bearded Zeus face the suffering expression of the god of the dead and the forelock of Hades. It would appear that the familiar, bearded, suffering face of Christ derives from this image of Serapis. In his function as sun-god, he was crowned with sun-rays and the kalathos (fruit-measure) as a symbol of fertility. Cerberus nestled by his side. Cerberus embodies the bestial, fiery, and destructive aspect of Serapis. It is in this signification that we find him in Poliphilo's mosaic of hell.

Serapis-Osiris is a foreshadowing of Christ, a god who dies and rises again, who takes upon him, in wise and suffering surrender, the sacrificial death so that life may be lived more abundantly. Like Christ, he is a saviour. It was through him that the mystery religions conceived the proud and paradoxical idea that man becomes fully whole and free when he loses himself in sacrifice. His figure embodies the transformation from desire to surrender, which Poliphilo also passes through when, drenched in tears and exhausted unto death, he rushes out of the Polyandrion and throws himself into his Polia's lap, not now to possess her, but to become whole through her.

The name of Pluto is mentioned only twice by Poliphilo, and with a certain dread. It is peculiar that he calls the god not only triple-bodied, but "the one who is within." *Internus*—does Poliphilo mean by that that Pluto dwells within his altar? Or can he mean that this Pluto is "the indwelling one," the "god in us"? It may be that the author of the *Hypnerotomachia* did not quite know what he meant, but the second interpretation is certainly the right one. After all, according to Poliphilo's account, Pluto's altar stands in the centre and at the deepest place. "In dreadful darkness" it represents the sanctuary hidden in the inmost centre, and is the place where the ultimate transformation is accomplished and the new way begins. Everything that happens descends to him by the path of change, and everything that happens arises again from him by the path of change. He is the hinge on which all events turn. Nor does Poliphilo alone experience transformation.

His nymph is transformed too. In receiving the name Polia she is recognized and acknowledged to be the high lady of courtly love. This is a moment of clarification in the process of the anima experience. Not only she herself is not seen in perfect clarity, but the task she implies is seen to be a task of courtly love, though of an entirely unprecedented kind, the goal of which is union with the anima. The alchemical symbol of the *conjunctio* which now makes its appearance brings confirmation of this. In her turn, however, Polia also loses something, namely her torch. The torch, the symbol of the fire of love, is plunged into the water. But water is the symbol of the great goddess herself, to whom all the fires of love belong. And it is Poliphilo who extinguishes the torch with his own hands, a symbol of an act of discrimination and insight. The moment the nymph-anima is clearly seen, it becomes possible to recognize the all-embracing whole of which she, born of water, is a part. Under the symbol of water, which unites the idea of the great goddess Venus and the ὕδωρ θεῖον of alchemy, it is the wholeness of the psyche on which (by the handing over of the torch) supreme value and supreme love are bestowed. Both the man and his anima participate equally in this turn of events. The nymph-anima becomes more human, just as her love becomes more human when she embraces her Poliphilo like a mother and a bride as he sinks into her lap in his deathly exhaustion. On the other hand, Poliphilo's love rises to the semblance of the divine in his self surrender to change. In this way, divine and earthly love are united and, united, turn towards the sea. And it is as if this intense reversal of the feeling of love were an appeal which is strong enough to be answered. The answer comes, as always in our dream-story, in a figure. It is Cupid in his golden bark.

The journey over the sea in Cupid's bark is remarkable in a number of ways. The author of the *Hypnerotomachia* here follows Dante's description of his crossing to Purgatory. There too a radiant angel appears, to waft the bark of Dante and Virgil forward with his opaline wings. But there he is but a fleeting vision. In the *Hypnerotomachia,* on the other hand, this passage is developed in a way which vividly recalls Goethe's *Faust.*

For that matter, the very events in the temple of Venus Physizoa with their flaming sorceries and magical illusions create an atmosphere not unlike that of the Festival at the Emperor's Court with its fireworks in Part II of *Faust.* On both occasions there is magic afoot which horrifies and fascinates. And on both occasions a "little spirit" emerges. Goethe's symbol for this spirit is the Boy Charioteer. In

Goethe himself, this "little spirit" always appeared as the lyric impulse which set him free to stream outward. In the Renaissance, the *spiritulo theosphato* appears rather as that power of creating visual forms which has bequeathed to us so many beautiful things.

Further, the lovers' journey in Cupid's bark contains many elements which recall Goethe's Classical *Walpurgisnacht* in Part II of *Faust*. In the Aegean Festival too, we see the ocean wonderfully animated by divine and magic figures which are surrounded by swans in the same way as in the *Hypnerotomachia*. ("Wonderful swans come floating through the bays in pure, majestic movement"—*Faust*.) And in *Faust* too, the classical ocean and the figures which people it are found by the help of a mysterious small being who bears some resemblance to Poliphilo's Cupid, namely Homunculus. What is lacking in the Classical *Walpurgisnacht* of *Faust*, however, is an adequate vessel symbolism such as is beautifully given by Cupid's bark in the *Hypnerotomachia*. In the corresponding scenes in *Faust*, Homunculus is alone in the phial—and frail indeed is the glass that contains him! Faust and Mephistopheles, who here appears as an anima, though in hideous form (Phorkyas), roam about alone without any real bond either between themselves or with Homunculus. Here again we touch on a point where the difference between *Faust* and the *Hypnerotomachia*, due to the difference of epoch, comes out clearly. To fathom this difference, we must turn to the scene in Wagner's laboratory which precedes the Classical *Walpurgisnacht* in *Faust*. There Mephistopheles says of Homunculus: "We are dependent in the end upon the creatures *we* have made." But this attribution is faulty; Homunculus is here regarded as a possession of the ego and his creation as a personal achievement. Goethe shared with his age the fallacy that he was doing things himself, and it stands in sharp contrast to the piety of Poliphilo, who ascribes all things to God's grace alone.

It is, however, only when the human being is enclosed in

humility as in an unbreakable vessel of piety that the divinity can come to his aid in so powerful a trinity as is symbolized in the *Hypnerotomachia* by the triple-bodied Pluto and the triple-headed Cerberus. Looking back, we can see that the hidden trinity has always been present, though in many guises, to the unsophisticated soul—in the triple-tongued dragon, the three golden statues, the three-sided obelisk. Thus Poliphilo, because he is so humble in himself, is guided and accompanied throughout his journey by a sacred trinity from the depths.

By the mediation of the nymph Polia and the profound transformation from desire to surrender that Poliphilo experiences in the place of tombs, what is human is brought close to the divine and the divine approaches the human. This divinity, this suprapersonal entity, was experienced as terrifying sorcery, as witchcraft and magic, as long as the human being confronted it passively, as an onlooker, as we saw in the events in the temple where Poliphilo was himself a mere spectator on the threshold. But as soon as the attitude becomes active, that is, as soon as the human being's love goes out towards it, the divine ceases to be terrifying magic and sends out its own spark of love to man in the form of a Cupid who wafts him onward as if on wings.

SECTION V

The Island of Cythera

(Psyche, attended by nymphs and matrons, comes to welcome Cupid's bark to the island of Cythera. Polia and Poliphilo are led in Cupid's triumphal progress to the amphitheatre in the middle of the island. The image of Serapis. The fountain of Venus is unveiled in the amphitheatre. The goddess speaks. Cupid transfixes Polia and Poliphilo with his arrow. Mars enters with the wolf. Nymphs lead the lovers to the fountain of Adonis. The grave of Adonis in the rose-bower.)

(Chapters 20 and 21) Poliphilo's story goes on to tell how the sea-voyage in Cupid's bark comes to an end, accompanied by the singing of the nymphs. It brings the lovers to the wonderful island of Cythera, the home of the goddess herself. The bark runs ashore on the shimmering sea-sand, and the first thing we read is a minute description of the island which, from the literary point of view, closely follows the description of Pomona's garden in Boccaccio's *Ameto,* except that the description in the *Hypnerotomachia* is infinitely more prolix and the mass of details of garden-planning almost unmanageable.

The island of Cythera rises, a perfect circle, above the crystal-clear water. Its entire circumference is bordered with a hedge of cypress and myrtle, and it is divided into twenty parts by avenues converging on the middle. It is further divided into concentric circles by colonnades and hedges (Fig. 25). The outermost circle is wooded with various deciduous trees and conifers; animals, wild and tame, satyrs, and fauns roam about in it in paradisial freedom. A balustrade of costly stone is followed by a region of meadows divided into squares by leafy arcades, whose columns and shady arches are overgrown with scented roses. The river which waters all the gardens on the island is so clear that

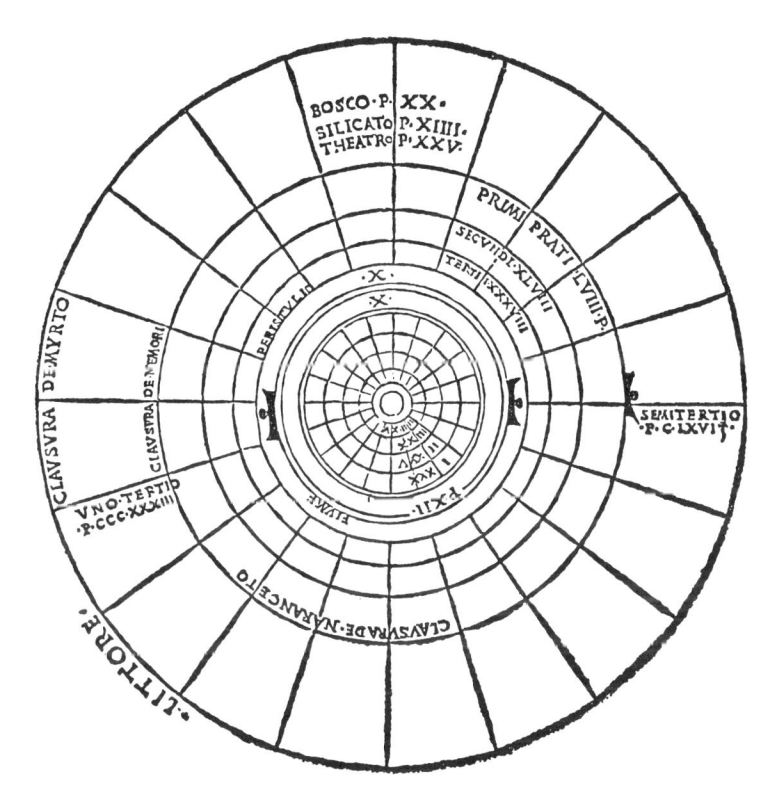

Fig. 25. Plan of the Island of Cythera

no object seen through it looks distorted, that is, there is no refraction. The iridescent fish which inhabit the water are all quite tame. Youths and maidens sail the waters in innumerable barks, carrying on a mimic warfare and filling the air with their shouts of jubilation. The river is spanned by twenty bridges corresponding to the twenty main avenues. On the other side of them there comes another region of meadows, then seven black and red steps leading up to a colonnade in which peacocks rest or spread their tails. Then come gardens, so bright, so artistically laid out, and so beautiful that they look like a Persian carpet. This region is peopled only by men and women dedicated to the service only of the great mother, Nature. Then again there come seven steps, followed by a kind of nursery garden where clipped ornamental trees are grown among mandala-shaped flower-beds like mosaics. Yet again seven steps, and now the flower-mosaics are enriched with figures and letters. Another seven steps lead up to a jasper balustrade with only one gate, which leads to a wood of costly trees where crystal springs babble and countless nymphs chatter, make music with youths, or busy themselves in rustic labours. Again seven steps, leading to a colonnade enclosing a large, innermost space, in the centre of which there is an amphitheatre. Quite apart from its wealth of suggestions for the art of gardening, this description is a positive text-book of botany. As a whole it is a curious mixture of poetry, art, and science.

(Chapter 22) Only now are we given an account of the actual arrival of Cupid's bark on the island. The little god is at once surrounded by all his nymphs, bearing his trophies on their lances. His lovely spouse Psyche also approaches with her attendants to bid him

Fig. 26
Cytheran Fashion-Plate

welcome. Poliphilo gives a minute description of all the beauty and elegance of the nymphs and of Psyche's attendants. We are spared not one detail, from top to toe, from necklace to skirt-hem. An illustration serves as a kind of Cytheran fashion-plate (Fig. 26). And this picture is described so accurately that it would be no great matter to cut out a pattern by it.

Poliphilo is hard beset by this mass display of feminine charms, so that at this last moment he is within an ace of being faithless to his Polia. Fortunately for him, the action proceeds. Poliphilo and Polia are fettered with garlands of roses and led to their place in Cupid's triumphal progress. This is the sixth procession of the kind which occurs throughout the course of the *Hypnerotomachia*.

The procession is headed by the nymphs in ranks of three. In addition to Cupid's armoury, his bow, quiver, arrows, and the bandage for his eyes, they carry three vases of sapphire, emerald, and earthenware. There are holes in the earthenware vase, a volatile vapour rises from it, and it bears the inscription: "All is fleeting." The nymph who carries Cupid's bandage has two most indecorous attendants. They are the only naked nymphs in the procession, and one of them holds up her long hair with her hand so that all may see her from behind. Cupid's golden chariot is drawn by four tame dragons. He is immediately followed by the two lovers in their rose-fetters with the nymph, their warder. After them comes Queen Psyche. Her robes have a special description all to themselves. (On the island of Cythera, Poliphilo seems hardly to be able to satisfy his soul with clothes. Every time we think he has finished, off he goes again.)

Fig. 27
Serapis in the
Serpent Circle

The procession of the nymphs, with its torches and candles,

is plentifully supplied with incense, holy water, and the sweetest music. The musicians also move in orderly ranks of three. Just in front of Cupid's dragon-chariot, two satyrs bear a three-headed, ithyphallic Hermes. These satyrs are accompanied by three nymphs. The first carries a golden vessel shaped like a woman's breast with milk dripping from it. The second carries the statues of two children, one complete, the other lacking head and arms. But the third carries a portentous figure that Poliphilo denotes as the "Egyptian Serapis" (Fig. 27). It consists of the heads of a lion, a dog, and a wolf, enclosed in a coiled snake, which emits powerful rays.

In this order the triumphal procession moves through the main avenue, between magnificent rose-hedges, and arrives at the centre of the island, which is occupied by an amphitheatre. This is a vast building in the style of the Colosseum, with colonnade rising above colonnade. Bases and beams are made of copper gilt, all the rest is constructed of Indian alabaster without joints, transparent as glass yet eternally durable. This superb edifice has never been blackened with smoke; it stands there flawless in its pristine purity.

Here Cupid descends from his chariot and enters the amphitheatre, accompanied only by Psyche, the lovers, and two warder-nymphs. All the rest remain outside. The floor of the interior consists of a single block of black obsidian, polished and shining, and when Poliphilo sets foot on it, he seems to be falling into an abyss or a dreadful black hollow. He is so startled that, although a nymph is leading him, he stumbles and slightly sprains his ankle. It is only by keeping his eyes on the walls that he can recover his senses and see how the sky and the clouds and the colonnades are reflected in the shining floor as if in a calm sea. Along the towering colonnades of the theatre there grow cypress and box, which form arcades overgrown with roses and jasmine. Here too there is a host of nymphs singing and dancing to the music made by other nymphs. The steps and columns are of costly stone or gold. Poliphilo, contemplating these splendours, is almost beside himself with wonder. All his senses are entranced, but his heart is aglow with love for Polia.

The rose-fetters of the lovers are now loosed, Psyche humbly hands Cupid his golden arrow, and Cupid presents Polia and Poliphilo to the fountain of his divine mother. (Chapter 23) This fountain of Venus occupies the exact centre of the amphitheatre. Its exterior is heptagonal, its interior circular, and its margin is hewn out of the same single block of black obsidian as the floor of the theatre (Fig. 28). The margin bears seven columns of precious stones. The fountain is canopied with a dome of pure crystal, on the summit of which there gleams a carbuncle as big as an ostrich egg. The inscription on the fountain runs:

ΩΣΠΕΡ ΣΠΙΝΘΗΡ ΚΗΛΗΘΜΟΣ
(Rapture is like the spark)

Between the two foremost columns of the fountain there hangs a costly curtain on which the word "Hymen" (= virginity) is embroidered.

Cupid now causes his golden arrow to be handed to Polia for her to rend the curtain, but Polia, in her timidity and inexperience, shrinks from the task. Smiling at her fears, the mischievous boy gives a sign for the arrow to be given to Poliphilo. Hardly has Poliphilo's hand closed on the magic arrow when a fierce desire to see the goddess streams through him, and, without a moment's hesitation, he tears blindly at the curtain. Then he sees that the rending of the curtain seems to have distressed his Polia.

Yet the goddess is already disclosed to the eyes of the lovers. In all her beauty, bright as a carbuncle and crowned with golden curls, she stands up to her hips in the clear, scented water of the fountain which, like the Cytheran river, causes no refraction. White doves flutter about her, in one hand she holds a shell full of roses, in the other a flaming torch. On the steps of the fountain leading into the water there grow herbs which help women in childbirth. To the right of the goddess there stand the three Graces, to her left the smiling young Bacchus and the maternal Ceres. Both hold wineskins from which sweet liquid drips into the water.

In ecstatic awe, Poliphilo kneels with Polia before the goddess. In his ragged garments, he feels utterly unworthy

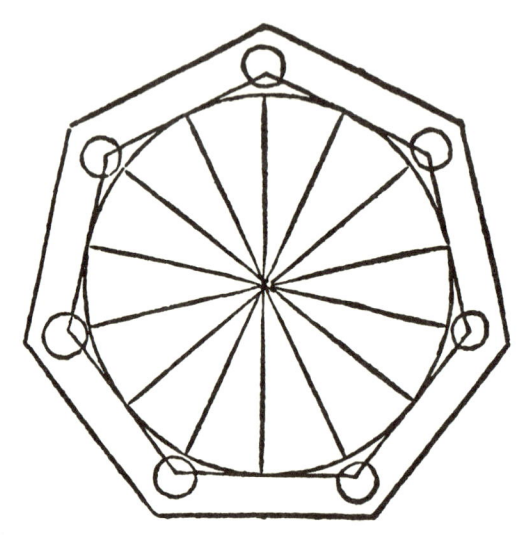

Fig. 28. Plan of the Fountain of Venus

of this grace and this strictly guarded mystery, and he wishes he could sink into the earth. But Venus commands the nymphs to cease their music, and all are silent while she addresses them in choice words. She turns to Polia as her faithful servant, and promises that her wish shall be fulfilled. Poliphilo shall be numbered among the true, faithful, and happy lovers. He shall be purged by the goddess of all common dross and purified of faults and weaknesses. Then she gives each of the lovers a ring set with the stone Anteros, which means Love Returned.

Cupid now draws his bow and shoots an arrow with such force that it pierces Poliphilo's heart and penetrates Polia's breast, where it remains. Cupid draws it out again and washes the blood from it in the fountain. But Poliphilo feels the fire of the divine arrow coursing through his whole being with terrible power. Not a nerve, not a vein in him but glows. His pulse flags, he is beside himself, he is like straw in a furnace. All his vital spirits stream out of the open wound in his heart, and he thinks of the hermaphrodite who lay in a spring in the embrace of his nymph, and felt their two bodies melting into one.

Venus, however, takes sea-water from her fountain in her hollowed hands and sprinkles the lovers with it. Poliphilo's dreadful anguish abates. The relief restores him to himself, he feels whole, renewed, given back to life. Nymphs now remove his rags and clothe him in new, white robes. The lovers kiss, all the bystanders kiss them too, for now they have been admitted to the holy collegium. The goddess bestows a sweet smile upon them, then whispers to them certain things which must not be repeated nor said aloud, for they are concerned with the strengthening of love, and their purpose is to unite the lovers' hearts in a single will. Then Venus gives the lovers her blessing.

At this moment the door of the amphitheatre opens, and a warrior enters. In power and majesty, he strides towards the fountain, beautiful, proud, and bold in his shining armour. His wolf follows at his heels, growling, with hackles up. At the fountain the warrior casts aside his armour and weapons and approaches the goddess, who embraces him tenderly. Thus the fountain becomes the stage for a divine love-scene. At the sight of it, the earthly lovers bid farewell, leaving the goddess in the temple with all her divine companions. Seven divinities remain by the fountain: Venus and Mars, Bacchus and Ceres, Cupid and Psyche—and the wolf.

(Chapter 24) Outside the amphitheatre, Poliphilo and

Polia find all Cupid's nymphs, who hurry towards them and tenderly surround them in a lovely circle. They bid Polia weave a rose-chaplet for Poliphilo, so that he, like her, may bear the sign of Venus. Polia at once begins to gather flowers, while the nymphs show the lovers all the splendours of the island. Finally, they lead them to another fountain which stands in a secluded garden, encircled with trees. The fountain is hexagonal, it is fed by a natural spring and is bordered with plain blocks of marble. Close by there is an arbour entwined with climbing roses, with seats around it and a tomb in the middle.

This is the grave of Adonis and the place where Venus tore her foot when hastening to the help of her darling, who had been mortally wounded by Mars. Cupid caught the blood trickling from the wound in a shell, and Venus' tears in roses. He then laid both in the grave of Adonis. The story of the beautiful darling of the gods is depicted on the tomb, showing him defeated by the jealous Mars, gored to death by the boar, and mourned by Venus. There are two inscriptions: one runs "Impure Sweetness," the other "The Festival of Adonis." A stream of water flows into the hexagonal basin from a spout in the form of a twisted serpent.

On the top of the tomb, however, a life-size, lifelike statue of Venus is enthroned in the guise of a young mother. She is suckling the infant Cupid, and mother and child gaze at each other as he sucks. The following distich is inscribed on the cornice: "Nay, cruel child, it is not milk thou suckst from thy mother's breast, but many a tear that thou must render back again, that she may weep for the dead Adonis."

The nymphs kiss the outstretched foot of the statue with profound reverence. Poliphilo and Polia do likewise, kissing the foot of the divine image too (Fig. 29). Then the nymphs tell the lovers the story of this sacred place, shrouded in deep mystery, yet of such great fame, where the blood and tears of the goddess flowed for her mortal lover. They relate too the yearly rite performed by the goddess by the grave of

Fig. 29. Statue of Venus as the Mother of Cupid

Adonis at the beginning of May. Cupid, Venus, and all the nymphs come to the grave. They pick all the roses from the arbour, yet the next morning they find fresh ones in bloom. But these are pure white. The rite proceeds with the bath of Venus in the fountain of Adonis, then the dirge for Adonis is sung. Cupid takes the blood and tears of the goddess from the grave of Adonis, and at that moment, all the white roses in the arbour turn red. Finally, the relics are replaced in the grave, and the ceremony ends with games, singing, and dancing.

Such is the nymphs' story. As they tell it, Poliphilo and

Fig. 30. The Fountain of Adonis

Polia leave the rose-bower with them, and they all sit down on the grass on the other side of the fountain (Fig. 30). The nymphs make music and chatter gaily, but Poliphilo nestles close to Polia and, for the first time, enjoys her kisses and caresses with a free mind. Then one of the nymphs approaches, all agog with curiosity. She and the others are now eager to know the whence and the whither, the what and the why—in short, the whole life-story of Polia. They have noticed that Polia's graceful and beautiful figure is not quite of the earth—there must be some share of divinity in it. That is why they wish to know all about her. So they ask Polia if she will not while away their hour of leisure by telling her story. Polia consents with a gracious inclination of her head, only a little sigh betraying her maidenly modesty. Poliphilo feels Polia's sigh in his inmost heart, for Polia's heart is, after all, his own. After a brief pause, Polia begins her story, weaving the rose-chaplet for Poliphilo as she speaks. Polia's story takes up nearly the whole of Part II of the *Hypnerotomachia*.

COMMENTARY TO SECTION V

The images in the foregoing section might again be interpreted in the alchemical sense, for they are rich in alchemical symbolism. Only to mention a few points, the various concentric rings on the island, for instance, signify the various stages in alchemical transmutation, the water is always denoted as ὕδωρ θεῖον, the amphitheatre is clearly described as the hermetic vessel. In the following commentary, however, no special account is given of the alchemical symbolism, since it would not appear to be essential.

The plan of the island of Cythera resembles that of the Mount of Purgatory in Dante. As in the *Hypnerotomachia*, we find in Dante concentric rings enclosing an outer, a middle, and an inner region. True, Dante's *Purgatorio* is conceived as a steep declivity, while the island of Cythera has only the gentle rise given by the sequence of five times seven steps. The innermost and highest region in Dante's *Purgatorio* encloses the earthly paradise with its two rivers —Lethe, the river of oblivion, and Eunoe, the river of remembrance. In the corresponding place in Poliphilo, we find the paradisal amphitheatre of Venus, and also two waters, the fountain of Venus corresponding to Dante's Lethe and the fountain of Adonis to Dante's Eunoe.

It is certainly surprising that Poliphilo's island of Cythera, the place of supreme delight, should be laid out on a similar plan to that of Dante's Purgatory. Since all the proceedings on the island are radically different from those in the *Purgatorio*, we must—indeed we have no choice but to—assume a parallelism of principle which comes out in the similarity of structure.

Now we must confess that Dante's Purgatory is an exceedingly tedious place. Nothing happens, nothing moves in it, and the almost respectable sinners sing so many hymns that they exhaust our sympathy. Neither infernally wicked nor divinely good, the Purgatory is a neither-nor, an intermediate stage. It is a twilight, a numbness marked by a certain colourless sanctimoniousness. Not until the innermost, highest region—that is, the earthly paradise—is reached are we given a passing relief with the appearance of Matelda and Beatrice and a vast vision of the Church Triumphant.

The state of affairs on the island of Cythera is precisely similar. This place of delight is also exceedingly dull. The very description of the island as a locality is confused and tedious to read. The interminable descriptions of women's fashions on Cythera are, of course, portentously boring, and the sweetly sentimental love-poetry expended on the whole is equally insipid. But the twilight and numbness of an intermediate stage find immediate expression in the figure of Cupid when, on the island, he has at first no light, no weapons, and no wings, and sits stiff and lifeless on his triumphal chariot in a way most unlike him.

It is true that this is no vision inspired by Christian theology, like Dante's, and what dawns on the horizon is not the heaven of a still somewhat pallid piety.[1] The sail in Cupid's bark over the ocean which is so densely peopled by ancient sea-gods does not lead to a mount of purification; on the

---

[1] The relevant alchemical symbol is the *congelatio albificatio,* which precedes the *albedo,* or, to use another image, the birth of the phoenix.

contrary, what is slowly manifested on Cythera is a true Mount of Venus. The first pale half-light which reaches Poliphilo from it flickers over his description, bathing it in an atmosphere of salacious sweetness which it was quite impossible to render in the summary. On the island itself, however, we enter upon the wide domain of the utterly unrestrained eroticism which characterized the civilization of classical times. Corruption is coupled with a static elegance to form a brilliant and obscene picture. Poliphilo has rendered this atmosphere so naturally and spontaneously that he has caught not only the inmost nature of the late classical age, but the brilliance of all *fins de siècle*. It is for that reason that his account also points far into the future, namely into our own eighteenth century. As a symbol of depravity we find on the island Poliphilo's Psyche with her spouse, the boy Cupid, and it takes no great power of imagination to grasp the implications of such an image. In actual fact the late classical age and the eighteenth century indulged freely in the most unseemly idea of the lady of fashion and her still half-fledged lover. We find it in the *Golden Ass* of Apuleius, and that writer, who understood his age extremely well, was perfectly consistent in putting the tale of Amor and Psyche into the mouth of an old bawd. In the eighteenth century the same idea found its most famous incarnation in the figures of the Countess and Cherubin in Beaumarchais' and Mozart's *Marriage of Figaro*.[2]

In comparison with the blind indiscriminateness of lust expressed in this symbol of Psyche and Cupid, the sensuality of the Middle Ages may be regarded as innocuous. All the wit, all the subtlety and elegance of late classical times are merely a thin veil spread over a sensuality which is utterly careless about the object of its desire, and in which the line

---

[2] Beaumarchais' two *Figaro* plays were followed by a third, which has remained almost unknown. It is set in a later time, and it turns out that the Countess has actually borne a child to Cherubin. The title of the play is *Le Père de famille*.

of demarcation between the human and the animal has vanished. It is, to put it mildly, the selfsame zoo.

Hence it is only to be expected that, as Cupid's proud triumphal procession moves through the fragrant gardens, it is the animal and not the human figures which are truly significant. It is the satyrs, the ancient goat-demons, which bring the only interesting symbol into the procession, and it is they who are characterized by animal attributes. We have the golden breast dripping with milk as the symbol of the goddess in her animal aspect, as the nourishing milch cow, while the animal aspect of generation is emphasized by the triple-headed, ithyphallic Hermes. The Hermes represents the fusion of Poliphilo's Priapus and Pluto. We might even translate this image literally by saying that generation and salvation are one and the same thing.

The greatest splendour, and therefore the greatest significance in Cupid's procession, however, is to be seen in that purely animal symbol that Poliphilo calls the Egyptian Serapis. The figure recalls Cerberus. Thus the hell-hound dominates the hour with fierce heat. As has already been pointed out, Cerberus may be denoted as the animal aspect of the god of the mysteries. Poliphilo himself hints at this, for the name of Arapis echoes in the very similar sound of Serapis. The three figures which are combined in the figure of the Serapis beast—the wolf, lion, and dog—recall the threefold nature of the god of the mysteries, deadly, sunny, and healing.[3] The three animals are also an allegory of the three aspects of time, past, present, and future. But whatever bears the impress of the three aspects of time is that which is from everlasting to everlasting, namely, the god and the beast. To put it otherwise, the beast is also the god, and it is in the beast that the god is closest to man and is most clearly visible. Here the Serapis beast is enclosed in

---

[3] The animal symbol of the wolf belongs to the night aspect of Apollo, the lion is a sun symbol, and the dog the animal of Aesculapius, the god of healing.

the shining snake-circle. It is placed in the centre of the magic circle as the sacred thing. As an alchemical symbol the snake circle is the uroboros (that which eats its own tail), a symbol both of the Great Work and its ruler, Mercury. Its lustre reveals it as the stone in which the opposites are reconciled. After the terrors of the underworld that Poliphilo experienced in the place of tombs, the light of the underworld, incorporated in the warmth of animal nature, shines through the equivocal twilight of the Mount of Venus as the saviour and the sun of the depths. That this is Poliphilo's actual meaning can be seen by the fact that he calls the beast Serapis. It is a seraph—a redeeming angel.

The importance of this Serapis figure cannot be overrated. The author of the *Hypnerotomachia* has placed it in the corresponding position to Dante's apocalyptic gryphon which appears in the earthly paradise of the *Divina Commedia* and draws the chariot of the Church as a symbol of the God-man, the redemption of all that is to be.

The meaning of all this symbolism is revealed later by the fountain of Venus in the rending of the curtain Hymen. Here, in contrast to the preceding suggestiveness, we have an almost crude sexual symbolism taken from the end of the *Romance of the Rose*. If we take into account the enormous spread of the *Romance* throughout the Latin world, Poliphilo's account must be taken as equivalent to a quotation. In the manner familiar to every reader of the *Romance*, he describes a defloration. But who is the virgin who is here made a "full-blown rose" as the *Romance* has it? Since Polia is distressed by the rending of the curtain and betrays her emotion, it can be none other than she.

This inference opens up significant perspectives. The veiled fountain of Venus would correspond to Polia before the defloration. But then the divine Venus in the fountain must in her turn be Polia, now unveiled. A lightning-swift reversal shows us the *conjunctio* of the man with his anima in her divine aspect. Thereby Polia is raised to the status of Venus, and Poliphilo's ecstasy is fulfilled in the anguish of his desire. He sees himself externalized in the figure of Mars. Therewith a climax is reached and a fulfilment that Poliphilo symbolizes by the sacred number of seven gods grouped round the fountain of Venus.

Among them, however, there is the wolf of the gods "which knows no compassion."
Every time the wolf appears in the *Hypnerotomachia*, it signifies destruction. We saw it for the first time in the maze of Queen Eleuterilida. There it embodied the death which is the end menacing the cycle of life. Now in a general way, the island of Cythera is an analogy to the realm of Queen Eleuterilida, just as, on the other hand, the place of tombs was analogous to the ruined city. On the island we have, just as in the realm of the Queen, a picture of nature, though what lives again for Poliphilo on the island is classical nature. The analogy between the two regions, however, holds good not only for the whole, but also for the details. The fountain of Venus, with the wolf appearing at the end, corresponds exactly to the Queen's maze with the wolf at the ineluctable centre. The element of death that is inseparable from the union of lovers has always been felt by human beings. Poliphilo's images represent that element in a sublimely candid yet reverent fashion. In this respect his story is worlds apart from the salacious close of the *Romance of the Rose*.

It is also very suggestive and important that Poliphilo's fountain of Venus should have its analogy in the Lethe of Dante's *Purgatorio*—that is, the river of oblivion. We might interpret this in the following way: the divinity of animal nature, which was manifest to the man of the early Renaissance in the classical acceptance of all things natural, contains the mortal danger (symbolized by the wolf) of complete self-loss. This is a very real danger, though we cannot know whether and how the monk Colonna felt it in himself. But in the Renaissance, it became a historical fact. We have only to think of the Borgias, who succumbed to that danger by wallowing like divine beasts in classical sensuality, by murdering, and by finally destroying themselves.

Yet "out of this nettle, danger, we pluck this flower, safety." In the realm of Queen Eleuterilida, the danger of the maze was overcome, since Poliphilo, with the help of Reason, rose above it and arrived in the last garden with the alchemical symbol in which the cycle of life is represented as a purposeful process of development. Corresponding to that symbol, we find on the island of Cythera a "last garden" too, namely the garden in which the fountain of Adonis flows. In Dante's *Purgatorio*, the Eunoe, the river of remembrance, would correspond to this fountain. The reference to Dante would seem to indicate that this time no process of reasoning will suffice to ward off the danger of submergence. What is needed is the power to remember that there is something which helps us to find our bearings in the dangerous situation of self-forgetting. Thus the faculty of memory is here stressed as quite peculiar and important, and so it is as long as it is concerned, not only with the personal past, but with the helping symbol. In the last garden of Queen Eleuterilida, the alchemical figure with the golden obelisk was a figure of the kind. Now, however, it appears in a totally different guise, namely as the grave of Adonis. We must therefore attempt to apprehend the significance of this image, and in order to do so, we must look back from a new standpoint on all that has happened on the island of Cythera.

If we keep firmly in mind the principal ideas underlying the elegant traceries of Poliphilo's description, the landing on Cythera and the triumphal progress of Cupid cannot fail to recall the procession of the worshippers of Isis in that famous eleventh chapter of the *Metamorphoses* of Apuleius, in which the Lucius-Ass is happily restored to his human shape and led to the temple of the goddess. The two processions have so many details in common—the gaily dressed women, the insignia of the participating gods, the vessels that are borne in the procession, and, last but not least, "the gods themselves who deign to walk on human feet," as Apuleius has it. And the procession of Isis includes a figure resembling Poliphilo's Serapis, "the messenger of the gods of the upper and lower world with his terrible, long-necked dog's head." This is Anubis, who bears the caduceus. What is absent from Poliphilo's account, however, is the humour which inspires the mummery preceding the procession of Isis. As becomes the mischievous god, the humour in Cupid's procession is felt rather than expressed, Poliphilo and Polia in their fetters of roses corresponding to the Ass healed by the rose-wreath. This analogy nevertheless casts an amusing and interesting light on the noble lovers of our story.

Further parallels to the eleventh chapter of Apuleius can be seen in the goddess's long and eloquent address in the Cytheran amphitheatre, in Poliphilo's white robe, which is presented to him as to Lucius, and also in the ceremony of the kissing of the foot of the statue by the fountain of Adonis. Further, in the amphitheatre on Cythera there is another curious allusion which also points to Apuleius. This is Poliphilo's sprained ankle. For there is somebody with a sprained ankle in Apuleius too, namely the priest who performs the second initiation of Lucius, in which the secrets of the "great god, the supreme father of the gods, the unconquerable Osiris" are disclosed. To judge from this description, the priest in question is the hierophant of a higher stage of the mysteries. If Poliphilo begins to limp in the theatre of Venus, that unquestionably suggests that he too is undergoing a higher initiation.

Regarded from the standpoint of the Isis mysteries, therefore, the action by the fountain of Venus represents a ἱερὸς γάμος, a sacred marriage, which is performed by the priest and priestess as representatives of the gods. Poliphilo has already seen the ἱερὸς γάμος in anticipation when, as an onlooker, he witnessed the sacrifice of the doves and the swans in the temple of Venus Physizoa. But what he there witnessed as a spectacle is now performed on himself. By the sacred action in the consecrated place, *something* in Polia stands revealed as Venus, *something* in Poliphilo becomes Mars, and when he comes to himself out of his godlike trance, he stands there in his white robe as "one twice born." He becomes a priest just as Polia becomes a priestess, and he is initiated into the mystery of the sacred marriage and the apotheosis. The mystery is that the sacred marriage does not mean an apotheosis but a divine service, and that man is made by it a vessel of the godhead, but not a god. This mystery can obviously be apprehended only when he to whom it is revealed, like Poliphilo and the old priest of Osiris in Apuleius, has stumbled over its abysmal seduction. Yet it is a mystery with which the human soul has been familiar from time immemorial, for the experience embodied in the vessel symbolism—that man cannot become God but can receive God like a vessel—is archetypal in character. It has been made everywhere and at all times; that is why it is contained as an archetypal image in the unconscious, which preserves the deposit of all universal human experience. When some emergency, such as the danger of self-forgetting in the present case, constellates the archetype, it emerges into visibility for him who has eyes to see it as a memory belonging to all mankind.

Thus the archetype of the vessel makes its appearance here as it did primarily in alchemy, in the symbol of the Adonis tomb. The tomb is vessel for the body of corruption, hence for the vilest and the most perishable part of man. In the tomb there lies the "clod of earth," the dead body which the suffering, tormented human being so often felt himself to be in life. His body itself seems to him to be a grave in which his immortal soul lies dead and coffined.[4] Thus the tomb with its dead is a symbol of all the wretchedness of man and his need of redemption; that is why it is also a place of mourning. Yet in the tomb beside which Poliphilo stands there lies one set apart—Adonis. Adonis is a figure which has much in common with Osiris. As Osiris was killed and torn to pieces by Seth, who also appeared in the shape of a black boar, he is killed by the boar of Mars. Like Osiris, he is said to have been originally a mortal man, born of the forbidden love of the king's daughter Myrrha for her father. The beauty of the young shepherd and huntsman then awakened the love of Venus, and he was killed by the jealousy of Mars. According to one version of the Adonis myth, Venus, who mourned him with blood and tears, caused him to come to life again. In another version he was also beloved by Proserpine, the queen of the underworld. Thus we once more encounter in the Adonis myth the name of the goddess which has already appeared in association with that of the triple-formed Pluto. A quarrel arose between Venus and Proserpine over Adonis which Jove settled by ordering the much-beloved youth to spend one third of the year with Proserpine and two thirds with Venus. When Adonis descends to Hades, winter covers the earth; his return to Venus in the upper world ushers in the spring.

The mortality and transience of the body's beauty, however, is more strongly stressed in the figure of Adonis than in that of Osiris. It is for that reason that in his cult there are dedicated to him the so-called "little gardens of Adonis," which are filled with quickly fading grasses. He incorporates

---

[4] Cf. the Orphic doctrine of the body as a tomb ($\sigma\omega\mu\alpha = \sigma\eta\mu\alpha$) mentioned by Plato (*Kratylos*, 400c, *Gorgias*, 493a, *Phaidon*, 70c).

what the Bible says of man: "Man that is born of a woman, is of few days, and full of trouble. He cometh forth like a flower, and is cut down; he fleeth also as a shadow, and continueth not." Yet it is this very mortal who was beloved of goddesses. They bestowed upon him that curious resurrection which is an alternation between waking and sleeping, and which moves upward as well as downward. Every year Adonis sinks into the depths as the lover of the goddess of the depths; every year he returns as the herald of spring and the bridegroom of Venus.

Thus the tomb of Adonis is the vessel of the body of corruption which holds a darling of the gods, a god dying and rising again, like Osiris. The mysterious life of the dead becomes visible to human eyes in the growth of vegetation, more especially in the roses which bloom on the grave and to which the blood and tears of Venus, when they are taken from the grave, give the red colour of life and love. In the *Hypnerotomachia* it is this symbolism which holds the foreground. On the one hand, the reddening of the roses is the sign for Adonis to rise again, on the other, there is a significant identity between those roses, Adonis, and the blood and tears of Venus which lie in Adonis's place in the tomb. All these things would appear to be symbols for one and the same thing.

In this case we can hardly avoid an alchemical interpretation. Adonis is the fruit of an incestuous union, and incest plays a leading part in the symbolism of the philosophers' stone, the self-begetting of which is often represented by an incestuous union (brother and sister, father and daughter, or mother and son). Adonis is a symbol of the philosophers' stone, just like the rose whose reddening corresponds to the stage of the *rubedo* which, in a large number of alchemical treatises, is the Great Work's goal. The red rose indicates that the labour is accomplished and also that the stone, like a risen god, has been born in ultimate purity out of the impurity of its primeval state. In actual fact the rose is a female symbol; in association with Adonis, it gives the impression of a union of male and female such as also occurs in the alchemical symbol of the hermaphrodite which is itself a synonym of the stone. Blood and tears are also to be taken as symbolic of the stone; they are the tincture which transforms the common stuff (the corpse) into gold (the risen Adonis). As so often happens in alchemy, a single principle, the stone, underlies all this intricate symbolism. Mysteriously begotten of itself, the stone of itself transforms itself in the hermetic vessel (the tomb) and can only be brought into the light of day by the divine fire (Cupid).

In the myth of Adonis as it is narrated in Poliphilo's dream, the conception of the blood and tears of Venus appears peculiarly important, for this blood and these tears are the form in which the contents of the tomb can be removed. We must therefore consider this point. The idea that the soul dwells in the blood goes back to very ancient times. It also appears in late classical times, though with certain differences. In Philo, for instance, the blood is the substance of the *anima vitalis,* in contrast to the *anima rationalis,* whose substance is the pneuma. Philo, however, regards pneuma and blood as a mixture in which the one cannot exist without the other.[5] These views are only touched on here in order to show the range of ideas and the sense in which the union of the two "bodily fluids" comes to mean the soul. The blood stands here for an inferior part of the soul, while the pneuma stands for a superior, light, and subtle part. In accordance with these views we may regard the blood and tears of Venus as sym-

[5] H. Leisegang, *Der Heilige Geist,* Leipzig, 1919, p. 83.

bolic of the wholeness of the soul, which comprises within itself heights and depths, light and darkness.[6] Venus herself, containing all the substance of the soul, would then figure as a world soul or *anima mundi*,[7] which, as an archetypal principle, remains invisible. It is only what is contained in the tomb of Adonis that can be made accessible. If we think, however, of the mysterious identity which, in this symbolism, exists between the blood and tears of Venus and Adonis, the contents of the tomb, personified in the figure of Adonis, are seen to be a symbol of that factor in which all the contents of the psyche, individual and suprapersonal, meet, hence a symbol of the self in which man finds at one and the same time his own most inward being and psychic wholeness. This agrees with the foregoing interpretation of the figure of Adonis as a symbol of the stone, for the stone is itself a symbol of the self. The resurrection of Adonis and his divine journey from Proserpine to Venus would then represent the self awakening to life and action by uniting the heaviness of animal nature and the subtlety of the spirit, the hither-worldliness of consciousness and the other-worldliness of the unconscious.

The place, however, in which the Self can awaken to life and action is the grave, and thus the body in the grave, as the place of resurrection, takes on a central significance. The body in the grave might be denoted as a vessel within a vessel, containing the self as the pearl of great price. This pearl can only be made accessible by the opening of the grave and the resurrection of the body, and Cupid alone can open the grave. Thus man can only find his self when he turns to this grave and gives fresh life to the body by love.

[6] Cf. also the Chinese conception of the duality of *sing* (being) and *ming* (life); in the human being this corresponds to the light *hun* soul and the dark *po* soul. See R. Wilhelm and C. G. Jung, *The Secret of the Golden Flower*.
[7] See C. G. Jung, *Psychology and Alchemy*.

As a vessel containing the blood and tears of Venus, as a fountain from which the spring of remembrance flows, the tomb of Adonis with its dead body offers an analogy to Poliphilo's fourth, Dionysian chariot, which showed him, in a setting of night, a vessel containing a divine liquid. But this time it is the human form which is associated with the vessel symbol, and in such a significant fashion that we might interpret it directly in this way:

The natural, corporeal man is like a grave containing a corpse which is, however, a dying and rising god-man. In man himself there lies dormant a saviour and mediator who with the wholeness of the psyche. The dead man in the may be brought to life by love, and can then unite him grave is a symbol of the inferior function. As long as it remains inanimate, the "world," that is, man's consciousness, is as sterile as the earth in winter. But if the inferior function is to awake and bring up the spring from the depths of the unconscious, the human being must open himself like a grave. He must look into himself and attain self-knowledge, or else his own centre will lie dead within him, and he will only experience the unconscious from time to time as a pale, spectral growth which springs from the grave like the white roses of death—as dreams and fantasies which cannot be put into action, and which are as frail and transient as the grasses on the little gardens of Adonis.

The tomb of Adonis with its manifold implications is a symbol of individuation, which also means the activation of the inferior function. This is experienced as a shadow, like the dead Adonis, but through it the light of the Self shimmers, secret and strange. Thus at the tomb of Adonis, Poliphilo is presented with a possibility fraught with meaning. Yet we do not see the grave opened. Cupid is not there to remove the goddess's blood and tears. Poliphilo's love does not go out to the dead man in his grave, for it is still the anima-Polia who holds all his attention captive. In a certain sense she stands between him and the grave.

For that reason Polia is now animated as never before. She begins her story, and that story occupies nearly the whole of Part II of the *Hypnerotomachia*. By the defloration, the virgin anima has conceived, and the weighty words she is to speak are, if it may be put in this way, the "spiritual child" of her sacred marriage with Poliphilo. As a mother giving birth to the word fraught with meaning, Polia, at the end of Part I of the *Hypnerotomachia*, resembles the statue of Venus the mother enthroned with the new-born Cupid on the tomb of Adonis. Or rather the statue of Venus is an aspect of Polia, who by her very existence closes the grave to Poliphilo. Yet at the same time Polia is also distinguished from Venus when she joins the group of nymphs by the fountain of Adonis, for by that she reveals herself as a nymph like the others. This double presentation of Polia expresses the fact that she really has a double meaning for Poliphilo. On the one hand, as a nymph, she is for him *his* soul; as Venus, on the other, she is the mirror of the unconscious that Poliphilo can only recognize through her. Indeed, by the fountain of Venus he actually heard the voice of the goddess only through her lips. The place where that happened is denoted by Poliphilo himself as a theatre. That means that the creative imagination is at work here, the man penetrating so intimately into the depths of his own soul that a curtain rises, and a rainbow-hued reflection of the hidden life of the archetypes appears before him.

In the events on the island of Cythera, the solution of a problem is presented such as Goethe's Faust also attempted by the side of Helen after the classical *Walpurgisnacht*. Like another Polia, Helen becomes by Faust the mother of a winged boy, Euphorion, who also incorporates the word, for Euphorion symbolizes poetry; he stands for the creative power of art.

On the other hand, when Dante's Beatrice appears on the

Mount of Purgatory, her language is her own. Her words are the teachings of Christian wisdom. Thus for Dante, the supreme revelation is clothed in the mantle of philosophy. For Goethe, it is contained in art, and we shall see in Part II of the *Hypnerotomachia* what form it takes for Poliphilo.

To the superficial reader, moreover, it may not at once become clear why so remarkable a break should occur at this precise point in the book, why the author was not content merely to begin a new chapter, but closes the first part to follow it up with a second which is not at all in proportion to it in length. To all intents and purposes, the action flows on without interruption; indeed, no fresh image or situation appears. Actually, the fundamental breach made by the division into two parts has nothing to do with the action of the dream but with its inner meaning, that is, with how Poliphilo the man comes to terms with his nymph-anima. From this standpoint, a first part has certainly come to an end and a second begins. Up to this point, his relationship to the nymph meant for Poliphilo a continuous transformation symbolized in his continual movement from place to place. Every transformation revealed a new goal, until the moment came when he could see that the nymph-anima was herself the goal, and could possess her as such. This manner of development by stages is by no means peculiar to Poliphilo's romance. On the contrary, it is characteristic of every man's experience of his anima. And the realization that the anima, and his union with her, is the goal must be so intense, or in other words so intimate, must penetrate to such depths, that only the symbol of the sexual act is adequate to represent it. But then the anima, as it were, is held in a strong and loving embrace, and the whole new development that follows ceases to be a transformation of the man's consciousness and becomes a transformation of the anima.

PART II

Part II of the *Hypnerotomachia* contains about half as many chapters as Part I. Some of them are quite short, some are filled with Poliphilo's protestations of love or with precise descriptions of the lovers' states of mind, illustrated by innumerable examples from classical legend. The actual contents may be very briefly summarized.

SECTION I

Polia's Story

(Chapters 1-12) Polia begins her story by saying that she is descended from the waters of Treviso, which are her kinsfolk. So she is born of water. Then she gives a vivid and lengthy description of herself, quite in the courtly manner, as the cruel lady who has obstinately spurned and tormented the lovesick Poliphilo. He first caught sight of her when she was on the brink of womanhood, as she was drying her golden hair in the sun on the roof of her palace, and from that moment on, the golden hair span round him a web of magic threads. He followed her like a servant and worshipped her steadfastly, but she would have nothing to do with him because she was quite incapable of love. Then the plague broke out in Treviso, and Polia too fell sick of it. To save her life, she dedicated herself to the goddess Diana, and thereupon she actually recovered. But from that moment on her life belonged to the goddess, and she took her part in the temple service of the chaste Diana along with other high-born maidens of the city.

It was in the temple of Diana that Poliphilo discovered his beloved again after a year had passed. In the hope of approaching her, he wrote her three long epistles, which Polia reproduces *in extenso* in her story. It would be superfluous to reproduce them here. They contain nothing but repetitions of protestations of love, and are early examples of the literary type of love-letter which became fashionable

Fig. 31. Polia Dragging Poliphilo into a Corner

at a later time in the sentimental romance.[1] But Poliphilo's letters merely troubled Polia's maidenly calm and therefore aroused her hatred. Under the guidance of Amor, Poliphilo succeeded in meeting the cruel beauty alone in the temple, and poured out his whole lovesick heart in her deaf ears. She paid no heed to him, and therefore the next day—he was already perishing from love—he ventured to repeat the attempt. As Polia once more remained obdurate, and did not even hear what he said, he sank to the ground before her eyes and fell into a deathlike trance. He is dead, thought Polia, but the thought left her unmoved. She dragged the senseless body of Poliphilo by the feet into a corner of the temple where nobody could find him, and left him lying

[1] Cf. Honoré d'Urfé's *Astrée*.

Fig. 32. Poliphilo in Polia's Lap

there (Fig. 31). True, the next day she took pity on him, but only because she realized that her own lovelessness was doing her harm. For in the night, she was assailed by two dreadful dreams [2] and was further frightened half out of her life by her cunning old bawd of a nurse, who told her the ghastly old story of the old man with the young bride. To preserve herself from evil—and for that reason only— Polia hurried back to the temple and fetched Poliphilo, who was still lying in his deathly swoon, out of his corner. She laid the cold and lifeless body of her unhappy lover across her lap. She wept, for the sight touched first her conscience,

[2] In the first, she sees Cupid, raging and fiery, burning and tearing to pieces two maidens; in the second, she is herself attacked by two horrible, half-animal devils. These two dreams, interpreted in the alchemical sense, are the *mortificatio* in its female form.

Fig. 33. The Lovers with the Priestess of Venus

and then her heart, and since pity is akin to love, she was soon embracing and kissing the swooning Poliphilo with all her heart. Love had begun to glow like a tiny spark in her icy heart, and with that change, poor Poliphilo awoke too (Fig. 32). At that moment, the priestess of Diana appeared in the temple. She found the lovers in a close embrace and drove them out of her temple with savage cudgellings. But that made no impression on Polia, for she was now entirely subjugated by love. Hand in hand with Poliphilo, she bravely made her way to the priestess of Venus, whom she once hated and despised (a parallel to the high priestess of Venus Physizoa in Part I), did homage to her, and confessed her evil ways and sins against love (Fig. 33). Polia then goes on to tell the listening nymphs by the fountain of Adonis how Poliphilo too told the priestess of Venus the story of

Fig. 34. In the Heaven of Venus

his sufferings up to the moment his pain struck him down in a swoon. Then she tells how, in that swoon, Poliphilo's soul fled from his lifeless body into the heaven of Venus, to whom he told his story of suffering. To solace Poliphilo, Cupid brought the image of Polia into heaven, and Poliphilo, sitting by the goddess's side, was permitted to see how Cupid pierced the image with his golden arrow (Fig. 34). Thereupon the image of Polia made obeisance, declared itself conquered, and pledged eternal troth to Poliphilo. In the company of the two divinities and the heavenly image of Polia, many secret and mystic visions were then vouchsafed to Poliphilo. His soul looked into Polia's eyes and was dazzled by their golden shafts as if by the sun's rays. Then the soul sped blissfully back to its body at the very moment it was restored to life by Polia.

Polia concludes her long story by describing how the priestess of Venus gave her blessing to her and Poliphilo as to a wedded couple.

COMMENTARY TO SECTION I

The matter of Polia's story is absolutely conventional and without originality. Literary borrowings and alchemical images are tacked together quite unsystematically. If we read Boccaccio's *Ameto,* which consists entirely of nymphs' stories of the same kind, we shall find that the present part of the *Hypnerotomachia* has borrowed not only its manner of narration and its atmosphere, but has taken whole sections from it verbatim. This second part is therefore a rather dull account of a commonplace love-affair, quite in the taste of the time and tricked out with a few high lights and some improprieties. It does no harm to the story to summarize it thus briefly, for apart from the end, where Poliphilo's soul and Polia's image are united by Cupid in the heaven of Venus, it contains literally nothing of interest.

Yet we can see a subtle connection between Polia's story and the contents of Part I of the *Hypnerotomachia,* since there is a whole series of parallels between them. Probably the most striking of them is that the turn for the better takes place in Part II, as it did in Part I, when Poliphilo is lying in his deathlike exhaustion in Polia's lap. Indeed, in a general way Polia repeats the love-story of herself and Poliphilo. Thus she gives a second account of the contents of Part I, but entirely from the feminine angle—and how utterly different it looks! Beauty and splendour have passed away with the wealth of significant images, and all that remains is a prosaic tale of human ordinariness. Even the exaltation of Part I has evaporated, and in its place the sphere of pure emotion, i.e. moods and passions of every kind, takes its place very volubly in the foreground. It is all as uninteresting as it could possibly be. We might dispose of it in a few words by simply saying that Part II of the *Hypnerotomachia* is a terrible disappointment as compared with Part I.

Thus when Polia begins her story, we are, in the literal sense of the word, "brought back to earth," and we begin to understand why, at the end of Part I, the wolf "who knows no compassion" follows on the heels of the divine hero. Everything that charmed us has been utterly destroyed. But the question at once arises—why? Nor must we lose sight of the fact that it is the anima herself who is telling the story. It seems significant that her voice should sound so uncompromisingly human. The poetic sublimity to which the first part of the dream raised us actually finds an excellent compensation in Polia's matter-of-factness, and everything is restored to its natural proportions by her prosaic, time-bound tale. Described by herself, Polia's figure loses all the ethereal delicacy and sweetness which she had in Poliphilo's eyes, and which made of her a very tedious angel. The anima does not describe herself at all as the man would like to have her. On the contrary, our final picture of her is that of a commonplace, rather unpleasant girl, capable of loving only herself. The gracious figure which led Poliphilo through the first part turns out to be an unkind, unreasonable tyrant who only turns to her lover when things are going badly for herself. She carries no torch, she has no wish to solace and no benevolence. She acts shrewishly and against the grain. And at the same time Poliphilo too is stripped of the romantic glamour which wrapped him round in the first part. We no longer see him as a hero who victoriously overcomes grievous hardships, but rather as a tool who is nearly brought to grief by the wiles of his anima. The story of Polia dragging away the senseless Poliphilo by his feet and throwing him into a corner is painfully undignified. Yet it is the faithful description of a man possessed by his anima. To be possessed by his anima is, unfortunately, a phase of development that no man can circumvent, for he can only realize the power of the soul when he has once been utterly at its mercy. And then again it is the anima, and she alone, who can release him from his wretched condition. He himself is "senseless," powerless; he has become utterly unconscious. He is no longer aware of what is happening to him, and it may only become apparent to those about him when his state of possession is painfully borne in upon them by his erratic moods, his eccentricities of behaviour, and every imaginable outburst of affect, positive and negative. If we ask such a man what is the matter with him, the very best we can hope for is a ranting idealization in the style of Part I of the *Hypnerotomachia*. And he will remain in that condition until the anima herself brings him to his senses with her cool kiss, and begins to speak herself.

As to anima-Polia's manner of speech, it is so far remote from the language of Poliphilo in Part I that we really imagine another being is speaking. For that matter, Polia's few utterances in Part I were already notable for their calm sobriety. But now, in Part II, it is that very sobriety which gives all she says its true significance. Her tale is characterized above all by its objectivity and candour.[3] She sees things as they are and tells what she sees. She relates her own deeds and misdeeds with perfect frankness and takes the responsibility for them without false contrition. In details, she shows a delightful power of observation, for instance when she says quite casually and openly that it was her best friend who raged most furiously against her when she was driven out of the temple of Diana. It does not surprise her—it simply was so, and she, the very epitome of all femininity, is perfectly familiar with the nature of women. By seeing things and people as they really are, by vividly portraying all their moods, she also sees herself with perfect detachment,

---

[3] It is for that reason that Boccaccio's sensuous realism is a particularly appropriate model.

and in that way her story becomes a portrayal of her own character too. She describes herself, with her good and bad qualities, simply as the thing that interests her most.

Summing up, we might say that Polia's story, for all its dulness, is important in several respects. The whole first part of the *Hypnerotomachia,* with its grandiose depiction of the archetypal content of psychic processes, here finds its complement and compensation on the personal, purely human side. What was seen in Part I *sub specie aeternitatis* here appears reflected in the clear eyes of the water nymph who sees everything from below. At the same time the under or dark side of the anima image is illuminated. We can see the malice, the callousness, and the egoism inseparable from it. Here we see the feminine as it is represented, for instance, in Chinese wisdom as Yin, which is associated with the shady side of the mountain, and whose symbol in the Western world is the cold-blooded serpent. And truly, as Polia tells her story, we can visualize the sinuousness of her way. Her leading is also a misleading, which in the end even costs the man the cruel loss of all his manhood. But then, along with the venom of destruction, she gives him the redeeming draught of new life.

Beyond all this, however, Polia's story is primarily a gospel of objectivity and truth to fact, and from this point of view we may find its special application to the man of the Renaissance as he is bodied forth in Poliphilo's dream. The Middle Ages were ignorant of this kind of objectivity, for they measured all things by the standard of Christian values. In Polia's story that kind of valuation is abandoned—she merely gives an account of fact without any "moral." Thus we may see that Polia, by her objectivity towards the appearance of the world and life, and by her faithful and unbiassed apprehension of existing facts as they are, becomes the first embodiment of an entirely new outlook. How can this outlook be defined? It has become familiar and valuable to the man of today, whose thought is largely empirical in character. He denotes the dispassionate faithfulness of observation and the objective evaluation of phenomena by the general name of "scientific." That term does not necessarily imply that a man is a scientist of a particular kind, but that he uses his capacities in such a way that science may grow out of them. It took time for men to learn to do so. It was not by thinking, but by living, by approaching the things they encountered from a fresh angle, that they began to see them in a new way. This is what Polia does in her story; hence in this sense, and perhaps with a somewhat bold transposition into modern terms, we may denote what she represents as the scientific attitude. Nor must we be disconcerted if this attitude makes its appearance in the telling of a tale of love. On the contrary, it is both witty and significant that, in this book of a lover, it should be the experience of love which is apprehended with scientific detachment as a phenomenon of reality. Polia might in a certain sense be regarded as a first personification of scientific method—yet not, as the monkish author imagined at the beginning of his book, as a scientific approach to antiquity, but as a scientific attitude towards reality.

Throughout the course of the story up to this point we have seen that the anima-Polia has preceded and guided her Poliphilo. In images, in actions, she has always shown him something which was later to acquire value for him and become his own action. Here her story becomes the exemplar of a method of observation that Poliphilo can later put into action himself. As the anima-Polia becomes the exemplar of a new attitude, and as, at the same time, the radiant figure is transformed into the drabness of everyday, she gives Poliphilo the man the opportunity of applying that outlook to himself and of seeing himself dispassionately. Coldness, selfishness, negative feeling, conflicting emotions —she acts them all for his behoof so that he may look into himself and see himself for what he really is, an ordinary, somewhat capricious, and unreasonable human being. Nothing could be more necessary than such an experience to the humanist with his vast aspirations (or for that matter to the man of today with his vast knowledge and skill). But he cannot go through that experience unless it is brought to him by the anima, unless he can first comprehend and accept it in her, because, for him, she confers value on what seems valueless, and because he loves her.

In this sense, and seen from Poliphilo's point of view, Part II of the *Hypnerotomachia* is a hymn to steadfast constancy. Since Poliphilo remains unwaveringly faithful to his beloved, and will not give her up, the coolness of feminine insight can unite, as its necessary complement, with the warmth of his consciousness, and bring him the refreshment from the watery depths that he needs.

In its general outlines, this revelation and opening of the depths is characteristic of the anima experience of every man, provided always that he advances so far on the path of his psychic development. Yet the specific content of that revelation will, of course, differ at different epochs. Thus for the man of the Renaissance it meant a new kind of objectivity in the contemplation of man and the world. And that mode of contemplation is certainly the gain that the man of the Renaissance acquired in his encounter with the classical world. The antique lack of prejudice with regard to physical nature became in him a lack of prejudice in respect of any object. Thereby he became a responsible person. And his own person as a phenomenon, his character, his personal qualities were now taken seriously as real facts like any other phenomena.[4] From his submergence in antiquity, which the man of the Renaissance experienced as a mystery, he brought back a new value, namely an outlook

[4] That is why the Renaissance was an age of biographies. Cf. the autobiography of Girolamo Cardano, the physician, who describes his own character exactly in the way defined above.

on the world and a new adaptation to the world. In psychological terms we might say that in this respect the *Hypnerotomachia* traces the process of the emergence of the persona, not only as a mask, but as a new relationship of man to the world.

This is the enrichment that Poliphilo experiences on his dream-journey. But it implies no final solution. The psychic life of man never stands still. Every goal reached is the fruit of the tree of the psyche which already bears within it the dark seed of fresh growth. Every end is a beginning, and no fulfilment is a true one which is not understood as a task to be performed. This task always makes its appearance in the next problem, which arises of itself from the goal just reached. And so it is with Poliphilo's dream, which has no happy ending with which to flatter the prejudice of consciousness. On the contrary, the whole concluding symbolism of the dream raises, with this first solution, cardinal problems of the inner life which are of the utmost importance to us, for they are universally human and not unknown in our own day. The symbolism before us, therefore, must now be examined for the specific problem it presents, since it is that problem which forms the transition to the last section of the dream. We shall then see what attitude Poliphilo the man takes up towards these new and vital problems.

While Part I of the *Hypnerotomachia* gives an account of a regression into the past which leads back to antiquity and finds its climax in the apotheosis of the ancient mystery cult, Part II signifies the return to the present and the descent into the banality of ordinary humanity. When the wanderer returns, he returns enriched; the humanist's idealization of classical antiquity has been dispelled and in its place there has come to life in the dreamer something of the unrestrained naturalism of antiquity as it really was. Enriched with that naturalism, he who was so divorced from reality at the beginning at last finds a contact with the world. At the same time, however, he finds himself; his figure fills out and becomes human, and he will now be able to live out his personal peculiarities just as they are and even in his monkish cowl. Further, he gains clear insight into the real meaning of the ideas which meant so much to him when he set out. In this connection, it is particularly significant that the symbolism of alchemy and the conception of courtly love enter into Polia's story too, and are transmuted into a new form. Both realms, as in Part I, coalesce in the idea of a marriage. Solemnized by Cupid in a very strange way, this marriage is the climax of Polia's story too. In alchemical terms, it points to a *conjunctio*, Poliphilo and Polia representing the archetypal opposites of male and female whose union and transmutation is the goal of the Great Work. But prior to this, both, again as in Part I, have been subjected to an alchemical process. They are, as the alchemists often describe, "mortified," and the symbols of this "mortification" are Poliphilo's swoon and Polia's nightmares. The volatile element is liberated from them in the form of Poliphilo's "soul" and Polia's "image," and the ascension to the heaven of Venus points to a *sublimatio*. Under the influence of the divine fire (Cupid), a *conjunctio* seems to have taken place, and the eternal spirit, Mercury, who holds sway over it, appears in the guise of Venus, that is, in female form, as occasionally happens in alchemical treatises.[5] Throughout these proceedings, the alchemical mysticism of numbers is evoked in the peculiar and changing constellation of the figures. In the course of Polia's story, we find the combination, first of the Two, then of Three, and finally of Four. The confrontation of Poliphilo with Polia in her cruelty is the first situation (the Two). The second is given with Polia and Poliphilo subordinated to a priestly figure, incorporated first in the priestess of

[5] See C. G. Jung, *Psychology and Alchemy,* Fig. 138, and "Der Geist Mercurius," *Eranos Year Book*, 1942.

Diana, then in the priestess of Venus, both of whom exercise an action which furthers the process (the Three). Finally, in a third situation we see Poliphilo's soul and Polia's image in the company of Venus and Cupid (the Four). This remarkable development of the figures could be rendered directly by the famous precept of Maria Prophetissa, which Jung has called a cardinal axiom of alchemy.[6] This saying, which summarizes the whole alchemical process in one hieroglyph, runs as follows:

The One becomes the Two, the Two the Three, and the One from the Third comes into being as the Fourth.

The development might be so rendered, yet with a certain reservation, since the One, the starting-point, is not visible, and the Four which arise at the end do not merge into unity. True, four figures are present, but they cannot attain perfection because there is no centre. The alchemical process as described by Polia does not end in a mandala based on the number four and fully centred. It certainly shows four figures as a climax, but their appearance is brief, and the whole finally returns to the second situation and the number three when Polia concludes her story by describing how the priestess of Venus gives her blessing to herself and Poliphilo. Hence it follows from Polia's faithful and unbiassed account that the alchemical Work could not be completed. In principle, the situation remains what it was when it first emerged into visibility in the temple of Venus Physizoa, and what led beyond it did not endure.

*Three we brought with us,
The fourth would not come.*[7]

If we wish to interpret this in psychological terms, it will be best for us to return to the symbolism of the first four triumphal chariots, where a quaternity was also represented

---

[6] See *Psychology and Alchemy*.
[7] *Faust*, Part II, Aegean Festival, the Kabires.

by the four elements, the fourth being described as a peculiar element of daemonic-divine character, self-contradictory like the ὕδωρ θεῖον of alchemism. Poliphilo felt some repulsion and horror at the sight of that fourth. At that point we interpreted the fourth chariot as a symbol of the inferior function, which seems alien and ghastly to the dreamer, yet which could unite him to the divine essence within himself. A very similar interpretation is given by the end of Polia's story. The situation in the heaven of Venus can be interpreted as a symbol of the united four functions. We need not here enter into the question of the allocation of the four functions among the four figures in the heaven of Venus since, as has already been pointed out, the image is evanescent. We can only say that the union of the four takes place in the heaven of Venus, hence in the world beyond—it may be in a heightened consciousness or in the unconscious—and not in the dreamer's real world. The development then finally reverts to the number-three, so that we know that the dreamer still lacks the fourth function, namely sensation. He still has no power of grasping reality direct, and he may still shudder at the strange creature in him which has that power. Hence, for all apprehension, which ranges from sensuous perception to the aesthetic enjoyment of reality, he is still dependent on the mediating function of his anima.

This consideration raises a question. What does a man look like who lacks the Fourth?

In the present connection, the answer to the question may be inferred from the symbolism used by Polia herself in her story, starting once again with the third situation in the heaven of Venus, where the goddess Venus, Cupid, Poliphilo's soul, and Polia's image come together. First we may follow the clear intimation given by the author, who points in a definite direction with the term "image" (*effigie*), applied to Polia. Here he is alluding to Platonic and Neoplatonic doctrines which, just at his own time, had aroused intense interest among scholars. Platonic philosophy had been rediscovered in the Western world in the course of the fifteenth century and, mingled with Neoplatonic conceptions, was passionately studied in Italy, especially at the Platonic Academy in Florence. We may take it for granted that this was not unknown to our author. With this allusion, therefore, he attacks philosophical problems which differ from the conceptions of alchemy. Firstly, it would appear absolutely right in the sense of Neoplatonic thought that the primordial One should not make any appearance in the story, for the One supreme godhead is, for the Neoplatonist, transcendental and only to be defined negatively as the Unknowable, Incomprehensible. The only thing knowable by man is the God-Spirit emanating from the One, which he beholds at moments of ecstasy and with which he can be united in a transient experience of mystic bliss. Seen from this standpoint, Poliphilo's swoon in the temple of Diana may be taken directly as a representation of the total surrender which is the first condition of ecstasy. The apparitions in the heaven of Venus may then be taken as the contents of the ecstatic revelation. We shall apprehend their significance best by turning to Platonic philosophy itself. Applied to Polia, the term "image" would mean that the dreamer recognizes the imaginary figure which has led him through his dream as an "idea" in the Platonic sense. He beholds the reality of the beloved which is "laid up in Heaven," and which his soul can remember from pre-natal knowledge. Cupid appears in this connection as the philosophic impulse, the love of the ideas, as the Eros described in Plato's *Symposium*. There Socrates calls him the great daemon who stands midway between the gods and men, between beauty and ugliness, between wisdom and foolishness and who leads men by the way of longing from the dark world of phenomena to the supreme ideas of the beautiful and the good. In Venus, the supreme idea is represented as beauty only [8] and corresponds to the prevailing bias of the Renaissance to give pride of place to the idea of the beautiful rather than to that of the good. Now in accordance with the symbolism under discussion, the way to supreme beauty does not lie through a multiplicity of ideas, but through the one idea of the beloved woman. If, at the same time, we recall the myth of the primordial, spherical hermaphrodite as related by Aristophanes in the *Symposium*, the idea of the beloved also recalls that "other half" from which man, originally whole and a sphere, was once torn, and for which he never ceases to yearn. Looked at in this way, it would certainly look as if the constellation of the figures in the heaven of Venus were intended to express that the soul of Poliphilo may attain immortal and supreme beauty under the inspiration of Eros if it takes for its sole aim the one idea of the beloved and, with the help of the great daemon, activates only this one pre-natal image.

If this is indeed the meaning, then even in Polia's story the conception of courtly love—somewhat in the sense of the Florentine *fedeli d'amore*—takes pride of place, and the dreamer takes it with him into his regeneration as a supreme value.

This sketch of the philosophical background is necessarily brief, since our object is not to expound Platonic or Neoplatonic doctrines but to catch the emotional atmosphere attendant upon them in our book. It is an atmosphere of enthusiastic striving after beauty, combined with the certainty that it can be attained through idealized love. The image in the heaven of Venus also shows Poliphilo the lover as a sage whose soul has turned in philosophical ardour to the world of pure ideas, and who lives, loves, and dies in beauty.

[8] From this point of view it closely follows Plotinus (*Enn.* I, 6); cf. Giordano Bruno, *Eroici Furori*.

This, then, is the portrait of the man who lacks the Fourth. He soars above the earthly, the commonplace, and, aiming at the highest, becomes wise, good, and beautiful. It is a splendid picture, and it would seem well worth while to sacrifice the contemptible Fourth in order to scale such heights. But there are two things we must not forget: firstly, that it is the anima-Polia who tells the story, and secondly, her manner of telling it. According to her account, the scene in the heaven of Venus is a dream within a dream, that is, a thing which, in psychic reality, has only the value of a phantom. That means that it is a coinage of the fantasy with which Poliphilo plays in his solitude without realizing its significance. To put it otherwise, it is an illusion, and the "secret and mystical visions" which were granted to Poliphilo in the heaven of Venus beyond what he sees with his own eyes are probably mere trickings-out of that illusion.

It is the nature of every illusion to sit in man's inmost heart like a dream within a dream. When he is alone, he takes the puppets out, and there, on that inner stage, they act the same play for him in a thousand variants. It is always satisfying because the cold wind of reality never blows on it. Yet it enters into reality nevertheless, for a man who, for instance, falls into a Platonic illusion about himself imagines that he has in him at any rate the makings of a Platonic sage. Thus the illusion inevitably comes to colour the human reality, and in the end the man ceases to live his own life, and lives that of a Platonic sage. The despised, commonplace, and worthless Fourth is then no longer at home within him, it attacks the wretched sage from without in a thousand devilries. For instance, those about him may appear foolish and wicked, and beneath his dignity. Even objects seem to be unpleasantly animated as if by spirits. They plague him with their mischief, and the body itself may begin to suffer.

This picture finds corroboration in a modern instance,

for it is important to realize that the enlightened man of our day is not proof against illusions and their consequences. The most vivid and most natural account of a self-imagined sage of the same kind as Poliphilo is to be found in Friedrich Theodor Vischer's *Auch Einer*,[9] a novel of quite outstanding psychological interest. Vischer knows him very well, for it is obvious that his hero is a piece of himself. For instance, in the course of his book, he makes him say:

"Man [i.e. himself], with the vaulted world of his head, with his radiant eyes, with the spirit that flashes its light into depths and distances, the feeling that rises to heaven on silver wings, the imagination that pours the golden stream of its fire over hill and dale and transfigures the mortal image of man into God [sic] with a will like a naked sword to rule by justice and to overcome, and with the devout patience that plants, tends and watches, so that the tree of life may grow and flourish and bear the divine fruit of all gentle culture, man with the angelic image of eternal beauty in his prescient, yearning breast . . ."

We may stop here, for the reader will have realized already that *Auch Einer* really feels that he too is a sage, led onward, like Poliphilo, by the "angelic image of eternal beauty." But alas! the vaulted world of his head harbours a permanent cold which brings on frightful fits of sneezing and coughing and makes him ridiculous. Further, all the objects which minister to his daily wants—studs, spectacles, watch, crockery—have united in a conspiracy against him. They play tricks on him, hide, break, and seem to be animated by a consciousness of their own and full of malice towards him. It is in vain for him to try to circumvent the conspiracy by giving it the technical term of "the malice of the object," or even to elaborate a mythical philosophy of the cold in the head. The enemies are not to be overcome by philosophy.

[9] This novel has not been translated into English. The title means roughly "One Kind of Man."

He quarrels viciously with everyone, loses his job, and wanders about Italy, sneezing, from one object of beauty to another.[10]

Finally he is killed in a fracas with a carter whom he sees maltreating his horse. He has never noticed that throughout his life he has been guilty of the grossest cruelty to animals, since, in his high-flown wisdom, he has denied his commonplace humanity. This *Auch Einer* too has, somewhere in the background, a figure of beauty not unlike Poliphilo's Polia. He gives her the name Cordelia, but he is determined only to love her from afar, and flees incontinently when she comes within his reach. That is an injustice and a wrong that Poliphilo does not commit. And that is why nothing can save *Auch Einer* from his blindness, and why no fiery daemon comes to his help with the golden arrow of love.[11]

To return to the *Hypnerotomachia*, it is interesting that at this point Cupid's arrow should only pierce Polia's breast, and that she should then declare herself conquered, and plight eternal troth. What can be inferred from this? We cannot avoid the suspicion that Polia is not quite innocent of complicity in Poliphilo's illusions. It may have suited her very well to play the "angelic image of eternal beauty." She has whispered to Poliphilo, "Thou art a sage," in order to display herself to him as a pure idea. But love knows the shifts and tricks of the anima. It is the lover's own constancy which overcomes the anima, so that she turns to him and plights her troth. Poliphilo returns from the illusory

---

[10] [Cf. Shakespeare, *Much Ado About Nothing*:
For there was never yet philosopher
That could endure the toothache patiently.—TRANS.]

[11] This German example may be of particular significance here, because the subsequent development of the German personality shows very clearly what dreadful destruction the splitting off of the Fourth may entail. But any nation or any individual which refuses to see its own reality and lives in an illusion is threatened by the same danger.

heaven of Venus to the final image in the temple of Venus, which showed him human imperfection as his own inward reality. It represents him as a man still struggling with his anima. Once more he is "betrothed" to her, once more his loving meditation must be concentrated on her. He must listen to her, for her part is not yet played out.

The insight that Poliphilo has gained from the images in Polia's story is, briefly summarized, that the idea of courtly love has been an illusion for him, and that it was not given to him to complete the Great Work of alchemy. Hence the return from the journey into antiquity and the descent into the commonplace means for Poliphilo a release from inward attachment to cherished ideas. It turns out that he has never really understood the symbolism of alchemy, therefore alchemy vanishes. And it turns out that the notion of courtly love in its traditional form has only been a kind of truancy of the imagination. Does that mean that courtly love vanishes from his sight too—that his anima vanishes?

If that were the case, it would mean that the end of the dream would bring his detachment from the anima figure of Polia. Then the long process of coming to terms with the lovely image that has deluded him so long would be complete. We should find ourselves facing the conclusion which belongs to all inner experience. The psyche is a constant process, a process of constant change, and what is left is not the image but the experience the image has conferred. But it is the anima alone that can teach the man the process of detachment from the anima and, as always, the final result depends on whether and in what way he understands her teaching.

SECTION II

The Assumption of Polia

(Chapters 13 and 14) As Polia finishes her story, she also completes the chaplet of roses she has woven for Poliphilo, and she now crowns him with it. The nymphs of the fountain of Adonis thank Polia for her story, then they bid the lovers farewell, and leave them to themselves. Once more the lovers pledge eternal love and troth. And now we may continue in Poliphilo's own words:

"Thereupon Polia cast her pure and milk-white arms about my neck and embraced me, pressing her coral lips to mine in a sweet, biting kiss. I hastened to return her kiss, and as I did so, a mortal desire overcame me. . . . But in the embrace of love, a wonderful, natural blush arose into her countenance and spread over her white cheeks. . . . And because she was oppressed by the utter sweetness, tears shone in her eyes like clear crystals, like round pearls, like the dew which Aurora strews on the clouds of dawn. Sighing like a heavenly image, like incense of musk and amber rising to give delight to the spirits of heaven, she dissolved into thin air, leaving nought behind her but a breath of heavenly fragrance. So, with my happy dream, she vanished from my sight, saying as she went: 'Poliphilo, most dear beloved, farewell!'

"Thus was my ineffable delight torn from me, the angelic spirit had vanished from my sight. . . . With a sigh, I awoke from my sweet dream, and, awaking, said: 'Farewell, then, my Polia!'"

COMMENTARY TO SECTION II

As we see, at the end of the *Hypnerotomachia*, the anima really vanishes. But first Poliphilo is abandoned by the nymphs of the fountain of Adonis who have listened with him to Polia's story. The multiplicity of nymphs or water-spirits may be regarded as a symbol of the collective unconscious, and their departure means that Poliphilo is taking leave of it too. The fountainhead vanishes also, the dreamer returns to himself.

Then Polia leaves him too, but in vanishing, she undergoes a further transfiguration. She glows like a rose, she becomes like a dewy cloud of morning, she is made divine and leaves behind her a breath of heavenly fragrance. No detail of this description should escape us, for it is in the details that we can see what Polia's disappearance means and what becomes of her.

There is only one female figure in the whole of the Christian cult which is adorned with such attributes and whose transfiguration is similarly described, and that is the Blessed Virgin Mary. She is the Peerless, Precious Rose, the Rose of Paradise or of Jericho. The poet Sedulius (*c.* 400) sings of her thus:

As on the thorny bush the tender rose gloweth in blossom,
Yet thornless, unwounding, is honoured more than its mother,
So from the root of Eve, Mary the Maiden springing,
Atoned here on earth for the sin of the maiden before her.

Mary too is like a cloud, a "transparent spring of refreshing rain," "verily a light cloud," a "lofty tent, full of lightning flashes." And she is the sweetest of balmy odours. The little book *Of the Death of Mary*, written at the end of the fourth century, relates how, at her passing, the room was filled with fragrance as her soul left her body. Her name is also interpreted as "myrrh of the sea."[1] A medieval hymn says:

---

[1] These attributes of the Virgin are taken from various German collections of early Christian hymns and other texts.

"She spread sweet perfumes about her, for He created her pouring forth sweet fragrance far and wide like cinnamon and fragrant balm and choice myrtle, for she was full of fragrance, so delicious by the repute of her humility, charity, unparallelled chastity, and all other virtues that all true believers, both here on the way and there at home, and all the heavenly hosts take their joy in her incomparable fragrance and cry astonied:

> *"Who is she that looketh forth as the morning,*
> *Fair as the moon,*
> *Clear as the sun,*
> *And terrible as an army with banners?"* [2]

If we consider these parallels—and they could be multiplied—it becomes obvious that Polia's disappearance is an assumption, and that she is here identified with the transfigured Virgin. Her betrothed is no longer Poliphilo, but Christ, the Virgin's Son. Béroalde de Verville, the French translator of the *Hypnerotomachia* in 1600, must have understood the matter in this way, for he has illuminated the initial letter of the short chapter describing Polia's departure with a significant miniature, showing Christ with the Cross, beckoning with His finger (see p. 210). He is calling Polia up to Him, and she becomes *sponsa veri sponsi*, the bride of the true Bridegroom.[2a] This is the Christian *conjunctio*, and it is similarly described in the book *Of the Death of Mary*:

"And as they [the disciples] prayed, thunder roared from Heaven, and there arose a dreadful noise as of chariots, and behold! there appeared the heavenly host of the Angels and Powers. And a voice like unto the voice of the Son of Man

[2] Radulph Ardens, *hom. in deip. ass.* from A. Salzer, *Die Sinnbilder und Beiworte Mariens*. [The verse is from the Song of Solomon vi. 10.—TRANS.]

[2a] Salzer, op. cit.

was heard, and the Seraphim made a circle round about the house. . . . And it befell that when the voice ceased, suddenly the sun and moon appeared about the house, and the Church of the first-born saints did stand by the house."

This powerful and beautiful picture points to a sacred marriage (ἱερὸς γάμος) which, like every mystery, is consummated in secret. But the visible image and symbol of it appear in the union of sun and moon. This means that the archetypal opposites of male and female, light and dark, divine and human, have become a dual unity. What appears in this early Christian picture is one of the profoundest conceptions of the pagan mystery cults, and it is to be found in exactly the same form in the symbolism of alchemy.[3]

We must not lose sight of these ideas if we are to understand the true significance of Polia's transfiguration. What we have to discover, first and foremost, is what our author means when, in his story, the anima-Polia takes the place of the Virgin Mary. For that is a thing we cannot simply take for granted.

If the anima who was, on her own showing, a "thorny bush" like Eve becomes a rose, a cloud in heaven, and a *sponsa,* she is doing what she has been doing all along—opening Poliphilo's eyes to something and pointing him the way. By rising to Christ, merged in the figure of the Blessed Virgin, she is turning his eyes to Christ and the union with Christ. At first sight this would seem to indicate an extremely simple solution to the problem, for, as Christ is embodied in the Church, Polia's assumption might simply mean that Poliphilo's soul is contained in the Church. For him, as for every Christian, the Church seems to stand in front of the divine and daemonic as the wardress of supreme

[3] The devout author of *Of the Death of Mary* seems to have grown uneasy, for he hastens to make a fresh start and to retell his story, this time duly veiled as the institution of Mary as mediator by Christ.

values and the shield against onslaughts from the depths. In accordance with the image, therefore, we may say that Polia, in vanishing, leads Poliphilo back to the Church. From this point of view it follows that the solution of the dream is Catholic and Christian, since the soul of the man of the Renaissance was, in spite of appearances, still an *anima naturaliter Christiana*.

In another respect, however, the solution of the dream is already somewhat remote from Christianity, since, with the nymph who turns into a cloud, an element absolutely alien to Christianity enters into it all the same. The identification of the transfigured Polia with Mary also signifies the fusion of the reawakened soul of antiquity with the Christian spirit represented by the Church. Polia is a female symbol which embodies no spiritual values at all, but simply the natural human qualities of man. Thus the original sharp line of demarcation drawn by Christianity between spirit and nature is partly obliterated. What this means, the author of the *Hypnerotomachia*, fortunately for the salvation of his own soul, could not discern. It is a symbol pregnant with significance for the future, which, to put it in the most general way, contains the germ of that worldliness of the church and divinization of nature and man which were to become a reality in modern Europe.

Even yet the matter is not exhausted. We are faced here with an extremely complicated symbolism which can only be disentangled fold by fold. The first thing to be said is that Polia does not vanish completely from Poliphilo's sight, for she leaves with him the chaplet of roses and her sweet, biting kiss. She, the rose, is still present in the chaplet, even though, in a sense, the one has become the many. What is worn on the head may be taken to symbolize what is in the head, i.e. a man's conscious thoughts and imaginings. According to this interpretation, the chaplet would mean that

Poliphilo's mind now bears the imprint of the anima. He no longer thinks as once he did, but as a man with a totally new attitude to life that Polia has given him. At the same time, the kiss and the chaplet are symbols of Poliphilo's coronation. Adorned with the chaplet and kissed by the daemonic-divine maiden, he stands there like some neophyte of antiquity who has passed through initiation and become the sharer in an ineffable mystery. Thus we can find no other interpretation than that Poliphilo, at the very moment of his return to the Church, is left standing in front of it as Polia's crowned neophyte.

It follows that, at the end of his dream, Poliphilo is left in a curiously equivocal situation which is worth consideration in more than one respect. He is a Christian because he finds his eternal salvation in the Church and in Christ alone. At the same time, through the influence of his anima, he is a personality with a life of his own which has nothing to do with the Church, and distinguishes him from all other Christians. There lies his personal mystery; it is there that his own views and ideas come into their own. In accordance with the symbolism of the dream, this life of his own stands in sharp opposition to the Church, and yet, since Polia becomes the *sponsa Christi*, it is inseparably bound up with Christianity. Poliphilo, therefore, is at one and the same time a Christian and a non-Christian.

It is important to realize this equivocality, for it is not peculiar to Poliphilo's dream. On the contrary, it is obvious that, for centuries past, a large number of cultivated men and women have lived in it. Even after the Renaissance, Europeans remained Christians, like Poliphilo, though more and more of them came to restrict their Christianity to the definite occasions prescribed by the Church or to cases of emergency. For the rest of the time they lived more or less in their own way, and thus it was the private lives of these people that moved into the foreground in a very significant fashion. What men did or were in themselves, apart from their religious or secular collectivity, became quite particularly interesting and important because they acted, in a way, as the neophyte of their own Polia. Personal inclinations and qualities developed, the result of which has sometimes been designated as cultivation, but more often as individuality or even personality. In the positive sense, the latter acted as character, originality, or charm. It flourished most exuberantly in the incomprehensible or even savage duality of the baroque, when men so often united within themselves much that was really saintly and much that was barbaric and unsaintly. The experience and conception of personality gave rise to new notions of the ideal human being, for instance, the Italian *gentiluomo,* the French *honnête homme,* the English gentleman. Of late, the opposition between Christian and non-Christian, which developed in the Renaissance and forced its way into the foreground in the age of the baroque, has become a little less obvious on the surface, but behind a persona which has often lost much of its meaning, it is still there and gives people their character. Thus the man of our day is the exponent of personal values in a way quite impossible before the Renaissance. The negative side of personality, however, is that it too often represents only a sector of the human whole, which is turned to the world and, being dependent on the world, only too often degenerates into a mask or a pose. This is probably due to the fact that the very foundation of modern individuality is equivocal, and that means halfness. A development was set going, a path entered upon, but it was never trodden to its end.

In corroboration, we had best turn back to the symbolism contained in Poliphilo's dream and see if we can penetrate yet deeper into it.

Polia's actions at the end of the dream are actually very simple, and may be very briefly summarized. She gives Poliphilo a chaplet of roses and kisses him, while showing him that what he sees in her is the *rosa mystica.* It is necessary to formulate her final action in this way, for there is here an inner, causal connection. The anima only appears as the bride of heaven at this point because Poliphilo sees her as such. With the chaplet of roses, the contents of the psyche that he has gained on his dream-journey through the mediation of the anima pass, so to speak, into Poliphilo's possession. A natural, open-minded attitude towards the world which was previously so unconscious in him that it seemed to lie buried in classical antiquity has thus become part of his consciousness. And yet another thing has entered into his consciousness—the fact that he has a character of his own which does not always correspond to his former ideals, and that he is a personality. Such knowledge represents a supreme value to him; it carries such conviction that it intoxicates the man like a kiss from his beloved, and he sees her who imparts it in a kind of glory. Poliphilo's journey by Polia's side represents the unfolding of his personal consciousness, and the wealth of images that have risen with it shows how important the full development of consciousness is for him as for all men. The reason it is so important is that the full consciousness of one's own personality is a first step beyond the personal and an approach to the suprapersonal. This fact is manifested in the assumption of Polia. If she appears as the bride of Christ, that must be taken to mean that the knowledge of one's own personality is almost as important as the knowledge of the suprapersonal, for it gives birth to it and leads up to it. From the psychological standpoint we might say that personal consciousness is the condition of individuation. For as soon as the personal consciousness has reached maturity, its scope and limitations present a problem to man. He must know what are his responsibilities, and up to what point he must say "that is I," and where he is exposed to influences which determine the course of his life, yet which he cannot attribute to himself.

When the development of consciousness has reached full term, this problem always arises in one form or the other, whether it is noticed or not. If a man is not aware of it, and does not live it out, he comes to an inward standstill. But if he becomes aware of it, he has to come to terms with all those contents of the psyche which are incompatible with his consciousness, and have hence remained unconscious. This process may be compared in a certain sense with an ascent to heaven. One's own darkness is raised into the light, and a more comprehensive self-knowledge is attained. At the same time, the suprapersonal factors of the psyche come to light, and man is released from his halfness by finding wholeness in his submission to that which is greater than his consciousness. Looked at from this point of view, the symbol of the *conjunctio* of Polia and Christ takes on a new and deeper meaning. Christ becomes the personification of the centre in which the striving soul of man (Polia) can experience both itself and wholeness. In other words, Christ is the symbol of the Self by which the opposites of consciousness and the unconscious are reconciled.

This is a conception which is by no means alien to Christian mysticism. A large number of Christian mystics have described it as the way to the experience of the Christ within. Thus Richard of St. Victor (*c.* 1175), for instance, writes in his *Benjamin Minor*:

"For the spirit which striveth to attain to the heights of knowledge the first task and undertaking must be perfect self-knowledge. To know thyself perfectly is a great height of knowledge. Perfect self-knowledge of the rational spirit is as a great and high mountain. This mountain ariseth above all worldly knowledge, and looketh down upon all wisdom and all knowledge of this world. . . . Learn to think, O man! Learn to think upon thyself, and thou shalt rise into thine own inward self. The more thou dost progress in self-knowledge, the farther shalt thou move beyond thyself. . . .

"First thou shalt climb, then stand still. There is toil in standing still, yet greater toil in climbing. Many have failed in that same climbing. . . .

"On the summit of this mountain, Jesus is transfigured, Moses and Elijah are beheld upon it, and both are known without signs. Upon that mountain the call of the Father to the Son is heard. Wouldst thou see Christ transfigured? . . . Wouldst thou see Moses and Elijah? Wouldst thou comprehend the Law and the Prophets without a teacher, with none to expound them? Climb the mountain, learn to know thyself. If thy soul shall long to know the hidden secret of the Father, climb the mountain, learn to know thyself."

Bernard of Clairvaux (1091–1153) has expressed the same thought with forceful concision and an almost gloomy determination:

"That is the curse that afflicteth the man that maketh himself guilty of ignorance of God. Shall I say of God or of himself? Without doubt, both. Both kinds of ignorance are to be condemned, and each sufficeth for a man's eternal destruction."

The equivalent of the conception of the experience of God through self-knowledge may be seen in the idea of the birth of God in man as expressed by Angelus Silesius (1624–1677):

Look, man, thy blessedness is there for thee to seize,
Wouldst thou bestir thyself, and cast aside thine ease.

Call not upon thy God, the fountain springs in thee,
Didst thou not stop its flow, it ever could spring free.

God became man in thee. If God thou willst not be,
Thou scornst His birth and death, which He did die for thee.

Then lead is turned to gold, and Fortune's wheel is stayed,
If I with God, through God, in God to God am made.[4]

[4] Angelus Silesius, *Der cherubinische Wandersmann.*

It is this transformation which Polia represents to Poliphilo as she rises to heaven; it is to this transformation and to the contemplation of the Christ within that she desires to bring him. But why does she vanish at that very moment from his sight, to become forever unattainable? Can it mean that transformation and the birth of God within are beyond Poliphilo's reach, after all?

No. When Polia vanishes, it only means that *this* transformation cannot be accomplished through the anima. Her disappearance symbolizes the fact that the anima is drained of all her contents and that, for the time being, her part is played out. She has now imparted to Poliphilo the knowledge of the unconscious. Her form is emptied, nothing tangible remains. Thus the departure of Polia symbolizes the phenomenon of the detachment from the anima, while at the same time a certain differentiation is hinted at.

To understand this, we must remember that the scene of Polia's assumption takes place by the grave of Adonis. Poliphilo is still standing in front of the unopened grave. When Polia floats upward, the female symbol is removed from the grave which, up to then, it had concealed. Thus the feminine is differentiated from the masculine symbol of Adonis, and as the female figure vanishes from the dreamer's sight, it becomes possible for the masculine symbol to emerge into visibility. The gaze can now detach itself from the heights left void by Polia's passing, and turn to the earth—namely the grave. But then divine love must be present, which can open the grave and take from it its strange, hidden contents.

The process of coming to terms with the anima forcibly constellates for the man the problem of the shadow and the inferior function. This fact is clearly presented in Poliphilo's dream by the symbolism of the grave of Adonis. It was already perceptible in Polia's story, for even there the emphasis lay on the recognition of shadow sides. But in the story, the shadows—and their recognition—lay with the anima. It was she who represented herself as selfish, domineering, and utterly callous. But in her assumption she has cast aside her shadows. She leaves them with the man, and he finds them now as his own shadow within him, as in a grave. The grave contains everything that cannot be fitted into the small sector of the conscious personality, and is therefore rejected, repressed, or buried along with everything that is as yet quite unknown to consciousness. In the vile husk of what is despised as all-too-human, the inferior function lies dormant in Poliphilo as in a grave. At the end of the dream, its symbol is the dead body of Adonis. But now there is added to it the other, equally valid symbol, namely that the contents of the grave can only be removed from it in the form of blood and tears. This is an image that speaks for itself. The activation of the inferior function means that tears must flow, and that pain and suffering are inevitable. For when the inferior function is activated, an abyss opens. It draws consciousness down into the dark realm of the unconscious, compelling it to descend into Hades, a descent analogous to Adonis' dark journey to the triple-bodied Pluto and Proserpine.

This is a mysterious symbolism which, in the dream, remains as closed as the grave of Adonis. We can do no more than suggest that Adonis and the triple-bodied Pluto, in becoming visible, present a quaternity. This would embody a wholeness that man can attain by individuation, or—to use an older term—self-knowledge. Adonis, the god-man, concealed in the repulsive husk of the corpse, appears here in a double sense as the Fourth; by this central image the world of consciousness, differentiated into three functions, may be completed, while on the other hand the unconscious, appearing in the form of a hidden trinity, may be brought closer to man.

What, however, is the meaning of this symbol of the hidden trinity? We have already encountered it in the course of Poliphilo's dream in many variants which need not be recalled here. But now, when the trinity of the underworld must be regarded as a counterpart of the Christian trinity, we must explicitly denote it as a daemonic trinity. If the grave of Adonis were to open, if the dead body were to come to life, would that mean that man would be touched by the daemonic? Must we imagine that he would then like Luther reach the point of hurling ink-pots at the devil? Maybe.

The pit of my own self cries ever out of me
To that pit which is God's. Which may the deeper be?[5]

Down in the depths, Proserpine stands by the side of the triple-formed Pluto—the female beside the male daemon, threatening to burst the quaternity asunder. In this connection, Proserpine can only be understood as the counterpart of Venus. Now in Poliphilo's dream, Venus is always what he calls her in Part I: Physizoa, living nature, hence a symbol of the vital, life-giving aspect of the unconscious. It is she who bestows colour on growth, she who sets the forward development in motion. But Proserpine, as her opposite, means inhibition, hesitation, and, when she bursts the quaternity asunder, death.[6] She incorporates the seduction and supreme danger which may be associated with the "resurrection of the body." Alchemy denotes that danger as the failure of the Great Work. In the symbolism of the *Hypnerotomachia*, that danger does not arise when Cupid opens the grave, that is to say, when a higher—or deeper—emotion of love is present which does not cling to the personal, and when the unconscious is experienced in the only

---

[5] Angelus Silesius, op. cit.

[6] Cf., for instance, the figure of the Venus of the underworld in Christian Rosenkreuz's *Chymische Hochzeit*, who brings punishment and imprisonment to any man who sees her. Another parallel is the Soteira in F. T. Vischer's *Auch Einer*, whom the hero sees in a grotto before he dies.

form accessible to man, namely in the inferior function and the inclusion of the shadow.

Poliphilo, however, at the end of his dream, has no inkling of the danger, nor does he see the goal. However profound the concluding symbolism of the dream may be, as far as the dreamer himself is concerned, we may only employ the outermost stratum in interpreting it. Since the dreamer pays no heed to the grave of Adonis, which vanishes at the end of his dream, we can ultimately see in him only a personality such as was described above, torn by the conflict of Christian and non-Christian. By his inward relationship to the anima, he has passed through an experience which comes to a standstill because he is not capable of tearing himself away from the image of the anima. He cannot do so even though the individual value, the intimate vitality which at first glowed in it, has vanished from the figure, and all that is left to him is the remote, very generalized idea of the mystic rose, which surpasses his powers.

The conclusion of the *Hypnerotomachia* offers no parallel to that of the *Divina Commedia*, which is purely dogmatic. The comparison with the superb final scene of *Faust*, on the other hand, is exceedingly interesting. The problems presented in the two run parallel. The "immortal" part of Faust turns entirely to the Mater Gloriosa, who veils the secret of bliss by enclosing within herself the whole world of the beyond. Like Polia the mystic rose, she is a symbol of the feminine and maternal aspect of the unconscious. She also contains the faint reflection of an anima image which once bore the name of Gretchen. The beauty and power of the poetry invest the final vision of Faust with such enchantment that it is difficult to reflect upon it. We are only too apt to forget that the preceding scene has just left

Mephistopheles, tricked by the angels, standing by the side of a grave. But Mephistopheles is the embodiment of the shadow-world, and if he is left behind, it is not he but Faust who is cheated, since he has now lost his link with the Mephistophelean depths. In spite of its lavish display of images, the final vision of Faust therefore remains a mere intuition without individual impress. It is taken from a general stock of ideas and can at best be related only to a future after death.

From the standpoint of content alone, and without respect to the difference in poetic value, the fundamental likeness between Part II of *Faust* as a whole and the *Hypnerotomachia* consists in the fact that an extremely important masculine symbol is crowded out of sight by the anima image. Just as Poliphilo forgets the grave of Adonis in the figure of Polia, Faust loses sight of Paris in his contemplation of Helen. But Paris is a counterpart to Poliphilo's Adonis, if only a partial one. He reflects his light, upward-striving aspect, the spring-like bridegroom of Venus. The other side of Adonis, which is turned towards the darkness of the underworld, is not contained in Faust's Paris. It has been absorbed into the figure of Mephistopheles, who embodies the shadow side of Faust and at the same time the realm of the daemonic in a general sense. In the *Hypnerotomachia*, everything, the light and the dark, the godlike and the daemonic aspect of the unconscious, and the access to it are all contained by implication in the image of the grave of Adonis. Looked at in this way, the image is germinal, and corresponds to an initial stage. In Part II of *Faust,* on the other hand, we have a growth developed upward and downward, and the figure which incorporates the heights as well as the possibility of yet greater heights is Paris. An important scene then demonstrates how Faust himself usurps the place of Paris. He becomes the spouse of a female figure of superhuman dimensions, and as the Helen of classical antiquity was a demigoddess, he himself becomes a demigod. The following scenes show the results of his usurpation. We are shown the sacrilege of this demigod which he can only overcome by damning and casting off the "remains of earth" as too "painful to bear," and soaring completely into the ether. Apparently the demigod there becomes a full god. But what remains of the human being in the actual world is the void, soulless body, whose symbol is the grave where hell holds sway. From Act III on, Part II of *Faust* becomes with increasing clarity the picture of an infatuation. Lured by the heavenly image of the anima, Faust transgresses the limits set for him. He misuses the shadow for his own purposes, then leaves it behind him. He shuts his eyes to his own reality, and therefore falls victim to the illusion of his own likeness to God.

In the *Hypnerotomachia* the evidence of infatuation is less crass if only because Poliphilo, to the very end, feels the anima image as something higher than himself, and therefore does no violence to it. He never loses sight of the suprapersonal element of the psyche in the image of the anima, and of the wretchedness of his human condition in respect of it. This is borne out by the beautiful and simple dedication of his dream book to Polia, which is here given as evidence of the spirit of humility in which the book was conceived:

Poliphilus Poliae S.P.D.

Oft have I thought, Polia, that the ancients dedicated their works to princes and patrons in order that they might thereby reap some reward, some favour, or some praise. No reason of the sort hath moved me, save perhaps the second, but knowing no more worthy princes than thee to whom to dedicate my Hypnerotomachia, I give it to thee, my great Empress, whose noble birth and incomparable beauty, whose high virtue and perfect courtesy have raised thee far above all nymphs of this age and have inflamed me with a particular love for thee, in which I burn and am wasted away. Take then this my gift, oh! most radiant of all beauties, vessel of all loveliness, renowned for the glory that there is in the sight of thee. It is thou who hast done this by thine own will, and hast imprinted thy heavenly counterfeit with golden arrows in the heart of him who is portrayed within. Therefore art thou the particular mistress of it. And therefore do I lay the work that now followeth before thy wise and learned judgment, for have I not relinquished the manner wherein I first wrote it and did write it again at thy command? Should it therefore be found wanting, should there be in it parts unfruitful or dry, which are unworthy of thy great nobility, it is thou alone who must bear the blame, most excellent instructress and sole ruler of my heart and my understanding. It is my belief that the gain and reward of the greatest talent will be for me thy lovingkindness, thy love and gracious mercy.

Vale

Quite apart from the general feeling of this dedication, there is a curious passage in it, namely that in which the writer states that he has not written as he wished but as he was commanded. Thus in the writing of the book, he did not feel himself a poet or writer, but a servant. For that reason, quite apart from the matter, the language and style are determined by the unconscious rather than by his conscious will. As was mentioned at the beginning of the present volume, the language is a very peculiar dialect of northern Italy, interspersed with fragments of Greek and Latin, which makes it very odd to read.[7] It is difficult to imagine what it must have cost this learned and distinguished monk to express himself in this medium at a time when Italian had long since become a highly developed literary language, and Latin was the only language to be recognized as civilized beside it. We can hardly doubt that he felt this language, which is quite without literary quality, as a barbarism. Yet he used it with humble constancy. What clings to his book in this peasant idiom is the earth. Under the compulsion of this mode of expression, the writing of the *Hypnerotomachia* must have meant suffering and an enrichment of inner

---

[7] This trait is characteristic. Works which arise from the encounter with the unconscious are always marked by linguistic and stylistic strangeness. Examples of this are certain alchemical treatises, poetically elaborated fantasies like *Faust* II, or Nietzsche's *Thus Spake Zarathustra*. [Blake's prophetic books might also be quoted.—TRANS.]

experience. Owing to it, his book has become ponderous and difficult to read, yet it is that very language which makes it touching.

All the same, the solution of the dream is unsatisfactory because there is a curious ambiguity about it. When Polia has vanished, and the grave has sunk into the earth, the unconscious seems to have voided itself, and hence one stage of development seems to have come to an end. There is no visible figure left to incorporate the spirit of the unconscious. Yet something remains, and that is the writer's enthusiasm which gives the dedication its atmosphere and which obviously survived the writing of the book. The *Hypnerotomachia* is unquestionably the product of an inspiration, and Polia's kiss may certainly be taken as its symbol. The kiss on the mouth is an image of a profound impression which can subsequently find expression. From this standpoint, Polia's kiss is the muse's kiss which inspires the man by a fleeting union with her. But at that very moment, the psychic image has already passed from sight, it takes flight and becomes the impulse to create. To give form to the anima experience in words and pictures is an imperative necessity, as the writer of the *Hypnerotomachia* has obviously felt it to be. The inspiration must be held fast and translated into terms of the real, life must proceed from it, for the reality of the anima is revealed in it too. Yet from the standpoint of inward growth, the creation of the work has only a provisional value.

One of the profoundest needs of man is to understand the psychic contents presented by the unconscious. And it would look as if the unconscious wished to be understood too, as if the anima only set the man so many riddles in order to make him solve them. But even when the dream has taken shape in the work, its riddle remains unsolved as long as the reflective spirit does not plunge into it and strive to understand its alien language. True, what man solves the riddle of his sphinx? The confused hieroglyphics of the unconscious are difficult to decipher. But although no direct path to understanding has been opened, a man can nevertheless realize that he does not understand his own work. This realization would impart a new direction to meditation, for then certain questions might arise. For instance, why do we dream and write things we do not understand? And is there any method by which understanding may be attained? With such questions, the problem of the meaning of the work would be raised.

Once the contents of the unconscious have been retained and given form, it is extremely important to put the right questions. They are, as it were, clues to the solution of the riddle. For as soon as we begin to question, we begin to realize how little we understand. This lack of understanding is torture to the intelligence, and that very torture in its turn activates the unconscious. New dreams may come in answer to the ceaseless questions, and so the riddles of the unconscious are solved step by step.

It becomes specially important to put the right questions when, after the unconscious has sunk back again, something remains behind, and that is very frequently or even normally the case. The process of inner development never comes to an end until death, and at the very moment when it appears to be complete, a new phase is setting in. This can be seen, for instance, in the very fact that something remains behind after "waking" from a dream, which need not be an image, but may be, as it was for the author of the *Hypnerotomachia,* a mood, an elevation of the spirit, a powerful impulse, in short, an inspiration. The symbols of this state at the end of the *Hypnerotomachia* are the sweet fragrance as of incense and amber which the anima leaves behind her, and a "mortal delight" in the author himself. Thus within him there is a goad, and about him there is a peculiar atmosphere, some wind is blowing upon him which he cannot comprehend.

In a general way, the sweet fragrance is an attribute of the Holy Ghost and intimates its presence. The Holy Ghost, as Hildegard of Bingen wrote, is "a holy wind, the fire of love, the sweet taste of the soul, which fills hearts with the fragrance of virtue." The image of the fragrance might therefore show that the anima has taken on a spiritual quality, that she has become a female pneuma, not unlike the higher Sophia of the Gnostics, but very unlike her former natural nature. This points back to ancient conceptions which can be found in Iranic texts. In the *Avesta* we read:

"At the end of the third night, when day is dawning, the soul of the righteous man feels that it is borne upward by flowers and perfumes, and it seems as if a sweet wind were blowing from the land of the south, sweeter than all other winds. . . . And in this wind it deems that its own *daena* is approaching in the form of a fair, radiant virgin."

Daena is interpreted as the spiritual soul of man and the embodiment of his religious feeling. When she has drawn near to the departed, she says to him:

"Verily, I am thou, O youth! the well-thinking, well-speaking, well-doing, well-selfed self of thine own person."

It is striking to see how closely this ancient Iranic tradition corresponds to Poliphilo's vision. He too is aware of the fragrance in the dawn as he awakes from sleep. By the symbol of the sweet scent, the revolution that the anima figure undergoes in her transfiguration invests her with a somewhat different meaning from that which she had when she was equated with the Mother of God. Or rather the significance is fundamentally the same, for Mary too, as the transfigured Bride of Heaven, becomes a female pneuma, and she too, as we have seen, possesses the attribute of fragrance. But there is a shift of emphasis. In Poliphilo's dream, the emphasis lies on inspiration as an awakening of the spirit, of the religious feeling which seeks a bond with the suprapersonal. In the fragrance, a premonition of the Self touches the human soul, and a longing for individuation is awakened. The spirit of love yearns for the grave of Adonis.

The stirring of "mortal delight," on the other hand, is most likely the natural reaction of the man to the presence of a female being. But how is it to find fulfilment here, and if that delight is felt for a vision, what are we to understand by that? The question is not unimportant. The man who is in a state of enthusiasm must feel startled by the glow within him, and the man who feels a "mortal delight" must needs ask, "Why is this happening to me?"

If the question is not asked, the enthusiasm is perpetuated, and the result is a vacant exaltation. The symbol of that mood is Polia's sweet fragrance in its negative aspect. Looked at from this standpoint, we might even say that it means no more than a certain rosy aura of incense which, being bound to nothing, can be attached to anything. It will serve to perfume ourselves or the work we have created. We can smell the anima's fragrance in an activity, an art, in definite persons, or even in our native country. There is hardly an aberration of taste which cannot be committed in this way, and committed heedlessly, for the sake of the "mortal delight" there is in them.

By means of this mood of consecration, contents of the unconscious, temporarily grasped but not yet understood, are projected into the object, and transitory things, ideas, or human beings are transformed into absolute values. Brightness floods one side of life, but somewhere the grave is all the darker for it. The grave of Adonis, as described in the *Hypnerotomachia*, is also the fountain from which water flows unceasingly. Contents of the unconscious flow unceasingly into consciousness; behind the brightness, shadows lurk, but the infatuated man cannot see them. Yet they are there, and fill with a dark daemonism all those aspects of the world and of life which are turned away from the rosy radiance of the anima.

Since the negative aspect of the vacant mood of consecration forms part of the concluding symbolism of the *Hypnerotomachia,* Poliphilo's adventure with his anima comes to an ambiguous end. We are left with an awkward impression of idealization and bedazzlement which cannot but give rise to misgivings. If we look back and try to discover where this unsatisfactory situation actually arose, we encounter the three great epistles addressed by Poliphilo to Polia while she was still a vestal in Diana's temple, which have not yet been discussed in this commentary. These three epistles mark the hardly perceptible moment at which the symbolism begins to become ambiguous, and at which we feel the first inkling of misleading and bedazzlement. In Polia's story, Poliphilo's ecstasy after the heaven of Venus is one instance of it. We must therefore ask whether the inner cause of the subsequent development may not lie in Poliphilo's epistles to Polia.

These epistles stand in striking contrast to the dedication of the *Hypnerotomachia* to Polia. In its pregnant concision, the dedication sounds thoroughly honest. It is a convincing expression of the writer's feeling and mood. The three epistles, on the other hand, are pure literature. To bear this out, we may turn to the beginning of the first:

"In overweening desire and utmost yearning to reveal the not moderate flame in my lovesick heart, that heart which, burning with its sublime and special love to thee, is consumed in longing, oh proud and revered nymph! sole miracle, perfect pattern of earthly beauty!—not with feeble words, no! with tears that have blotted the writing on this papyrus, I yield to the honourable and permitted boldness, though without rashness, and in the grievous oppression born of constant provocation and the invasion of an obstinate torment of love, to reveal to thee the unbelievable passion, the sincere tenderness that I feel for thee, my sweet good, my sweet hope, sole refreshment in the torments whereof thou knowest nought, in the longing thou canst not conceive. It is in a trembling voice, with reverent words, with humble prayers, that I commend myself to thee at this most grievous moment of my state in which I find myself, my heart pierced with arrows, and implore thy aid that my intemperate flame may be tempered. O Polia! light divine, adored goddess! Turn not a deaf ear, I beseech thee, to my just prayers, my vows. It is with bended head, beseeching, consumed with burning love, that I call upon thee, call to thee, that thou mayst make haste to bring me thy healing succour, thy powerful aid, thy necessary release, while yet there is time. It is because my heart is torn from my breast by the fangs of thy starlike eyes that the cause of this disordered and unlovely epistle has come into being, that I write to thee in the confusion which love hath engendered in me. . . ."

This opening will do, for the contents of all three epistles are the same. It goes on in the same style for page after page, with the same ejaculations and complaints and in the same affected style. It may be that such epistles were esteemed as a literary delicacy by the Renaissance, which may have regarded such stilted confessions of love in such a connection as a novelty. And the writer had one eye on the world when he wrote them. He may have hoped to impress it by the skill of his phrasing no less than by his extraordinary sufferings. In any case, his literary exertions in the epistles give us the impression that his yearnings are aimed as much at the reading public as at the anima.

This is particularly remarkable since it is clear from the rest of the book that the writer means it seriously, and that he is no mere rhetorician. Yet in writing the epistles, he has obviously reached a point at which it becomes clear that, for all his seriousness and honesty, there is something in him that is—different. If, at the critical moment, he can find nothing but literature to write to his beloved, he would seem, at the bottom of his heart, to doubt her reality and to fear, or to hope, that she is, after all, mere literature. The idea is frivolous, for if the anima is mere literature, things are easy for the man, and she can be disposed of, possibly to the writer's benefit as regards his public. But there is more behind this than mere frivolity. There is in all probability a hidden resistance to the anima. In this respect Poliphilo's thousandfold repeated and extravagant asseverations of his love become suspect. It looks as if the ardent vows were necessary to shout down some secret voice raised in opposition, which casts doubt on this extremely uncomfortable love affair and refuses to obey the anima. Further, the *reductio ad absurdum* of the divinization of the beloved gives us further grounds for suspicion. It is so absolutely out of place with regard to the fairylike creature who is presented to us so clearly with all her feminine charms and wiles. Can it be that Poliphilo is turning Polia into a goddess so that he may feel inexpressibly elevated as the bearer of an illustrious love? Or must he raise her so high because there is something in him that will have none of her? Exaggerations always point to a hidden purpose or to a contrary current which is struggling to make headway and can only be concealed by violence.

It is curious that Poliphilo should never wonder why Polia is so cruel and why she will have nothing to do with him. Why does it never occur to him to reflect whether the grounds for it do not lie in himself? It is one of the functions of the anima to show a man his own being. If she calls herself cruel and malicious, it is because the man is cruel and malicious towards his own soul. It is cruel and malicious to turn her into mere literature and sell her to the world for the "mortal delight" of his vanity as a writer. It is cruel and malicious to tell her lies, to stand before her in the pose of humble adoration when it is the man's business to know that there is something within him that doubts her and wards her off. It would not cost him much to own up, for on the other hand he has all the good things that have accompanied him throughout his dream-journey. He has known what it is to be under safe guidance from within, and he could take his stand on that when doubt and resistance threaten to disturb his peace.

In the process of coming to terms with the anima, there comes a moment when something is required of a man which goes beyond love and is based on religion in the Latin sense of the word, that is, on the profound regard for the numinous. In the symbolism of the *Hypnerotomachia,* it is the moment at which Poliphilo begins to write. At that moment, he should open his heart to the anima *religiose,* so that she, in her turn, may reveal to him what can lead him beyond doubt and resistance. But an achievement of such a kind presupposes two things: Firstly, the man must admit the anima to be as real as an actual woman. That should be possible, for she awakens his love and desire in exactly the same way as a real woman. Secondly, he must be willing to note what is going on in him, because otherwise the only thing that will issue will be fine phrases. But at that moment, his "grave of Adonis" opens. He is confronted with the equivocal promptings of his own heart and with the defects of his morality. He learns how hypocritically and selfishly he can behave at times, and how unscrupulously he can sell himself to the world. If he does not open his heart in this way to the anima, he may remain elevated above his shadow sides as an apparent lover and idealist, but then all that is equivocal in him will appear in his anima.

When that happens, she has nothing to give him but insecurity and ambiguity. It lies, moreover, in the iridescence of her nature that she can, with one and the same gesture, lead the man to illumination and seduce him into infatuation. She always embodies both his Venus and his Proserpine.

That is why he needs the link with his "grave of Adonis." He must recognize within himself the No beside the Yes, the dark promptings beside the light, for in these contradictions the shadow is making itself known to him. He must not attempt to leave that shadow behind him, because it is from that angle that he can also see through his anima. The man who has discovered the shadow within him will recognize the daemon when it approaches him in the shape of woman. He will then be free to choose between the double gifts the anima has to offer him.

Epilogue

The *Hypnerotomachia* was written at the end of the fifteenth century. That is a long time ago, and we might venture to hope that the picture of the human psyche presented in it would by now be obsolete. That, however, is far from being the case. On the contrary, the resemblance between Poliphilo and many cultivated men of our time is remarkable. Like him, they have passed through a first stage of development and have become conscious personalities. Today they are even too well-adjusted to the world outside them, and too deeply attracted by it. But whether they realize it or not, a faint odour of anima clings to most of them still, and it is unfortunately only too obvious that the men of our time linger far too long by their "tomb of Adonis." Hell has broken loose because too many conscious beings, all over the world, fail to see the darkness in themselves. In the individual, that darkness certainly presents a serious problem, but it brings its own reward, for in the individual, the shadows themselves are the path which leads to the supra personal aspects of the psyche, just as Adonis has his bond with both heaven and the underworld. From this point of view, however, the problem of the shadow can only be tackled by the individual, and if he is, for instance, to improve social or political conditions, he must begin with himself. Since he does not do so, the incense fragrance of the anima envelops the world, causing exaltation and destruction at one and the same time.

This situation is rendered graver by the fact that psychic

problems have grown dangerously acute since the beginning of the modern age. The end of the *Hypnerotomachia* showed us the author in a strangely equivocal state, which seemed to be characteristic not only of his own but of the coming age. We saw him as a Catholic who yet, as the neophyte of his Polia, remained standing outside the Church. The psychic situation of modern man is characterized by a breach. The man of today cannot be described as one hesitating before the next step, one hanging back, who cannot yet struggle out of his halfness into wholeness. He is a man who cannot take the next step at all, because there is no bridge between the opposites of which his being is composed. As regards the "normal" side of his nature, it no longer bears the impress of Christian values, as it did in the *Hypnerotomachia*. He is contained in no hierarchical order, whether of this world or the next; no church embraces him. Therefore he is contained in a collective, secular consciousness consisting of the most multifarious systems of thought and feeling, some quite loose, some firmer in structure. His consciousness is determined by science, art, and—there is no other way to put it—in place of religion, the current morality of his time. On that foundation every individual lives like thousands of others. Further, every individual shares with his contemporaries a specific kind of unconsciousness. He projects just as they do, has similar illusions, and is widely identified with his fellow countrymen. Hence the parallel to the Christian of the *Hypnerotomachia* in our own day is the collective human being whose consciousness is adapted to the secular world of his age. Thus he becomes a worldling who can feel as much at home in New York as in London, Paris, or Cairo.

It would seem as if, since the Renaissance, development had proceeded in such a way that the secular personality, which Poliphilo experienced in a mysterious initiation by the anima, had become common property. The very thing which was private and mysterious at the time of the Renaissance is now within reach of everybody. Everybody, for instance, who has been to school till the age of twelve, has then learned a trade and taken up a profession (if it is only, in the case of women, housework), and is possessed of a conscious, more or less stereotyped culture which, by its very nature, can be further formed by the daily press. That culture may be utterly dreary, or it may be stimulating; the one thing that it is no longer is private. The landmarks of this development are the public buildings which have taken their place beside the churches, and serve the purposes of art, trade and industry, administration, education, or entertainment, and give concrete form to the demand for equality among men. They are of a size and splendour which were once reserved to the churches and the palaces of princes. In psychological terms, the development of nations into democracies is based on the existence of the collective consciousness which floodlights every citizen. Everyone has his share of light, large or small. That is the basis of his freedom of thought and action, which he puts into practice personally. But his thoughts and actions are all the same entirely collective in character, for which reason everyone can share in everybody else's freedom of thought and action.

The wider collective consciousness spreads, however, the shallower it grows and the less import it has for the further development of the psyche. We may, of course, say that we are not interested in any such development, that we do not need it and would prefer to do without. It is true that the further development of the psyche first sets in with dark and painful problems. Collective consciousness, which means uniform and steady light, is *ipso facto* hostile to problems and repudiates them. But men have no choice in the matter, for psychic development is a natural happening which forces its way onward with dreadful power if men do not consciously make room for it first. As a compensation to this shallow consciousness, the unconscious is activated and the shadow cast by every man, in so far as it is light (i.e. possesses consciousness), grows steadily in importance. The shadow contains everything that can renew and enrich a shallow consciousness. From this point of view the problem of the shadow is a modern problem. In the *Hypnerotomachia* we only find it hinted at as something in the future that cannot be resolved in the dream. Today, the imperative need of a solution has made itself felt, and the problem of the shadow has even, to a certain extent, become the cardinal problem of our day. The shadow and the inferior function are not merely the elements by which a shallow consciousness may be enriched. They are the bridge between the opposites which compose the being of man, the cement by which consciousness and the unconscious cohere. In modern man, the inferior function and the shadow have been activated, whether he is aware of it or not. If he does not become aware of it, he loses his own reality. He runs the risk of arrogating to himself as his own property not only the wisdom and the light of the world, but also the wisdom of the unconscious which shines forth from the darkness. Thus in the end he finds himself in a situation like that described, for instance, at the end of Goethe's *Faust* or in Vischer's *Auch Einer*. He is borne aloft in an apotheosis, but beneath him the lemurs are cowering round an open grave.

The way of the shadow and the inferior function is the only legitimate way to the anima. Where man has jumped over his shadow, the relation to the anima bears the stamp of the illegitimate. In that case a man who may be a pattern of decency and good will in his outer life becomes the desecrator of the holy of holies within him. Then the image of the anima darkens. Just as the man cheated her of his shadow, she cheats him with illusions. She turns her seductive side towards him and becomes his Proserpine. She creates hindrances and hesitation, turns him more and more into a shadow, till the hell of the triple-headed Cerberus yawns before him. Transformation approaches in the guise of catastrophes in outer life, and the sweet fragrance of incense which proclaims a premature apotheosis yields to the smell of death on the battlefields of the world.

The inner development of women takes a course parallel to that of men, and their inner situation today is very like that of the men. Their intense participation in the collective consciousness of our time comes out most clearly, perhaps, in the fact of woman suffrage. There is certainly no obvious reason why women should not vote, just like the men, since the contents of their consciousness and their unconscious implications coincide very largely with those of the men.

The "other side" of women's life is governed by the animus instead of the anima, and manifests itself in preconceived opinions and fanatical activities. As in the man, there stands behind it the archetypal image of a psychopompos such as appears most clearly, for instance, in Greek mythology in the figure of Hermes. An analysis of that divinity—in its phallic aspect, as god of the winds, as servant and messenger of the gods, as robber, cheat, and thief, as god of trade and speech, as inventor, as the guide of souls and the dead, as protector of heroes and saviour of divine children, and as god of dreams and sleep—might be instructive for the comprehension of the male element in women. As the anima incorporates the breath of the man's soul, watery and cloud-like, the animus incorporates the ghostlike mind of women. Those emotions and passions which are, in a sense, the "outriders" of every content of the psyche, are often much more distinctly visible in women than in men. That is why the "mana personalities" appearing in the world attract with peculiar force their passionate adoration or equally passionate hatred. But the passion is not really for the man in question, but for the archetypal image projected on to him. We might say in a general way that women, even when they are very independent (or at any rate feel very independent), tend to transfer spiritual leadership to a man. Because their spiritual activity lies more in darkness, they let men act for them. By mysterious machinations they foment men's illusions, and when a man is borne aloft in some premature apotheosis, we shall often find, on closer inquiry, that it is a woman who has sent him up there.

We might even wonder whether the extraordinary power and greatness in which the image of the Leader has appeared all over the world of today has not been occasioned mainly by the secret, quite unconscious action of women. They really need a leader if they are to find their way out of the world of a flattened and dissipated consciousness. But the source of renewal, for them as for men, cannot lie in the outer world. For the woman too, the only legitimate way out of the slavery of one-sidedness is individuation. It leads through the uneasy and slippery region of the shadow, behind which there stands a daemon with a magic wand, possessed of great knowledge and smiling a kindly, crafty smile, the messenger and servant of the gods.

Thus men and women in the world of today are faced with the same problems. Those problems will remain insoluble as long as men and women cannot see that they bear within them an image of leadership which points them imperiously on to the next requirements of their inner development. Those demands are never theories; they are, as in the *Hypnerotomachia,* tasks which must be performed.

Since they concern the inner life, those tasks certainly bring their own problems with them; they are, moreover, absolutely private in kind. To perform them, the men and women of today must first relearn that there are in the humblest, most simple of lives secrets that cannot be divulged. That in itself would be an exceedingly difficult task, for it runs counter to the collective consciousness, which values publications and discussions as a supreme value and will admit nothing that cannot be put into print and made known to everybody. Collective consciousness is hostile to the individual secret; it forbids any individual peculiarity. In doing so, people overlook the fact that an individual peculiarity confers no place apart on the man who consciously lives it. By really experiencing within him, not only his own peculiarities, but also what is common to all men, the individual will, on the contrary, be better equipped to find his true place in the world, and will not be so prone to burden it with the shadows that surround him. He will know that he cannot discharge his burdens on to anyone but himself. They may be hard to bear, he may stumble at times, and he may lose the godlike self-assurance of those who see no shadows in themselves. But he will at any rate stand in human reality and real life, which has, from time immemorial, been insecure and problematic.

Security will then no longer reside in the outer world and the ego: it will be perpetually reborn of the encounter with the images that well up from the unconscious. It will come as a reward to the man who really turns to the image of the anima without losing himself in it. If the man of today were ready to obey the call of his psyche with due reflection, he would find the true modern form of courtly love. After all, his consciousness is developed highly enough for him to be able to reflect both on himself and her. The man who reflects will notice when the fragrance of incense titillates his nostrils. The anima is just like any other woman. She wants to be loved and taken seriously, but she is quite pleased when the man sees through her.

But the anima is not only a woman like any other. She is like the moon too. In her opening phase she rises like a tender crescent in the night sky, and looks like a mysterious girl. She becomes animated when the patient sufferer in the ragged clouts casts himself at her feet. She receives him like some kindly Nausicaa, bathes him, and leads him into the king's hall. Then she is as the full moon. She becomes an

Artemis in bridal robes and calls to her beloved brother. She pours her milky liquid over hill and distant vale. Then she can be heard hunting, she comes with a rout of bears and panthers. And then she wanes. There is no moisture left in her, and her torch smokes. Then she vanishes, and it is time for the man to hurry home and see in his mirror his own wreath-crowned, smoke-blackened head.

Publisher's Note

Since this book was written, the writings of C. G. Jung cited here in footnotes have been published as volumes of *The Collected Works,* trans. R. F. C. Hull, ed. H. Read, M. Fordham, G. Adler, Wm. McGuire, Bollingen Series XX, vols. 1-20 (Princeton: Princeton University Press and London: Routledge and Kegan Paul, 1953 ff.), paragraph numbers.

The following gives *CW* volume numbers (and paragraph numbers, where applicable) for the works Linda Fierz-David refers to. The pages where she cites Jung are in parentheses.

Psychology and Alchemy (9, 24, 44, 62, 81, 82, 83, 85, 118, 126, 129, 142, 183, 201, 202) is *CW* 12. Note 5 on pp. 82-83 refers to § § 122 ff. and § 249.

"The Relation of the Ego to the Unconscious" (55, 111) is in *CW* 7.

Psychological Types (58, 111) is *CW* 6.

Two Essays on Analytical Psychology (83) is now included in *CW* 7. The material quoted as on p. 265 is § 399; that quoted as p. 268 is § 404.

Psychology and Religion (91) is found in *CW* 11, § § 1-168. "Zur Psychologie der Trinitätsidee" (92) is found in *CW* 11, § § 169-295.

"Uber die Archetypen des kollektiven Unbewussten" (111, 128) is in *CW* 9, i, § § 1-86.

"Bemerkungen zu den Visionen des Zosimos" (142) is in *CW* 13, § § 85-144. *The Secret of the Golden Flower* (183) is in *CW* 13, § § 1-84. "Der Geist Mercurius" appears in *CW* 13, § § 239-303.

A corrected version of Jung's foreword to this book is now in *CW* 18, § § 1749-1752.

We want especially to thank William McGuire, formerly of Princeton University Press, for his assistance in our republishing this book.

J.H.
M.H.S.

ON THE ANIMA FROM SPRING

ANIMA AS FATE   Cornelia Brunner

The first translation into English of a 1963 work published as a study from the Jung-Institute, Zürich, written by a respected Swiss analyst and one of C. G. Jung's longtime associates. The first part of the book explores the notion of the anima, the contrasexual aspect of a man's psyche, in the works of Rider Haggard, particularly in his celebrated novel *She*. This part also provides background and a psychological evaluation of the author's adventurous life and many travels. The book's second part traces the development of the anima in a series of dreams that a middleaged physician experienced over a period of several years. Preface by C. G. Jung. (xv, 277 pp., ISBN 508–8)

ANIMA: AN ANATOMY OF A PERSONIFIED NOTION   James Hillman

Anima and Eros, Anima and Feeling, Anima and the Feminine, Anima and Psyche, Mediatrix of the Unknown, Integration of the Anima, etc.—ten succinct chapters, accompanied by relevant quotations from Jung (on left-hand pages facing Hillman's essay), which clarify the moods, persons, and definitions of the most subtle and elusive aspect of psychology and of life. Illustrated. (188 pp., ISBN 316-6)

ANIMUS AND ANIMA   Emma Jung

Two classic papers on the elemental persons of the psyche. Examines both animus and anima as they appear in behavior, fantasies, dreams, and mythology. Accessible, incisive, and with plenty of practical counsel, this book maps a way toward the union of opposites and the emergence of the Self. Includes a picture of the author. (94 pp., ISBN 301-8)

PAGAN MEDITATIONS   Ginette Paris

An appreciation of three Greek Goddesses as values of importance to our twentieth-century collective life: Aphrodite as civilized sexuality and beauty; Artemis as solitude, ecological significance, and a perspective on abortion; and Hestia as warm hearth, security, and stability. As the author's contribution to *imaginative* feminism, this book addresses both the meditative interior of each person and the community of culture. (204 pp., ISBN 330–1)

GODDESSES OF SUN AND MOON   Karl Kerényi

Karl Kerényi, a colleague of C. G. Jung's and one of the major mythographers of this century, here takes a novel look at four unusual feminine configurations depicted in Greek mythology. The vision that emerges restores passionate feminine consciousness to its rightful place both in politics and in the economy of the psyche. The four papers explore the mythemes of Circe, the enchantress; Medea, the murderess; Aphrodite, the golden one; and Niobe of the Moon. Together they lend a deep psychological orientation to some of the most puzzling and controversial issues of our day: feminism, the occult, aesthetics, madness, dreams, even terrorism. (84 pp., ISBN 211–9)

ISBN prefix: 0–88214–
Spring Publications, Inc.   P.O. Box 222069   Dallas, TX 75222